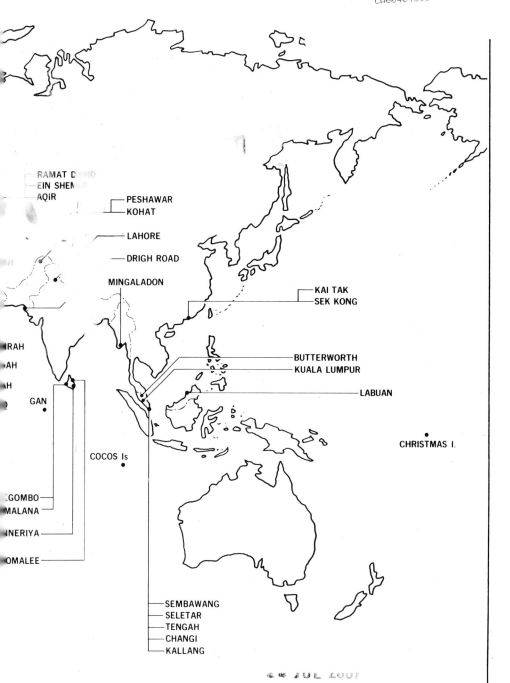

RAMAT DAVID
EIN SHEMER
AQIR

PESHAWAR
KOHAT

LAHORE

DRIGH ROAD

MINGALADON

KAI TAK
SEK KONG

RAH
AH
AH

GAN

BUTTERWORTH
KUALA LUMPUR

LABUAN

CHRISTMAS I.

COCOS Is

GOMBO
MALANA

NERIYA

OMALEE

SEMBAWANG
SELETAR
TENGAH
CHANGI
KALLANG

Principal British Military Overseas Airfields

ACTION STATIONS

OVERSEAS

Patrick Stephens Limited, a member of the Haynes Publishing Group, has published authoritative, quality books for enthusiasts for more than twenty years. During that time the company has established a reputation as one of the world's leading publishers of books on aviation, maritime, military, model-making, motor cycling, motoring, motor racing, railway and railway modelling subjects. Readers or authors with suggestions for books they would like to see published are invited to write to: The Editorial Director, Patrick Stephens Limited, Sparkford, Nr Yeovil, Somerset, BA22 7JJ.

ACTION STATIONS
OVERSEAS

Sqn Ldr Tony Fairbairn

Patrick Stephens Limited

For Amanda

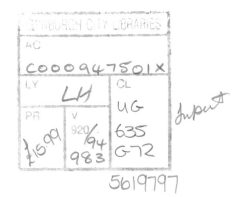

© Tony Fairbairn 1991

First published in 1991

*British Library Cataloguing in Publication
Data*

Fairbairn, Tony
  Action stations overseas: Britain's military
  airfields abroad.
  1. Overseas military bases
  I. Title
  355.7

  ISBN 1-85260-319-4

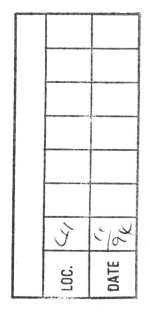

*Patrick Stephens Limited is a member of
the Haynes Publishing Group P.L.C.,
Sparkford, Nr Yeovil, Somerset, BA22 7JJ.*

Typeset by Burns and Smith Ltd, Derby
Printed in Great Britain

10 9 8 7 6 5 4 3 2 1

Contents

Acknowledgements

The fruition of this project depended on the interest and generosity of many individuals, but first and foremost I would like to acknowledge the part played by the MoD Air Historical Branch, without which my task would quite simply have been impossible. In particular Sebastian Cox was unstinting in his help over administrative arrangements, Peter Singleton pointed the way to some of the older photographs, and Richard King ferretted out a constant flow of vital raw material with patience and enthusiasm.

Certain other stalwarts 'in the business' gave freely of their time and material, and here I should like to mention Chris Ashworth, Steve Bond, Mike Bowyer, Chaz Bowyer, Peter Green, Burne James, Wg Cdr C. 'Jeff' Jefford, Fred Lake at the MoD Library in London, Paddy Porter, Bruce Robertson, Sqn Ldr Peter Russell-Smith, and Ray Sturtivant.

Offers of photographs and other material assistance, for which I am extremely grateful, also came from the following: Paddy Alton, N. Bailey-Underwood, C. Baxter, J. Beel, A. Bradbury, F. Brown, Air Cdr J.P.R. Browne CBE, S. Burge, C. Butcher, Wg Cdr R.I. Campbell, Sqn Ldr A. Cant, A. Chapman, J. Colver, P. Cook, R. Cook, R. Cottrell, K. Cox, Sqn Ldr Simon Crockatt, Brian Cull, Simon Culverhouse, M. Dalton, Flt Lt C. Evans, R. Ewington, Maj Mike Fallon of the Public Information Branch — HQ South West District, F. Galea of the National War Museum Association — Malta GC, Sqn Ldr R.B. Glover, the late B. Goldsmith, A. Harding, R. Hayward, Don Healey, Flt Lt Paul Hickley of 60 Sqn, Gerry Hinton and Philip Rowe at the Atomic Weapons Establishment, Aldermaston, Flt Lt J.C. Holt of 10 Sqn, Capt A. Hudson — 660 Sqn AAC, J. Hughes, Wg Cdr Mel James, J. Keward, W. Killick, S. Kingham, J. Lindop, M. Lines, Wg Cdr D.D. Martin OBE, K. Le Masurier, C. Mayes, P. Moat, Flt Lt M. Morris , Museum of Army Flying, Middle Wallop, Bill Overton, L. Packham, J. Pickering, Capt Barry Priest, Public Relations Staffs at HQ Strike Command and HQ RAF Support Command, A. Reid, C. Richardson, B. Robinson, Robbie Shaw, Sqn Ldr Mike Shepherd-Smith of RAF Unit Goose Bay, C. Simlett, Dave Skinner, G. Speed, Josephine Swain, T. Sykes, THEM DAYS Inc (for permission to quote from 'On the Goose'), J. Thompson, Ivor Turnnidge and the RAF Airfield Construction Branch Association, J. Le Vien, R. Walker, G. White, and the RAF Wittering Photographic Section. Finally I must flag up my long-suffering family, consisting of my wife Amanda (I promise to start washing the car again!), and sons Jonathan and Spike — thank you for mowing the lawn, guys.

Introduction

My own introduction to the world of overseas military airfields took place in the early 1960s when I was still a teenager and the family began packing up its bags in England to join my father, then an RAF pilot, at Changi, Singapore. The flight out east was an exhausting 30-plus hour epic from Stansted aboard a British United Airways Britannia that took us via Istanbul and Bombay into Singapore's now defunct Paya Lebar airport. On the ground at Paya Lebar we climbed wearily into the waiting Ford Anglia for the drive to temporary accommodation at the Dragon Inn Hotel on the East Coast Road. The journey is etched on my memory for its mind-boggling medley of sights, sounds, smells and temperatures.

At that time, Singapore was a hive of military flying activity, for the Malaysian Confrontation was looming, and as an aviation enthusiast since the age of four, I set to work with a will in my spare time, armed with notebook and recently-acquired Kodak Sterling bellows camera. Standard practice was to catch a Changi bus down to the airfield, where there was a seemingly endless flow of aircraft. I later discovered that the lofty, flat-topped concrete structure from which I conducted my clandestine photography was in fact one of the magazines for Changi's infamous, and impotent, Second World War 15-inch guns.

During my two years at Changi I saw many memorable sights, both on the ground and in the air: entire squadrons arriving to take part in the Confrontation operations; a representative of every FEAF aircraft type, drawn up for inspection by HRH Prince Philip during his Far Eastern tour; and the mighty aircraft carriers of the day, *Eagle* and *Victorious*, clearly visible from Changi's grass padang, decks crammed with Scimitars and Sea Vixens, as they slipped through the Straits of Johore on their way to the nearby naval base. As an ATC cadet there were flights from Seletar aboard 209 Sqn Scottish Aviation Pioneers, which nimbly alighted on tiny Malayan jungle strips, and a low-level cross-country sortie in a 215 Sqn Argosy. Heady stuff to look back on, as my departing British Eagle Britannia lifted off from a monsoon-saturated Paya Lebar to return me to the United Kingdom.

Some years later, having joined the Royal Air Force myself, I was lucky enough to be posted to Akrotiri in Cyprus, when that base was home for what amounted to a complete air force. But my Mediterranean assignment had the added bonus of periodic detachments to the Persian Gulf, and in particular to the staging post airfield of Masirah, with its distinctive 'moonscape' desert environment, its extraordinary lifestyle and its unforgettable camaradie. Arriving at Masirah on the occasion of my first visit I was directed to my accommodation - a tent - where I stowed my suitcase under my camp-bed. Work began each day at 7 a.m., and after flying had finished at around 2 p.m. there was ample opportunity to relax on the Station's nine-hole golf course with its 'browns' (as opposed to greens!) of oiled sand, or down at the sailing club, with transport to the beach provided by the diminutive Masirah State Railway. In the evening there were cooling 'Green Charlies' (cans of Carlsberg beer) followed perhaps by a Combined Services Entertainment show or a detachment party at the 'Crazy Horse Saloon' (basically an up-market shed – bring your own food and drink). On the far side of the airfield was a tiny isolated branch of Khimji's Store, crammed with luxury goods, where I bought my first Rolex Oyster for £32. Laundry was no problem here – you simply bundled up soiled clothing on the bottom of your bed in the morning and it was returned that evening, having been collected by Ali Dhobi and immaculately washed, dried and pressed during the day at the Station's Arab laundry.

Masirah and countless other overseas airfields like it have now passed into RAF history, the crucial part they played in numerous military campaigns in which Great Britain found itself embroiled down the years largely forgotten. For this reason, and because of my own life-long interest in RAF stations, I decided to set down the potted histories of at least the larger overseas airfields. The task of researching the station histories from official records was an absorbing but often humbling experience, for although my own time overseas was for the most part peaceful and comfortable, it became clear that less fortunate souls before me had worked, fought and in many cases died in extremes of climate and terrain that made life at home in the United Kingdom seem positively humdrum. The selection of stations is, of course, my own and my one regret is that lack of space prevents me from doing them greater justice. For the sake of continuity and historical accuracy I have, throughout the text, used contemporary country names – e.g. 'Ceylon'. I hope the finished product is a useful and relevant addition to the series, and one which brings together between two covers something of the grandeur and operational vitality of the principal British overseas military airfields, the majority of which really did see action at one time or another.

Tony Fairbairn
Wittering

Glossary

AAC Army Air Corps.
AAR Air-to-air Refuelling.
AACU Anti-Aircraft Cooperation Unit.
ADIZ Air Defence Identification Zone.
AFB Air Force Base.
AFME Air Forces Middle East.
AHQ Air Headquarters.
ANZUK Australia, New Zealand, United Kingdom.
AOC Air Officer Commanding.
AOP Air Observation Post.
APC Armament Practice Camp.
APS Armament Practice School.
APSF Aden Protectorate Support Flight.
A/S Anti-submarine.
ASV Air-to-Surface Vessel.
BAOR British Army of Occupation in the Rhine.
Batavia Old name for Jakarta, capital of Indonesia.
BFBS British Forces Broadcasting Services.
Cab Rank Patrols Standing patrol of fighter-bombers armed with cannon, bombs or rockets, usually maintained in the vicinity of a land battle.
Comms Communications.
CENTO Central Treaty Organization.
CFB Canadian Forces Base.
CT Communist Terrorist.
EACF East African Communications Flight.
East Indies Indonesia.
ECM Electronic Counter-measures.
FAA Fleet Air Arm.
FEAF Far East Air Force.
FECS Far East Communications Squadron.
FCU Ferry Control Unit.
FRADU Fleet Requirements and Air Direction Unit.
FRU Fleet Requirements Unit.
FTS Flying Training School.
HAS Hardened Aircraft Shelter.
HCU Heavy Conversion Unit.
HKAAF Hong Kong Auxiliary Air Force.

KAAU Kenya Auxiliary Air Unit.
LABS Low Altitude Bombing Strike.
MCU Marine Craft Unit.
MECS Middle East Communications Squadron.
METS Middle East Training School.
MRR Maritime Radar Reconnaissance.
MU Maintenance Unit.
NAS Naval Air Station.
NEAF Near East Air Force.
OCU Operational Conversion Unit.
OTU Operational Training Unit.
PR Photographic Reconnaissance.
PSP Pierced Steel Planking.
QRA Quick Reaction Alert.
RAE Royal Aircraft Establishment.
RAFG Royal Air Force Germany.
RASC Royal Army Service Corps.
RCT Royal Corps of Transport.
Recce Reconnaissance.
RHKAAF Royal Hong Kong Auxiliary Air Force.
Rhubarb Sorties Small-scale fighter or fighter-bomber attacks on ground targets of opportunity.
RMAF Royal Malaysian Air Force.
RNAF Royal Netherlands Air Force.
SAC Strategic Air Command.
SAM Surface-to-Air Missile.
SRAF Southern Rhodesian Air Force.
SAAF South African Air Force.
SACEUR Supreme Allied Commander Europe.
SAR Search and Rescue.
SAS Special Air Service.
SD Special Duties.
SFTS Service Flying Training School.
SOAF Sultan of Oman's Air Force.
SOE Special Operations Executive.
SP Staging Post.
TAF Tactical Air Force.
TCW Troop Carrier Wing.
UNFICYP United Nations Force in Cyprus.

The airfields

Abu Sueir, Egypt

For much of its long career Abu Sueir was synonymous with flying training, and a site close to the Sweetwater Canal and the main Port Said railway was first chosen as far back as September 1917. It was used as a training base during the First World War, and No 4 Flying Training School was formed here in April 1921 with Avro 504Ks for initial training, and Bristol Fighters and de Havilland 9As for advanced instruction. Other types used by the School included the Vickers Vimy and the Armstrong Whit-

worth Atlas, formations of the latter making training flights to Iraq in 1932. These early years also embraced a period in the bomber role, for between September 1919 and February 1920 it was home for the Handley Page 0/400s of No 214 Sqn. In August 1938 work began on buildings for the storage and maintenance of aircraft, and in November 1938 No 102 Mainten-ance Unit was established for that task. The MU also provided general stores and fuel.

Abu Sueir formed as a station proper on 2 September 1939 with the departure of 4 FTS to Habbaniya. At about the same time

DH10 at Abu Sueir in 1920. (MoD Crown Copyright)

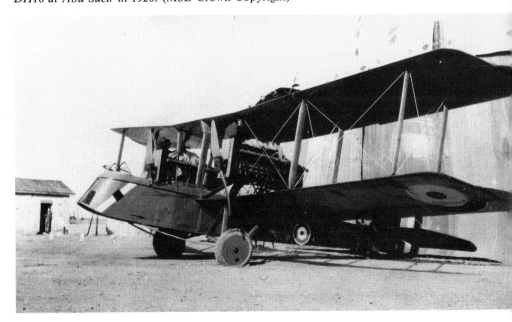

4 FTS on parade at Abu Sueir — Vickers Vimys in the background. (G Speed)

a Subsidiary Repair Unit began arriving and was soon patching up Lysanders, Blenheims, Ansons, Wellesleys, Gladiators and Gordons. No 102 MU, on the other hand, was responsible for modifications to the types it stored which included Hawker Hardys, Vickers Vincents, Gloster Gauntlets and Gladiators in addition to Lysanders. Seven Hinds were modified for the South African AF. By May 1941 the MU was established with seven Ansons and six Fairey Gordons, the latter forming a Target Towing Flight. The Pilot Pool, meanwhile, was carrying out *ab initio*

flying training for medical officers, in addition to refresher and conversion courses for regular aircrew.

During 1940 and 1941 several fighter squadrons used the Station for short reorganizational periods, including No 80 with Gladiators, No 450 (an Australian Hurricane unit), No 272 flying Beaufighters, and No 213 also on Hurricanes. After Abu Sueir's vital repair facilities were badly damaged in a Luftwaffe attack in July 1941, garages and workshops were taken over in Cairo, and the resources of the university were even utilized. A more

DH9A trainers of 4 FTS Abu Sueir. (P Green)

Hawker Hart (T) K4896 of 4 FTS Abu Sueir. (R Ashworth)

permanent fighter presence began with the arrival in November 1941 of No 89 Sqn and its Beaufighters. The 'Beaus' scored the following March when Squadron Leader D. S. Pain in X7671 shot down a Heinkel 111. The tally mounted in April, when the Station was bombed, with three enemy destroyed, one probable and two damaged. Two Wellington squadrons, Nos 37 and 70, arrived in June 1942, and during their five month stay took part in many raids on German Army positions in North Africa, leading up to the Battle of El Alamein in October. No 203 Sqn was also on strength over this period, flying Martin Marylands and later Baltimores.

Plans were now in hand for a return to the training role but before this took place the USAAF put in a brief appearance. First to arrive was the 315th Service Group, followed a few days later (in November 1942) by the B-24 Librators of the 376th Bomb Group, which attacked Axis naval targets as part of the effort to cut enemy supply lines to Africa. The Stars and Stripes were packed away in February 1943, but on the seventeenth of that month, No 73 Operational Training Unit formed, with Spitfires, Hurricanes, Kittyhawks, Tomahawks, Harvards, Blenheims and Harts. The training activity resulted in incidents practically every day; in July, for example, Spitfire I K9873 bent its propeller blades on a sand dune during a strafing attack, Spitfire Vb EP327 spun in fatally during a tight turn at low height, damaging the Station church, and Kittyhawk AK583 dived into the ground with its pilot from 10,000 feet. Pilots from numerous countries, including Canada, Australia, Turkey, Egypt and South Africa, were trained; the

Yugoslav students attracted a visit by the King of Yugoslavia in his personal Tiger Moth to view facilities in November. The first two Boulton Paul Defiants (AA498 and '509) were received in January 1944, and the Fairchild Argus was also added to the inventory. The CO at this point was one Group Captain John Grandy, later to become Chief of the Air Staff. Even the instructors had their problems, and records relate that in June 1944 Sergeant J. H. Ross (RNZAF) allowed Spitfire Vc EE749 to collide with a totem pole at the end of No 2 runway!

Later in June, No 73 OTU moved to Fayid and the Station closed for the construction work needed to prepare it for use as a Liberator Heavy Conversion Unit. The first two Liberator VIs arrived from Palestine in July and No 1675 HCU was in business, with cross-country Bullseye exercises, special route and practice bombing, searchlight cooperation, and day/night sorties to such targets as Cyprus, Sollum and Mersa Matruh. The odd leaflet-dropping mission to Crete was added for good measure. With the completion of the last Liberator course and the closure of the HCU in October 1945, RAF Abu Sueir reformed and welcomed two Liberator VI squadrons, Nos 40 and 104, from Italy. Both these squadrons re-equipped with Lancaster B VIIs the following January, before moving on to Shallufa in the summer of 1946. During that year Headquarters Middle East Air Force moved out of Cairo and was split between Abu Sueir and Ismailia, this remaining the situation until the HQ as a whole transferred to Nicosia in December 1954.

Political events now began to influence

208 Sqn Meteor FR9s at the top of a loop, from their base at Abu Sueir c. 1951/52. (via A Thomas)

the Station's role and, following the Egyptian Government's policy of non-cooperation in the Canal Zone, No 208 Sqn's Meteor FR9s, which had arrived in October 1951, were tasked with photographing Egyptian troop and vehicle concentrations. A sister recce squadron, No 13 with Meteor PR10s, took up post in January 1955, both units moving on to Mediterranean bases in early 1956. Abu Sueir closed in April of that year.

Akrotiri, Cyprus

Just outside the Station, on a peninsula at the southern tip of Cyprus, is Akrotiri's famous salt lake where pink flamingos mass at migration time, and one of these birds is shown in the Station badge. Although a comparatively young base, by the beginning of the 1970s it had assumed the mantle of the largest operational station in the RAF, and was described in a contemporary official guide as '... our most important multi-role base overseas.'

Formed on 1 October 1955, some six months after EOKA (the Greek Cypriot underground movement) had launched its armed struggle for union with Greece, the first unit to move in was 103 MU, whose role was that of a Third Line Servicing unit, repairing everything from aircraft to kettles. That was in November, but the following month two Prentices arrived

from Nicosia to form a Station Flight. Then, in mid-January 1956 the first visiting Hastings landed, followed six days later by the first jet aircraft, a Meteor flown by the AOC. At the end of the month the Station gained its first permanent squadron, No 13, which flew in its Meteor PR10s from Egypt. By February, visiting Hastings, Valettas, Pembrokes and Ansons were carrying out transport and general communications flying, while in March a second Meteor squadron, No 208 flying the FR9 version, took up post. At about the same time No 3 Wing RAF Regiment was established, the task of its two squadrons being to provide light anti-aircraft defence of the base. A third fighter squadron was added in April with the arrival of No 6's Venom FB4s. During the month the first Anson arrived to replace the Prentices on the Station Flight, while in May No 13 Sqn began to re-equip with Canberra PR7s.

The EOKA movement made its presence felt during the night of 7/8 June 1956 when time bombs exploded in Station buildings, and others were found wedged against the doors of a hangar containing Meteors and Venoms. But the Suez Crisis loomed even larger, and resulted in several changes to Akrotiri's order of battle. No 208 Sqn, whose Meteors lacked the range to operate effectively over Egypt, was despatched to Malta (in August) to make way for two additional Venom squadrons, No 8 from

Habbaniya and No 249 from Amman. At the same time, the first elements of two French Air Force squadrons, 3 Escadre with F-84Fs from Rheims and 33 Escadre on the RF-84F at Cognac, began arriving to operate alongside the RAF units in the Suez campaign, known as Operation Musketeer. No 13 Sqn began flying recce missions on 28 October, during the course of which an intercepting MiG damaged the elevator of a Canberra. At this point Nos 6, 8 and 249 Sqns remained on standby, but during the period 1-6 November all aircraft, including the French F-84s, mounted many sorties in support of the allied landings at Port Said. One of 8 Sqn's Venoms was lost when it hit a rise on the approach to its target at low-level.

No 73 (Venom) Sqn replaced No 8 (posted to Aden) in December, while in March 1957 No 32 Sqn moved across from Nicosia, having re-equipped with Canberra B2s in the UK. No 73 similarly re-equipped with the Canberra in March. The Middle East Communications Sqn (MECS), with its Pembrokes and Meteors, was based here from May, and on 29 June No 6 Sqn flew a final 'figure six' formation of Venoms to mark their replacement by Canberras. Earlier in the month 90 Sqn had sent in a detachment of Valiants from the UK, while

73 Sqn had sent a detachment out to Turkey.

The return of 249 Sqn (with Canberras) in October 1957 meant that the Station now had four squadrons of the aircraft operating in the bomber role, plus one in the photo-reconnaissance role. In addition to exercising with the US 6th Fleet in the Mediterranean, the Canberras mounted detachments to bases in Libya and Kenya. During the summer of 1958 two Shackletons of 38 Sqn flew over from their detachment base at Nicosia, which was somewhat overcrowded, to begin Island Patrols from Akrotiri. In November a number of Hawker Hunters, a gift to Jordan, staged through.

Following Britain's withdrawal from Iraq in 1959, and CENTO replacing the Baghdad Pact, Akrotiri's importance increased considerably, both as a staging post to the Middle East and Far East, and in providing the main air striking force for CENTO. The Canberras began participating in many CENTO exercises, providing the 'attacking force', for example, to test the air defences of Turkey, Iran and Pakistan. Exchange visits were made with Royal Rhodesian AF Canberra squadrons, while nearer at hand, Akrotiri's aircraft were able to use the Episkopi bombing

Canberra B2 WH638 of 73 Sqn at Akrotiri in 1960. (P Russell-Smith)

Lightning F3 XR749 'Q' of 56 Sqn at Akrotiri in December 1969. Behind is XP743 'G'.
(P Russell-Smith)

range which had now opened a few miles up the coast. The Station also had its own Para Medic team which carried out practice drops over the Ladies Mile beach.

During the latter part of 1959, deliveries to Akrotiri's squadrons began of the improved Canberra B6, the old B2s being ferried back to Benson in the UK. MECS activities, on the other hand, included the use of the Vickers Varsity for casevac flights as far away as El Adem. The early months of 1960 saw visits not only by such Hunter squadrons as 19, 66 and 43, but also detachments of Canberras from Germany, Valiants from the UK, together with RN Scimitars, Sea Vixens and Gannets from HMS *Ark Royal* for joint Service exercises. Another RAF/Army exercise (Swiftsure) in May attracted Beverleys from Abingdon, plus Hastings from the UK and Nicosia. Five Victors of 15 Sqn began a five-week attachment in September, their place being taken in November by four Vulcans of 617 Sqn.

The units at Akrotiri became even more diverse with the arrival in March 1964 of 29 Sqn's Javelin FAW9s in the air defence role, followed a month later by 1563 Flight with Whirlwind helicopters for search and rescue. No 13 (PR) Sqn, on the other hand, left for Malta in September 1965. The Canberra Trials and Tactical Evaluation

Unit was here from January 1966 to December 1968, while in July 1966 No 70 Sqn tranferred its Hastings from Nicosia. All the major branches of air activity were thus now represented on the Station, and that of air defence was made even more potent when, in April 1967, No 29 Sqn was replaced by No 56 Sqn with Lightning F3s.

The re-equipment programme continued apace, with 70 Sqn relinquishing its ageing Hastings, which it had flown for eleven years, in favour of the more versatile Argosy in November 1967. This turbo-prop transport, its clamshell rear doors useful for air-dropping, was used for both logistic supply and search and rescue work. In one of their stranger tasks, No 70's Argosys had International Red Cross markings applied over their national insignia for diplomatic reasons when airlifting supplies into Jordan after political unrest in the country in 1970. But perhaps the most significant change was the disbandment of the Canberra squadrons in 1969 and their replacement by two Vulcan squadrons. A special ceremony was held in January to mark the departure of Nos 6, 32, 73 and 249 Sqns which, since 1966, had formed the so-called Akrotiri Strike Wing, and the British Aircraft Corporation presented a solid silver model of the Canberra to the Station to commemorate the occasion. The two

Vulcan B2 squadrons fresh from the UK were 9 and 35, which now made up the NEAF Bomber Wing and which were a powerful weapon in the CENTO armoury. Regular deployments were made to Masirah in the Persian Gulf, together with occasional detachments to Iranian bases.

Late in 1970 No 70 Sqn began to receive Hercules although the Argosys lingered on for long enough to inspire contemporary cartoons depicting No 70 (Argules) Sqn! For their part No 56 Sqn took over No 74 Sqn's Lightning F6s as the latter unit was returning to the UK from Singapore. The Mk 6 Lightning's susceptibility to engine fires led at least one 56 Sqn pilot to present the Safety Equipment Section with a crate of Keo beer after successfully ejecting over the sea. No 1563 Flight, on the other hand, reformed its Whirlwind HAR10s into 84 Sqn. The change was effected in January 1972 and resulted in a HQ/Search and Rescue Flight at Akrotiri with yellow-painted aircraft, plus a detached Flight at Nicosia which took over the UN support role from 230 Sqn detachment and which operated camouflaged aircraft bearing UN markings. No 13 Sqn, still flying Canberras in the Photo reconnaissance role, returned from Malta for a spell lasting from January to October 1972. During its brief stay, the unit fitted in a memorable detachment to the New Hebrides. Sadly, one of the Canberras stalled and crashed during its landing approach following a practice flypast to mark the Squadron's departure.

The Station was now at a peak in its strength, which was fortunate since a peak effort was required in July and August 1974 when, in the largest peacetime airlift since the Berlin Airlift, well over 22,000 people of nearly 50 nationalities were flown out from the base, and a vast amount of refugee aid was handled following the Turkish invasion of the northern part of the island on 20 July. The Station itself was reinforced by 12 Phantoms from Nos 6 and 41 Sqns, in case of need. During the year, Akrotiri also played a significant supporting role in the Suez Canal clearance operations, including the off-loading of US Navy helicopters from C-5A Galaxies and their preparation for flying after reassembly.

In fact 1974 was a decisive year for several reasons, not least of which was Defence Minister Roy Mason's announcement to Parliament that December of major reductions to RAF units in Cyprus. Swiftly implemented, these resulted in the departure of 9 Sqn to Waddington, 35 Sqn to Scampton, 56 Sqn to Wattisham, and 70 Sqn to Lyneham, all in January 1975. No 103 MU had already disbanded, and 84 Sqn now remained as the only RAF resident flying unit on the station. But in the meantime air operations of a less overt nature had quietly begun, and in February 1975 the *Washington Post* revealed the presence of Lockheed U-2Rs at Akrotiri. Based here to keep a watchful eye on the Middle East, one of these aircraft crashed on the Station in December 1977 causing considerable damage.

Westland Wessex HAR2 XS498 of 84 Sqn comes to rest at Akrotiri after a sortie over Cyprus — August 1988. Note harlequin motif on the tail, and less visible scorpion squadron marking on the nose. (T Fairbairn)

No 5 Sqn Tornado F3s at Akrotiri for Armament Practice Camp — August 1988.
Nearest camera is ZE732 'CH' while behind is ZE780 'CF'. (T Fairbairn)

Since then the Station's main role has been to host front-line RAF squadrons from Strike Command and RAFG for Armament Practice Camps, and to act as a fair-weather training venue for such units as the Red Arrows. No 100 Sqn at Wyton has maintained a standing detachment of its target facilities Canberras for the use of the APCs, which also result in visits from supporting Hercules transports and VC10 tankers. There is a regular schedule of TriStar trooping flights. The steady pattern of APC activity was interrupted in September 1984 when a number of aircraft were deployed to the Station to provide air support for the British Forces in the Lebanon (BRITFORLEB). These comprised six Buccaneers of 12 and 208 Sqns, plus three Chinooks of 7 and 18 Sqns, the Buccaneers flying a number of low-level sorties over Beirut. No 84 Sqn, which had re-equipped with the sturdier Wessex back in early 1982, relinquished the UNFICYP support task to the Army Air Corps in October 1986. At that point the AAC was flying Alouettes, but Akrotiri handled its replacement Gazelles which were airlifted to the island by RAF Hercules in 1988.

Aqir, Palestine

Just before the outbreak of the Second World War, financial authority was given for the construction of an airfield capable of housing two permanent bomber squadrons, at Aqir, some ten miles north-west of Lydda. Work started in the late summer of 1939 and proceeded according to plan, enabling the Station to open in February 1941. The airfield underwent further development later on, eventually becoming an important base in the lines of communication to Iraq, and was ultimately used as a repair centre for the expanded air forces in Palestine and Syria.

The first flying squadron to be based here was No 6 in the army cooperation role, which used the base for a matter of days in February 1941. Equipped with Lysanders, 6 Sqn was at this point off operations. Of more significance, 250 Sqn formed here on 1 April 1941 with Curtiss Tomahawks from 'K' Flight, an ex-Gladiator unit, before moving on at the end of May to take part in the Allied action against Vichy French Forces in Syria, which began in June of that year. Between April and September a number of other squadrons spent brief periods here in connection with the Syrian campaign, including 11, 45, 55, 84, and 211 (all Blenheims), together with 80 and 450 on Hurricanes.

The principal non-operational unit here at this period was 123 Maintenance Unit, which was based at Aqir from June 1941 until February 1942. The MU's role was that of an Ammunition Storage Depot.

With the surrender of the Vichy forces and the occupation of Syria in July 1941, Aqir's squadrons had all moved on by the end of September, but the following month saw the formation here of 335 Sqn on Hurricane Is (which remained until December). October also saw the establishment of 74 OTU, whose role was to give final training to army cooperation Hurricane pilots before they were posted to operational units. The OTU's first two Hurricanes, Z4640 and Z4795, arrived from Egypt on the 19th of the month, and the Unit as a whole was based here until autumn 1943, during which time Harvards (e.g. AJ816, '839 and '840) were also used.

Apart from the OTU a number of other units operated from Aqir during the Middle East crisis of mid-summer 1942 when Rommel pushed the Eighth Army back to El Alamein. These included a detachment of Halifaxes of 10 Sqn from the UK, which was joined by 227 Sqn (non-operational) to act as a servicing unit, and a detachment of UK-based 76 Sqn, also using Halifaxes.

In August 1942 a Liberator II bomber unit, No 159 Sqn, arrived here from St Jean, and then, in a rather confusing and scantily documented administrative move, was renumbered 160 Sqn later in the month. Servicing facilities were provided by personnel from a number of other squadrons which were without aircraft at that time, the Liberators operating against targets along the North African coast and against Axis shipping in the Mediterranean. No 160 left for India in early November. One of the squadrons helping to service the 159/160 Sqn Liberators was No 454 which was properly established here with Blenheim Vs, nominally as a light bomber unit, at the end of September before leaving for Iraq the following month.

By mid-1943 74 OTU had added photo-recce courses to its syllabus and was training USAAC, Turkish, RAAF, SAAF and Egyptian pilots. It moved to Petah Tiqva, another Palestine airfield, on 20 September, but was replaced by 76 OTU which formed here on 1 October for medium bomber crew training using Wellington Ics, IIIs and Xs, plus Defiants for target-towing. With the ending of the Second World War, 76 OTU became redundant and was disbanded on 30 July 1945. Prior to the end of the war, sporadic

operational flying at Aqir was carried out by detachments of squadrons based largely in Egypt, including 294 Sqn (Wellingtons), 680 Sqn (flying PR Mosquitoes and Baltimores), and 221 Sqn (Wellington XIIIs on sea and desert rescue duties).

Aqir's diversity of roles was further widened by the establishment, in January 1945, of 160 Maintenance Unit. Based here until November 1947 its main function was that of an Aircraft Repair Unit and after the war it was responsible, for example, for scrapping numbers of Vickers Warwicks which had become surplus in the Middle East.

The back end of 1945 saw two Liberator VI squadrons (37 and 70) based here between October and December, now operating mainly in the transport role. In fact the end of the war had brought a general increase in transport activity through the Station and to provide ASR coverage for such flights, detachments of 294 Sqn's Warwicks and 621 Sqn's Wellingtons were positioned a Aqir. The latter unit moved here *in toto* during April 1946, relinquishing its Warwick Vs for Lancaster ASR IIIs at the same time, and then transferring to Ein Shemer in June. Between March and June 1946 two Spitfire squadrons, 208 with Mk VIIIs and 32 with Mk IXs, were based here for internal security duties before moving on to other airfields in Palestine.

This period saw a marked increase in tension between the Arab and Jewish communities, and as a result British paratroops were stationed in the Middle East. One of the transport squadrons involved in airlifting these troops, No 620 Sqn, was based at Aqir with its Halifax VIIs from June 1946. Dakotas and then Halifax IXs were received, taking part in searches for illegal shipping to Palestine, before 620

One of Aqir's Dakotas KG522 — c. 1946.
(K Le Masurier)

Halifax A9 RT789 at 160 MU Aqir in late 1946. (K Le Masurier)

was renumbered 113 Sqn in September 1946. No 113 disbanded here on 1 April 1947.

Using Airspeed Horsas, the Army trained glider pilots during the years 1946-7, but the last RAF flying squadron to serve here was No 215, which was on strength for most of November 1947. Formed the previous August in Egypt to fly the Middle East transport routes with Dakotas, it returned there after its brief sojourn in Palestine. In preparation for the British withdrawal from Palestine generally, RAF Station Aqir was closed on 15 January 1948.

Ascension, South Atlantic

Without Ascension Island, Britain would have been hard pressed indeed to have conducted the campaign that culminated in the successful end to the Falklands War. Located in such a vital position in the South Atlantic, it provided an indispensable theatre airhead from which to mount a wide range of air operations, both during and after the conflict.

Although Ascension Island is a British Dependency, the airfield itself, known as Wideawake, was constructed by the Americans during the Second World War as a staging post for their aircraft flying between Brazil and Africa. Later on, it was developed to accept US transport aircraft supporting the NASA tracking station which had been constructed on the island. Britain's right to use the airfield under a 1962 agreement was invoked at the start of the war in April 1982. At that stage, however, its facilities, both technical and domestic, were inadequate to accept the

heavy traffic which Operation Corporate would incur. In particular, fuel and water were in short supply and there was a lack of living accommodation. These problems were tackled by the installation of pillow tanks for aviation fuel, and the provision of tents, and later fold-up huts, the design of which led to the name 'Concertina City'.

Wideawake then became possibly the busiest airfield in the world as men and equipment began pouring in by air. At the same time, vital stores from ships of the Task Force anchored off Ascension were ferried to the airfield using an RN Wessex which had been airlifted south, together with a Chinook which had arrived on board the container ship *Atlantic Conveyor*. An RAF Sea King was later airlifted in by Heavylift Belfast, and began operating in the search and rescue role.

The first aircraft to be deployed on a formal detachment basis were the Nimrod MR1s of 42 Sqn on 6 April. Their tasks included providing communications links and surface search ahead of the Fleet, activities which were made more interesting by the presence of Soviet intelligence vessels. The Nimrods were followed on 18 April by five Victor tankers, together with four more the next day, which immediately began flying not air-to-air refuelling (AAR) sorties, but maritime radar reconnaissance (MRR) missions in support of a small naval force which had been detached from the main Task Force to head for South Georgia. Following the arrival of Nimrod MR2s, modified for AAR and equipped with Searchwater radar, the Victors were able to revert to their more familiar AAR role, although their MRR capability (for which they had been specially modified) was retained. By the end of April, Hercules were making regular airdrops to ships at sea, and Vulcans had arrived to make their input to proceedings.

The first Vulcan sortie of Operation Black Buck took place on 1 May, when at 0235 hours Flight Lieutenant Martin Withers took off in XM607 to bomb Stanley airfield in the longest-ranging bomb raid in aviation history. A second Black Buck raid was mounted on 4 May, and in addition the Vulcans flew anti-radar attacks throughout the course of the conflict. Each mission required intricate AAR support from up to 18 Victor tankers. Thus, with the start of Vulcan sorties the Victors' workload increased enormously, crews being required to fly at five times their normal rate. In addition to topping up RAF Harrier GR3s flying direct from

England to Ascension during 3–6 May, the tankers began refuelling Nimrods in early May and Hercules towards the middle of the month. RN Sea Harriers had arrived earlier and six of these, together with six of the RAF GR3s, flew aboard the *Atlantic Conveyor* which then sailed to join the carrier Task Group. The departure of the RAF Harriers left a gap in the air defence of the island which was now filled by three Phantoms which flew direct from the UK, again with Victor tanker support.

Following the recapture of the Falklands, Ascension's role remained as a vital staging post on the resupply route to the islands. Initially this was a tortuous process due to the lack of a serviceable runway at Stanley. Passengers and airportable freight were flown from the UK to Ascension by VC10, Hercules and Heavylift Belfast. Passengers and routine freight were then transferred (by Ascension-based helicopter) to vessels moored at sea off the island for onward movement to the Falklands. High priority freight, on the other hand, was loaded on to Hercules at Ascension to be airdropped at Stanley. The Hercules employed on this task had been specially modified to enable them to be air-to-air refuelled. During one such 'round

trip' on 18 June, 70 Sqn's Flight Lieutenant Terry Locke and crew flying XV179 undertook a flight lasting 28 hours 4 minutes – a record for the 'Herc'. During the sortie, the purpose of which was to drop missile spares to a Rapier Unit on Sapper Hill, East Falklands, 179 was refuelled twice by Victor tanker. The disparity of Hercules and Victor airspeeds made this a tricky operation – which was later overcome by the introduction of Ascension-based Hercules tankers which were then used to refuel the 'airbridge' Hercules transports. The gruelling airdrops ended in late June, when Stanley's runway opened to Hercules traffic.

Ascension's link with the UK was given a shot in the arm in 1983 when British Airways Boeing 747s began to appear on the route in place of RAF VC10s. The turnround of the first 'Jumbo' drew much interest, its take-off producing a vast cloud of volcanic dust which engulfed the MV *Keren* anchored off the end of the runway. Heavylift Belfasts were running a twice-weekly schedule at this point and the year also saw the arrival of the inaugural TriStar. When the Mount Pleasant runway, capable of accepting wide-bodied jets, opened in May 1985 the Falkands were at

British Airways Boeing 747 taking off spectacularly from Ascension in 1983. (S Crockatt)

Hercules XV204, framed by the wing of Heavylift Belfast, at Ascension in 1983. Overhead a Wessex ferries stores to a ship moored off the coast. (S Crockatt)

last linked in some comfort by air to Ascension and thus the world at large.

Today (1991) Ascension has settled into a steady routine as a rather pleasant staging post where RAF TriStars and Hercules rub shoulders with USAF C-141s. This, together with its benign climate, makes it an agreeable spot in which to serve. But for a growing number of individuals (the author included!) who have completed a 'real' South Atlantic tour – in the Falklands – it is remembered as the first stepping stone in that long but keenly anticipated journey back home to the UK.

Belize

The second smallest country on the American continent, Belize lies on the east coast of the Central American isthmus, bordered by Mexico to the north and Guatemala to the south and west. A British dependency, known until June 1973 as British Honduras, it received its independence in September 1981. The presence of British forces is due to Guatemala's long-standing claim to the country, which first led to the deployment of British troops here in 1948. The immediate threat receded, but tension heightened on a number of occasions, and faced with the possibility of an invasion by Guatemala in 1975, RAF Pumas and

Harriers were flown in to help defend the country against any aggression. These aircraft are based at Belize International Airport, the location of the headquarters of all British forces at what is known as Airport Camp. A Wing Commander acts as Air Commander for the RAF elements.

The first RAF aircraft to appear were three Pumas of 33 Sqn which were flown in aboard two Belfast transports on 11 October 1975. These were operational by the 15th, and there has been a Puma detachment, later designated 1563 Flight, even since, drawn from both 33 Sqn and 230 OCU in the UK. Next came the Harriers, six aircraft provided by 1 Sqn and 233 OCU at Wittering, which flew out from the UK on 5 November. The Harriers remained until 19 April 1976, when an easing of tension permitted their withdrawal and they were airlifted home by Belfast and Hercules. Following another deterioration in the political situation, a further six Harriers were deployed on 5 July 1977, maintaining an unbroken presence in the guise of 1417 Flight, using the resources of both the UK and the Germany Harrier squadrons. The Army added its own Scout AH1 helicopters operating mainly in support of the Force HQ, and an RAF Regiment Rapier missile squadron was established for short range air defence. Westland/Aérospatiale Gaz-

Above *Puma HC1 ZA938 'CW' of 33 Sqn reflecting the sun at Belize International Airport.* (J Webber)

Below *1417 Flight Harrier GR3 XZ998 'G' in its hide at Belize International Airport.* (J Webber)

elles replaced the Scouts in November 1979.

Operating from two self-contained hides at Airport Camp, and at a constant state of operational readiness, the Harriers perform in the air defence, close air support and reconnaissance roles, photographs taken on recce missions being processed by a Reconnaissance Intelligence Centre. Frequent patrols are flown in Belizean airspace, and training sorties are mounted using practice bombs, 30 mm cannon and 38 mm SNEB rockets on local ranges. Whenever possible, joint exercises are conducted with the Army, the Gazelles acting as Forward Air Controllers. The helicopters also provide recce and resupply support for the Army Battlegroups (made up of infantry units), and act as Air Observation Posts for the artillery.

The Pumas, on the other hand, not only support the Army, transporting troops, supplies and light guns, but also provide search and rescue casualty evacuation facilities, including the airlift of Belize civilians in emergencies. Considerable assistance generally is given to the local civil community, the Pumas for example flying in surgical teams to otherwise inaccessible villages in the interior. 1563 Flight has also responded to international disasters, and two Pumas were sent to Palanquero, Colombia in November 1985 following the Nevado Del Ruiz volcanic eruption. The helicopters airlifted casualties and medical supplies, while the Belize Tactical Air Operations Centre provided a communications link wherever it was needed.

Air transport support for the forces based in Belize is provided by scheduled RAF Hercules and VC10s, though for a while Red Coat Air Cargo operated a Ministry of Defence freight contract using Britannias. How long these forces will remain in the country is currently (October 1989) anybody's guess.

Benina, Libya

Located outside Benghazi in that part of Libya known as Cyrenaica, Benina first appears in the air warfare history books in December 1940, when, as a large Italian base in North Africa, it was raided by RAF Blenheims. By February 1941 Cyrenaica was in British hands, bringing in a detachment of Blenheims from 55 Sqn, then based at Heliopolis, Egypt, and 3 Sqn RAAF with Hurricanes for air defence. With the arrival of the Germans in North Africa that month and the subsequent loss

of Cyrenaica, it was not until January 1942 that the RAF was back, again in the shape of No 55's Blenheims, joined by the Hurricanes of 260 Sqn. Scores of wrecked German aircraft were found on the airfield. Before the year was out several other Hurricane squadrons, including Nos 238, 33 and 274, had arrived for brief periods.

In December 1942 No 245 Wing disbanded at Kilo 40, its personnel leaving to take over RAF Station Benina. The following month saw brief stays by two distinguished Middle East bomber squadrons, Nos 37 and 70, both with Wellingtons. During the early part of 1943 there was considerable activity, particularly in the way of transport aircraft, both British and American. The eighteen B-24 Liberators of the 98th Bomb Group which arrived in February would, six months later, be slogging it out over Ploesti. Another Liberator, this time from the 376th Bomb Group, caused some anxiety in September by making several down-wind approaches, but it eventually landed safely! Between April and August No 162 Sqn was here, summoned with its Wellingtons to augment the Western Desert bombing force. A weather service for these units was provided by the Gladiators of No 1563 Meteorological Flight.

Two fighter squadrons used the airfield for operations in January 1944, No 33 with Spitfire Vcs and No 335 (Hellenic) with Mk Vbs, while in April the first Yugoslav squadron in the RAF was formed here with Hurricane IICs. This was No 352 Sqn, followed in July by a second similar unit, No 351 Sqn. By the middle of the year the flow of traffic was such that a Reception Flight had been formed to carry out daily inspections and maintenance. Its customers were Beaufighters, Baltimores, C-46 Commandos, C-47 Dakotas (RAF and US), Lockheed Lodestars, Marauders, Martinets, Mitchells, Proctors, Spitfire Vs and IXs, Hurricanes, Warwicks, Wellingtons and Ansons. Sea and desert rescue duties were performed by a detachment of 221 Sqn Wellington XIIIs during 1945.

The start of 1946 saw Benina with a number of diverse functions: it was handling Middle East transport aircraft, there was a Communications Flight with a Baltimore and a Proctor, air/sea/desert rescue duties were covered by a detachment of 621 Sqn's Warwicks, and No 1563 Met Flight was daily plodding skyward in Spitfire Vcs. In addition, the Aircraft Safety Centre, Cyrenaica was located here with responsibility for aerial lighthouses and the two long-range Fairmile launches of No 101 Marine Craft Unit based in the port of Benghazi. The Station was allotted its own Anson PH612 in July. The diversity of aircraft types handled ranged from BA Swallow G-AECA being flown to South Africa, through Bristol Wayfarer G-AHJD operated by Airwork on contract to the Sudan Government, to B-17 Flying Fortress of the 365th Bomb Group photo-surveying the Tripoli-Benghazi area.

The pattern for 1947 was, if anything, more exotic. The Crown Prince of Egypt landed in his Proctor SU-ACH (the following year he burst a tyre here while taxiing in his Miles Gemini), Handley Page Haltons of London Air Motor Services rubbed shoulders with French Air Force Marylands and Ansons, not to mention the routine BOAC Yorks and Dakotas. When BOAC York G-AGNP force-landed 30 miles to the south due to lack of fuel, Benina despatched a supply of aviation gasoline to enable the aircraft to complete its journey. In fact such was the civilian activity that BOAC staff took over much of the signals work, while Shell staff took over refuelling of aircraft. On the military side, visitors included RAF aircraft from the Malta, Middle East, East African, and Levant Communications Flights.

By the very nature of this air traffic, there were many instances of machines being overdue, and any visiting aircraft that happened to be on the airfield at the time would be asked to carry out an air search of the surrounding desert. Thus, in January 1948 an RN Expediter of No 728 Sqn (Malta) was ordered up to locate a missing de Havilland Dove on delivery to the Egyptian Air Force. Often the visitors would have serviceability problems requiring attention. For example, when Tempest NX201 landed in December 1949, *en route* to Manston, it was found to have consumed five gallons of oil in 55 minutes. A spare oil feed pipe was flown in. Mosquito RG299 landed with fuel leaking into the cockpit, but what proved to be a badly distorted filler pipe was soon remedied.

One of the last incidents of Benina's career as an RAF station, and sadly one for which it is well remembered, was the tragic accident to Hastings TG574 of No 53 Sqn in 1950. Returning home to the United Kingdom from Singapore, the aircraft had taken off from El Adem on the night of 20 December *en route* for Castel Benito, when one of its engines shed a propellor blade. This smashed its way into the fuselage,

severing the tail control rods and mortally wounding the resting co-pilot. Perilously close to losing control of the stricken machine the captain, Flight Lieutenant Graham Tunnadine, made for Benina, which he would normally have overflown. With great skill Tunnadine lined up on the runway lights, only to lose sight of them at the last moment when they were obscured by a hillock. The Hastings then hit the ground about 400 yards short of the runway, bounced and lost its starboard wing which was ripped off. The ensuing impact killed the four crew members on the flight deck, though more than twenty passengers were able to scramble out comparatively unscathed. Tunnadine and his crew were awarded the King's Commendation for Valuable Service in the Air.

From April 1951 the main task was the handover of the airfield's facilities to the Foreign Office Administration of African Territories, and the Station closed in September of that year.

Brüggen, Germany

'The task of this Station in peace is to train for war – Don't you forget it', proclaimed the terse notice at the entrance to RAF Brüggen, a succint reminder, if indeed one were needed, of the role of this important strike/attack base in RAFG. Begun in 1952, construction was completed twelve months later in July 1953, in time for the first squadron to move in during the month. This was No 112, formerly at Jever, with Vampire FB5s. Operating principally in the fighter/ground attack role, the Squadron's Vampires were soon sporting the distinctive 'sharks's teeth' markings already made famous on the Luftwaffe Bf 110s of II/ZG 76 and the Curtiss Tomahawks and Kittyhawks which 112 flew in the Western Desert in the Second World War. Exercises took up a large proportion of the flying hours, and for these 112 maintained a high degree of mobility within the 2nd TAF.

Another important unit to be taken on strength during 1953 was the General Equipment Park, which in 1960 became the more familiar 431 Maintenance Unit. But Brüggen was principally a fighter station, and to confirm this 112 Sqn was joined, in August 1953, by 130 Sqn which reformed here with North American Sabre F4s. This swept-wing 700 mph fighter was a considerable improvement on the Vampire and 112 Sqn took delivery of its own Sabres in January 1954. When two further Sabre squadrons, Nos 67 and 71 were relocated from Wildenrath in July 1955, Brüggen could boast a potent interceptor Wing at a period of rather tense East-West relations. The Sabre, though, was an interim measure pending the availability of the British-built Hawker Hunter, which was duly issued to all four squadrons in April and May 1956. These squadrons, however, did not last for long, and as a result of a general pruning of the 2nd TAF all four were disbanded on 31 May 1957.

Having lost all its flying squadrons in one fell swoop, it was a matter of only days before replacement units began moving in, and units with widely-ranging roles at that. First to arrive (in June, from Laarbruch) was 80 Sqn whose task was to carry out high and low-level strategic and tactical reconnaissance for the 2nd TAF using its Canberra PR7s. Next unit in (during July) was 87 Sqn which, alongside 68 Sqn based elsewhere, was providing the 2nd TAF's night fighter capability with Meteor NF11s. Finally, at the other end of the operational spectrum, came 213 Sqn in August with Canberra B(I)6s for light bombing and night intruder work. This period of varied operations came to an end in 1969 when all three squadrons disbanded *in situ*, No 80 in September followed by 87 and 213 in December.

A new era began in 1970 when no less than three Phantom FGR2 squadrons reformed on the Station, the first of which was No 14 on 1 July and which was also the first such unit in RAFG. Nos 17 and 2 had followed suit by the end of the year, while a fourth, No 31, was added in July 1971. Replacing the Canberras in the Command, the Phantoms combined the photo-reconnaissance role (No 2 Sqn) with a powerful ground attack capability.

A more economic (single seat and lower thrust) ground attack aircraft lay in the Jaguar, which began to replace the Phantom in this role at Brüggen in December 1975 when 14 Sqn reformed with the type. Using the overlapping 'Designate' squadron system to maintain continuity of front-line forces, 17 Sqn similarly re-equipped in February 1976, followed by 31 Sqn in June. A fourth squadron, No 20, reformed here on Jaguars in March 1977 after disbanding at Wildenrath as a Harrier unit. With its very sophisticated nav/attack system (NAVWASS) and Westing-house/Ferranti laser rangefinder, the Jaguar became a classic ground attack type in the Hunter mould. Brüggen's Jaguars also had a nuclear strike potential and in this role the aircraft had a greater range than the Phantom. No 2 Sqn, on the other hand, continued to specialize in tactical reconnaissance, all squadrons eventually operating from newly constructed

17 Sqn Phantom FGR2 XV468 'B' at Brüggen in June 1971. (P Russell-Smith)

Hardened Aircraft Shelters on the Station. In addition to exercises in Europe the Jaguars flew as far afield as Canada, with 20 Sqn being the first (together with 6 Sqn from the UK) to participate in the Maple Flag series at Cold Lake, Alberta in October–November 1979.

Tornado GR1s then replaced the Jaguars on an overlap basis at Brüggen, with 31 Sqn the first to become operational on the type in November 1984. 17 Sqn was next, in March 1985, followed by 15 Sqn eight months later. Meanwhile, in June 1984, 20 Sqn had moved out to Laarbruch to become a Tornado unit itself, but in October 1986 the number of Tornado squadrons was made up to four with the arrival from Honington, UK, of 9 Sqn. Each squadron has twelve or thirteen aircraft, including two with dual controls for continuation training, and each aircraft carries individual and squadron code letters on its fin.

Since April 1976 Brüggen has had the services of 37 Sqn, RAF Regiment with its Rapier short-range SAMs for Low-Level Air Defence. In addition, 25 Sqn on Bloodhound II missiles was headquartered here from January 1981, returning to the UK (Wyton) in March 1983. Outranking them all in terms of longevity of tenure, though, is 431 MU which reports directly to HQ RAFG and which is divided into four squadrons. Cat 3 aircraft repairs and modifications are handled by the MU's Aircraft Engineering Sqn, while the Propulsion Sqn is responsible for the repair of Tornado and Jaguar engines. MT and general engineering support fall to the Mechanical Engineering Ground Sqn, and last but by no means least the Supply Sqn stores and issues a wide range of equipment and spares, including conventional explosives.

Butterworth, Malaya

In December 1941 British airfields in Northern Malaya came under heavy Japanese air attack, and the situation was becoming desperate. By the 8th, the airfields of Singora and Patani, just over the border in Thailand, were in enemy hands and an allied attack on them was essential if the Japanese raids originating from them were to be stemmed. Accordingly, on 9 December, the remaining machines from two badly depleted Blenheim squadrons, Nos 34 and 62, attempted two counter-attacks. The first mission was successful, but just before the

second could be launched. Japanese bombers arrived overhead as the Blenheims were preparing to take off. Only one Blenheim, piloted by Flight Lieutenant A. S. K. Scarf, was able to leave the ground. Undaunted by the vulnerability of his solitary aircraft, Scarf headed for his target, the aircraft at Singora. There, in spite of being attacked by fighters, he dropped his bombs but was hit in the back and left arm and mortally wounded. Struggling to maintain consciousness, he turned back to the Malayan border and although now very weak from loss of blood, he managed to put the Blenheim down in a padi field near Alor Star. His navigator was unhurt but Scarf himself died that night from his wounds. His actions were recognized five years later in the award of the Victoria Cross, Malaya's first.

The airfield from which Scarf had struggled into the air was Butterworth, situated at the northern end of Malaya's west coast. Opening in October 1941 the Station was still under Care and Maintenance when Japanese air raids began in December. It was to this somewhat inadequate environment that a number of flying units were sent to consolidate during December, including Nos 27, 34 and 62 Sqns (all Blenheims), together with the Brewster Buffaloes of 21 Sqn, RAAF. Later in the day of Scarf's fateful mission the Station suffered yet another low-level attack, in which aircraft on the ground were picked off one by one. So bad was the position that 62 Sqn, with two serviceable machines, was withdrawn to Taiping while 21 Sqn's six marginally effective Buffaloes were sent to Ipoh. No 27 Sqn, a Blenheim night fighter unit, had no machines to send anywhere.

After the war in the Pacific the Station reformed in January 1946 and for six months was the HQ for 231 Air Sea Rescue Unit, whose motor launches carried out anti-smuggling patrols in local waters. Another arrival at the beginning of the year was 47 Sqn whose period of tenure, with Mosquito FBVIs, was even shorter. Later in the year it was announced that the future role of the Station, which was already handling transitting Yorks, Expediters, Mosquitoes, Spitfires, Beaufighters, Mitchells and Dakotas, would be that of a permanent staging post and heavy bomber airfield. Accordingly, a York of 511 Sqn from the UK arrived in October to carry out take-off tests. By the end of 1946 1300 Meteorological Flight was established for daily PAMPA weather sorties. Lack of wood for repairs grounded the Mosquitoes for a long time, and training sorties in the Flight's Harvard were all that could be managed.

By March 1947 some civilian traffic was being handled; an Airspeed Consul of Malayan Airways made several visits while surveying proposed air routes, and other callers included South Eastern Airways and Orient Airways. Vickers Viking G–AJJN passed through on a test flight to New Zealand in April, while in May RN Seafires and Fireflies disembarked from HMS *Theseus* for local flying. Equipped with Beaufighters and Harvards, 27 Armament Practice Camp was established here in early 1949 as a training facility for FEAF's front-line squadrons.

Although the Malayan Emergency had begun in mid-1948, Butterworth did not become heavily involved until the spring of 1950, when it began hosting detachments of fighters and light bombers needed to provide air support in Northern Malaya. One of the first such units to be taken on strength was 33 Sqn (in May) with Tempest F2s which carried out rocket attacks on bandit positions. By early 1951 the poor serviceability of the Tempests, the last in

RAF service, led to their replacement by de Havilland Hornets. During the first week of Operation Sword (which lasted from July 1953 to March 1954), the Hornets took part in attacks on known terrorist camps in Malaya. Since Butterworth was only 30 miles away, 33 Sqn was able to put its Hornets over the target area continually during daylight. In 1954, as part of Operation Eclipse, the Hornets struck at targets pinpointed by Austers. In addition to Beaufighters, Brigands and Vampires, the Station also handled Yorks, Dakotas, Austers, and the occasional Lincoln from Singapore. Operating alongside these regular forces was the Penang Squadron of the Malayan Auxiliary Air Force which, with Tiger Moths, Harvards and later Chipmunks, mounted low-level reconnaissance sorties over a seven-year period beginning in 1950

The succession of detachments reached a milestone in February 1955 with the arrival of four Canberra B6s of 101 Sqn from the UK – the first RAF jet bomber squadron to fly on war operations. No 101 was succeeded by Canberra detachments from 617, 12, and 9 Sqns, which in effect replaced the earlier Lincoln detachments at Tengah.

Rocket-armed Hornets of 33 Sqn about to take off from Butterworth on a strike against communist terrorists in the Malayan jungle. (A Wallace via P Porter)

On the last day of March 1955, 33 Sqn amalgamated with another Far East Hornet squadron, No 45 at Tengah, under the latter's numberplate and based at Butterworth. However, the Squadron soon began retraining on the jet Vampire prior to re-equipping with Venoms in October, when it also moved to Hong Kong. The Hornets were flown to Seletar for scrapping, but sadly not before two had collided and crashed into a padi field within sight of Butterworth.

In a changing political and military scene, Butterworth was handed over on 1 July 1958 to the RAAF which had plans to use it as the base for a fighter and bomber Wing under the build-up of the Commonwealth Strategic Reserve in Malaya. Nos 2 and 3 Sqns (Canberras and Sabres respectively) of the RAAF arrived in November, joining small, periodic detachments of RAF Bomber Command Valiants. A further RAAF Sabre squadron, No 77, was added in 1959, intended but not needed for the Firedog campaign, which was drawing to a close. Although the airfield was now under RAAF ownership, RAF units continued to be based here. No 110 Sqn with Sycamore and Whirlwind helicopters moved in during September 1959, tasked with resupplying forward postions and casualty evacuation, finally departing for Seletar in 1964, while in 1960 it became home for 52 Sqn's Valettas, which remained until April 1966. The late 1950s and 1960s also saw many Bomber Command Vulcan detachments from the UK mounted in response to both Firedog (Vulcan B1s) and the later Indonesian Confrontation (Vulcan B2s). Later still it was used by the RAAF's 3 and 75 Sqns on Mirage IIIs in the fighter/ground attack role, together with Dakotas of 38 Sqn on search and rescue and utility work.

Calafrana/Kalafrana, Malta

During the latter half of 1915 the Germans had some fifteen submarines operating in the Mediterranean area, initially in the Aegean but later futher west in the Mediterranean itself. After the sensational sinking of the battleships *Triumph* and *Majestic* off the Dardenelles by the *U-21*, it was clear that some form of countermeasure was necessary to protect the shipping route between Gibraltar and the Aegean. Senior Naval Officer Malta suggested basing a small airship on the island, but the Admiralty felt that seaplanes, or better still flying boats, would

be more effective in patrolling the area. A survey undertaken to find a suitable site for a 'seaplane shed' and slipway soon identified a location on the western shore of Marsa Scirocco Bay. The Admiralty authorized work to start at the end of January 1916, and the base opened the following July.

At the end of July five Curtiss H4 Small America flying boats were flown out from Felixstowe to begin patrolling the approaches to Malta, and if not overwhelmingly effective in their occasional attacks on enemy submaries, they undoubtedly proved their worth in reporting the presence of the subs to convoys. In March 1917 three Short Type 184 seaplanes arrived from Dundee as replacements for the Americas, several of which had been written off, while on 27 June two small FBA two-seat flying boats were added. Later in the summer yet more FBAs (three) and 184s (six) were taken on charge to make up numbers. Patrols to locate the growing number of hostile submarines were mounted throughout 1917.

On 1 April 1918 Calafrana became an RAF seaplane base under the command of Colonel C. J. R. Randall, and during the summer two DH9s took off from the nearby Marsa sports ground to search for submarines when the sea state prevented seaplane operations. The DH9s were reportedly the first shore-based operational aircraft in Malta. Naturally enough the RAF presence now began to increase, and in August 268 Sqn formed here from one of the ex-RNAS seaplane Flights. Equipped with Short 184s and 320s, the Squadron flew anti-submarine patrols in the Central Mediterranean, until its disbandment in October 1919. No 268 was joined by 267 Sqn which formed in October 1918, again from ex-RN resources, but equipped initially with Felixstowe F2As and Short 184s. No 267's role was aerial support for the Mediterranean fleet, but from its base here one of the Squadron's F2As named 'Neptune' undertook a particularly epic flight to Gibraltar in May 1922. Felixstowe F3s and Fairey IIIDs were successively received, before disbandment in August 1923.

Following a reorganization of the RAF in Malta, Calafrana became a self-accounting unit on 1 August 1923, comprising an HQ and a resident Flight, No 481, which took over 267 Sqn's men and machines. Throughout the 1920s many of the Fleet Fighter and Spotter Flights'

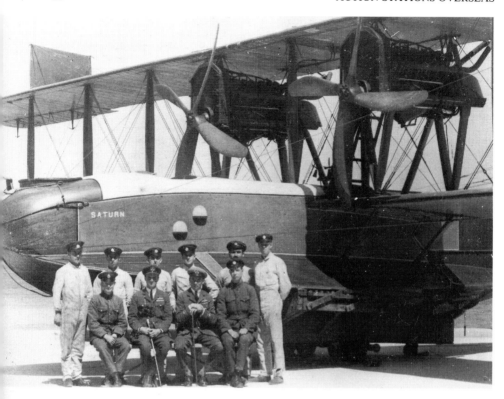

Felixstowe F2A of 267 Sqn Calafrana in 1922. (MoD Crown Copyright)

seaplanes disembarked to Calafrana from their parent ships anchored in Grand Harbour, but on 1 January 1929 481 Flight, now operating Fairey IIIDs, was re-numbered as 202 Sqn, remaining in Malta until moving on to Gibraltar at the outbreak of the Second World War. In addition to its primary role of coastal reconnaissance, No 202 set off on an Eastern Mediterranean cruise in July 1931 and an even more ambitious flight to Khartoum the following year.

Throughout the 1930s the Station, known at this stage as RAF Base Cala-frana, handled many visiting seaplanes and flying boats. For example in July 1930 a composite Flight of four Fairey IIIFs and two Blackburn Ripons disembarked from HMS *Glorious*, while in February 1931 three Short Rangoons of 203 Sqn staged through on their way from England to Basrah, Iraq. In May 1932 there were visits from flying boats of France's 3rd and 4th Aviation Regiments, and in August one of three 204 Sqn Supermarine Southamptons which had arrived from Naples and Corfu required

engine changes and overhaul. No 209 Sqn flew out Blackburn Iris S1593 from the UK in June 1933 to begin a detachment which included a cruise of the Greek Islands in November. Tragically, one of two Short Singapores of 210 Sqn which left Naples for Calafrana in February 1935, *en route* to Singapore, crashed in the Sicilian mountains killing all nine occupants.

On the civil front, Short Kent flying boats of Imperial Airways operating the Brindisi-Alexandria route began to call in from March 1935, having been temporarily diverted from Athens 'due to a revolution there'! Two months later 202 Sqn took delivery of Supermarine Scapas, which were soon engaged in anti-submarine patrols for the Mediterranean fleet.

In December 1936 the spelling of the Station name was altered to 'Kalafrana', in accordance with local ordinances. Earlier in the year, on 15 July, no less than four Fleet Air Arm Catapult Flights had been formed with Kalafrana as their dis-embarked base. These were Nos 701 (Hawker Ospreys, Fairey IIIFs, Blackburn

Sharks, Fairey Seals and Swordfish); 705 (Swordfish and Sharks); 711 (Ospreys then Walruses); and 713 (Ospreys then Fairey Seafoxes). (The Flights all achieved squadron status in 1939, but were amalgamated into 700 Sqn elsewhere in early 1940.)

During September 1937, Short Singapores of 209 and 210 Sqns operated briefly from the base on anti-piracy patrols, for the benefit of British shipping during the Spanish Civil War. The patrols were continued by 202 Sqn. By May 1939 the Station was overhauling and repairing the Saro Londons with which 202 Sqn was now equipped, together with machines from Gibraltar. In addition, there were visits by UK-based Sunderlands of 228 Sqn. Plans were already in hand for 202 Sqn to move to Gibraltar, and these were put into effect in September 1939.

The base received its first bombs of the war in June 1940, which included a direct hit on the north slipway. Sunderlands of 228 (based here from September 1940–March 1941) and 230 Sqns had recently begun patrols in cooperation with the Navy, and in July they tangled with enemy fighters. A London (K5261), attached from 202 Sqn for A/S patrols, was attacked by

Italian Fiat CR 42s, one of which was shot down. By the beginning of July there had been numerous high-level raids on Malta as a whole, but on 4 July the Station defences were able to open up on the first low-level raider on nearby Hal Far, as it overflew Kalafrana. The following day a French Latécoère 298B torpedo-carrying floatplane arrived from Bizerta, the crew of two saying they wished to serve in the RAF. In November the Sunderlands escorted in a delivery flight of Hurricanes, while the Latécoère carried out three photo recce sorties. During the month one of the Sunderlands failed to return.

February 1941 found 228's Sunderlands undertaking communications flights between the Middle East and Gibraltar, but on a more irregular note a captured Heinkel 115 floatplane arrived from the UK in June to begin clandestine operations. The Heinkel was lost on 22 September, and although wreckage was spotted some 20 miles off Malta, no trace was found of the crew. Around this time a Rescue Flight was based here whose types included the Walrus flying boat and float-equipped Swordfish.

Flying boats were particularly vulnerable to enemy action and whilst on the slipway, Sunderland W3996 received a direct hit

Fairey IIIFs of 202 Sqn at Calafrana in June 1935. (202 Sqn via R C B Ashworth)

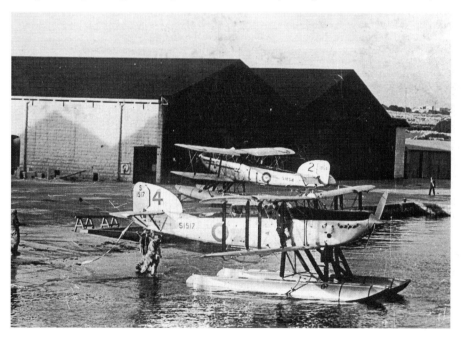

Sunderland N9021 at Kalafrana in April 1939. (via R C B Ashworth)

from a bomb in February 1942. T9046 was damaged in a low-level attack by two Me 109s later in the month, and sank in a storm the following day. Throughout the year the Marine Craft Section did sterling work rescuing downed crews with its high-speed launches. By February 1943 alerts were still being sounded, but no raids actually materialized. Sunderland EJ131 of 230 Sqn had carried out four A/S patrols in January but in February the number dwindled to two with no ops at all after that. Three USAAF Catalinas arrived for ASR work in July, and one Hurricane pilot was picked up. The remaining war years were quiet for Kalafrana, and on 30 June 1946 the base was handed over to the Royal Navy. There is no recorded use for it after that date.

Castel Benito/Idris, Libya

RAF Idris received its official station badge in July 1958. Depicting a terrestrial globe girdled by a chain and centred by a springing gazelle, the badge symbolized the close ties between the Station and the aircraft of RAF Transport Command, which were such regular users of the airfield at that point. Up until July 1952, however, the airfield had been known by its more familiar wartime title of Castel Benito (the change to 'Idris' was made at the request of the Libyans), and it is from the war years

that its RAF history dates.

Captured from the retreating Axis powers in January 1943 after the Battle of El Alamein, prior to that it had been an Italian showpiece airfield located some 20 miles inland from Tripoli. When it formed on 17 February 1943 it was relatively unscathed from Allied attacks, though certain facilities had been sabotaged by its previous Axis tenants. The new landlord was the Western Desert Air Force whose operational squadrons here in January/February included, wholly or partly, Nos 92, 145, 417 and 1 (SAAF) all with Spitfires, No 73 with Hurricanes, No 89 on Beaufighters, Nos 112, 250 and 450 all using the Kittyhawk, while the USAAF's 12th Bomb Group had flown in its B–25 Mitchells.

Following hard on the heels of these early units came (most of them only briefly) a detachment of 680 Sqn (a photo recce unit with Spitfires and Beaufighters), 6 Sqn (Hurricanes), 117 and 216 Sqns (both Hudsons), and from the USAAF the 316th Troop Carrier Group (Dakotas) together with the 316th Fighter Sqn (part of the 79th Fighter Group) on Curtiss P–40 Warhawks. Later, in August, came a detachment of Beaufighters from No 108 Sqn in Malta. For the remainder of the war years no permanent units were based here, though the flow of the transients remained

Castel Benito's own Anson C19, VL306, pictured in November 1949. (P Cook)

considerable – there were 776 in January 1944, for example.

With the ending of hostilities the Station was actively involved in the repatriation of troops by air from the Far East, in the process of which Stirling V PJ950 crashed just after take-off, and Liberator VIII KN758 from Bassingbourn was written off after undershooting. In an effort to make life pleasanter for visitors the Station Baltimore was despatched to Rome in February 1946, to bring back paintings and reproductions for the walls of the aircrew buffet and the transit hotel! In April of that year the Station replaced Luqa (Malta) as a trunk route staging post for BOAC and RAF Transport Command.

The Italian connection was revived with the visit, in October 1946, of Commandante Ragazzi to discuss the possibility of an airline operation over a route embracing Padua-Rome-Catania-Castel Benito. The airline was to be known as Alitalia. From July 1947, BOAC handled all civil aircraft passing through. Travelling somewhat faster than the commerical types was Canberra B2 WD962 which, arriving to carry out ejection seat trials, set a new record of 2 hr 41 min 49.5 sec between London and Castel Benito.

The many units utilizing the Station's Tarhuna weapons range included Malta-based Vampire squadrons, both RAF and RAAF, while in October 1952 two Austers of 651 Sqn were detached in for spotting duties. Regular weekend visits were made by UK-based Valettas carrying student navigators and later on, Varsities in the same role would become equally familiar. The Mau Mau Campaign saw the Station processing Hastings airlifting troops from the United Kingdom to Kenya (Operation Nicotine) in March 1953.

Already a popular venue for trials and record-breaking attempts, Idris now began to specialize in this activity with the arrival in September 1953 of Supermarine Swift F4 WK198, flown by Mike Lithgow, for a successful bid on the World's Absolute Air Speed Record. Canberra B2 WH699 Aries IV, from RAF Flying College, Manby, sped through in December 1953 on its record-breaking flight from London to Capetown, while in September 1954 Britannia prototype G–ALBO flew in for tropical trials.

In one of its more unusual roles the Station Anson was fitted out for locust spraying in June 1955 following a request for assistance from the Libyan authorities after their own Piper Cub had been grounded for an engine change. At the same time three Austers of 1908 AOP Flight based at Idris were active in the comms and recce roles on behalf of locust control officers in outlying desert districts,

Hawker Sea Furies of 804 Sqn RN at Castel Benito in November 1950. (P Cook)

which frequently involved landing on difficult desert tracks.

Idris became an important trials airfield in June with the permanent relocation here from Khartoum of the Tropical Experimental Unit, airlifted in by Hastings TG500 and '502, to together with York MW234. (The unit operated at that time under the auspices of the Ministry of Supply.) The trials programme for 1955 began immediately with the arrival of Auster AOP9 WZ677 aboard a Bristol Freighter. Other new types to sweat it out during 1955 included Sea Venoms WM575 and WZ894 (supported by Bristol Freighter XJ470 from A&AEE, Boscombe Down), Blackburn Beverley XB262 with Westland Whirlwind XD164, Fairey Gannet WN372, Vickers Valiant WP205, and Canberra (B(I)8 WT326. Otherwise full of interest, the year was marred by the loss of BOAC Argonaut G-ALHL, which crashed some 900 yards from the runway threshold in September.

Throughout the 1950s there were periodic Canberra detachments from both the United Kingdom (Nos 18, 109 and 12 Sqns) and Germany (No 69 Sqn). Finally, until its closure in late 1966, Idris retained the dual roles of staging post and location for the Tropical Experimental Unit, whose title and controlling authority had meanwhile evolved into Overseas Experimental Unit and Ministry of Aviation respectively.

Celle, Germany

Built in 1935, Celle was used as a Luftwaffe training base until Germany's defeat in 1945. It was then taken over by the RAF and in the immediate post-war hurly-burly hosted several squadrons, some of which remained here for less than a week in the course of their restless progress around Germany. First in were the Auster Vs of 659 Sqn which, arriving on 14 April 1945, used the place for a mere 24 hours. The AOP Austers were replaced on 16/17 April by three squadrons of Spitfire XIVs, Nos 41, 350 and 130, which remained until early May. While based here the Spitfires met up with patrolling Soviet Yak fighters and were engaged in fierce dogfights with FW 190s, 350 Sqn destroying five out of a group of fifteen of the German fighters which were encountered on 20 April. Celle's stepping-stone role continued with the brief appearance between 6 and 9 May of 486 Sqn (Tempest Vs), 137 Sqn (Typhoons) and 414 Sqn (Spitfire XIVs).

The arrival of 35 Wing, comprising Nos, 2, 4 and 268 Sqns on 30 May 1945, bestowed a rather more permanent atmosphere on Celle than hitherto. The role of the Wing was photo-reconnaissance, and of its constituent Squadrons Nos 2 and 268 were flying the Spitfire XIV while No 4 still operated the Typhoon FR1b. From mid-

June to mid-September the airfield was unserviceable, and during this time Celle's flying squadrons operated from Hustedt. Meanwhile organizational changes were being made: at the end of August, 4 Sqn disbanded to become the high level Flight of 2 Sqn, while on 19 September 268 Sqn was renumbered as 16 Sqn, re-equipped with Spitfire XIXs in the process. September also saw 2 Sqn taking delivery of Spitfire XIs, which it flew until they were replaced by PR19s in March 1946. No 16 Sqn disbanded on 1 April.

Thus by mid-1946 only No 2 Sqn remained of 35 Wing's orginal three squadrons, with the result that on 22 June the Wing was disbanded, RAF Station Celle forming in its place on the same date. A delightful insight into the informality of the times is provided by the following entry in the Station records for 7 June 1946: 'The AOA [Air Officer in charge of Adminis-tration] took his Mosquito up to Sylt in the morning, returning after lunch.' 2 Sqn's principal activity at this point was the reconnaissance of the whole of the British Zone of Germany, mainly on behalf of the Army. Based alongside 2 Sqn was 1401 Meteorological Flight using Spitfire XIs, 84 Group Communications Flight with the Anson, Proctor and Savoia Marchetti 73, and 652 AOP Sqn on Auster Vs. The Comms Flight's duties took its aircraft all over the Continent and even to the UK – for example, to Gatwick with individuals bound for the Victory Parade in London. No 652's role, on the other hand, was artillery cooperation, and the Squadron added Auster VIs for the work in September.

After spending brief periods at Sylt, 2 Sqn finally departed from Wunstorf in April 1947, and following the loss of 652 Sqn to Lüneburg in December the airfield closed for a time. However, this inactivity was short-lived, for in mid-September 1948, when Operation Plainfare (the Berlin Airlift) had already been running for some two and a half months, the RAF began converting the Station into an Airlift base. Approximately 2,000 Geman workers were employed on the extensive building programme, which included a runway and PSP loading apron, and by mid-December Celle was ready to play a central part in the Operation as a Combined Airlift Task Force despatching base. This enabled the 317th Troop Carrier Wing, which had been operating its Douglas C–54s out of Wiesbaden, to move to Celle, and on 16 December the first C–54 left for beleaguered Berlin, carrying food and coal. The 317th TCW flew its 288th and last sortie on 31 July 1949.

The successful conclusion of the Airlift and the departure of the US C–54s enabled RAF units to begin moving back in, which they did from mid-September 1949 in the form of an entire Mosquito Wing. Nos 4, 11, 14 and 98 Sqns made up the Wing which was soon busy exercising with Bomber Command on simulated attacks on strongly defended targets, the defending force being provided by Fighter Command together with Dutch and Belgian fighters. In July 1950, 14 and 98 Sqns took part in the Farnborough Air Display over in England, in which the Mosquitoes re-enacted the attack on Amiens prison, while the following month No 98 flew to Castel Benito for Middle East exercises.

Throughout 1950 Celle gradually relin-quished its Mosquito squadrons, 14 and 98 finally leaving for Fassberg at the beginning of November, making way for a more modern fighter – the Vampire. Three squadrons of the diminutive jet had been taken on strength before the year was out and these were No 16 (from Gütersloh), plus Nos 93 and 94 which reformed here in November and December respectively. Early the following year the Station was tasked with providing a Battle Flight of six Vampires, and it was decided that the whole of Flying Wing HQ should operate from mobile vehicles, initial trials of this *modus operandi* providing some useful lessons. When 93 Sqn moved to Jever in March 1952 its place was taken by yet another Vampire FB5 squadron, No 145, which reformed here and took its turn for Battle Flight duties along with various RAuxAF fighters squadrons visiting the Station for their summer camps. (Nos 600 and 615 were here in May 1952, for example.) No 94 Sqn had, meanwhile, formed an aerobatic team which, in May 1952, visited the RNAF base at Leeuwarden in Holland to give a display in front of Prince Bernhard.

Operations with the Vampire continued apace with the Celle Wing leading the Coronation Flypast over Düsseldorf in June 1953. In August of that year trials on behalf of HQ 2nd TAF were carried out on the limitations of the Vampire at varying heights, airspeeds and power settings. Then, in January 1954, the first Venoms arrived to replace Vampires with 16 Sqn, and throughout the year 94 and 145 Sqns similarly re-equipped. The emphasis in role now shifted to ground attack, but the

Above *Fg Off Ian Campbell gives his 94 Sqn Vampire its pre-flight checks prior to a sortie from Celle in 1953.* (Wg Cdr R I Campbell)

Below *94 Sqn pilots in front of their first Venom FB1 at Celle* c. *January 1954. At right is Sqn Ldr Bower — 94's CO.* (Wg Cdr R I Campbell)

Venom proved troublesome and was dogged by electrical faults. Flame-outs also caused concern, with WE412 being written off and fatally injuring is pilot in August 1955, resulting in another visit by the de Havilland technical staff to try and sort out the problems. The situation had improved sufficiently by October for eighteen Venoms to take part in Exercise Foxpaw, a simulated bomber raid on East Anglia.

In April 1957 the Station Commander addressed personnel on the subject of the current defence cuts and how they would effect 2nd TAF. Celle itself was to close as a RAF station. The first of the Station's squadrons to suffer the effects of the contractions was No 16, which disbanded in June. By August facilities were being handed over to the German Air Force, and the following month Dornier 27s began operating from the base. A big parade, attended by the CinC 2nd TAF, was held on 9 September, which included an aerobatic display by 94 Sqn and a flypast by all station aircraft. Under the NATO exchange scheme 94 Sqn managed to squeeze in an exchange visit with the RCAF's 421 Sqn Sabres at Grostenquin before disappearing under the terms of its September disbandment. The remaining Squadron, No 145, was similarly disposed of in October. When the Germans took over responsibility for the base on 1 December 1957 the RAF became a lodger unit, and on that date Celle as an RAF station ceased to exist.

Changi, Singapore

'Changi is a beautiful station, with lovely buildings set amongst flowering trees on green slopes commanding fine views of the Straits of Johore.' Thus, the Station Commander described Changi at the ceremony to mark its closure in December 1971.

Unlike the other major Singapore stations, Changi began life not as an airfield but as an army artillery base located to cover the eastern sea approaches to the Straits of Johore. Covered in jungle and swamp, the area was first surveyed in 1927 and work then began to prepare it for the siting of 15-inch artillery guns. After some three years of construction activity, work was suspended due to the Great Depression in Britain, but was resumed again in 1934 after Japan's occupation of Manchuria led to a reappraisal of British defence policy. By 1941 'Fortress Changi' as the Japanese

later termed it had been completed.

With the Japanese advance down Malaya came the bitter realization that the mighty guns, which had been sited to ward off a seaborne attack, were useless. Changi's troops were therefore withdrawn to defend the city itself against Japanese forces which landed in Singapore in February 1942, and the 15-inch guns were destroyed, having played no part in the war.

Following the surrender of Singapore, the Japense decided to add an airfield to the excellent facilities of the Changi garrison. The plan was to construct two intersecting earth landing strips, one running north/south and the other east/west. Work was begun by a 'Ground Levelling Party' of POWs - so named in deference to the Geneva Convention - in 1943, and the initial force of about 800 men was gradually expanded to include survivors from the Thailand railway. Soil and rock to fill swamp areas was moved in hand trucks along a network of narrow-gauge railways. Japanese aircraft began to operate from the airfield in late 1944, many arriving in crates and being assembled in hangars constructed by the Japanese, which remained in use long after the war. Numerous box-type dispersals were laid down around the airfield, but these saw little use before the Japanese surrender in 1945. As far as the Second World War is concerned the name of Changi will, sadly, always be synonymous with the appalling prison camp conditions endured for more than three years by countless POWs, Service and civilian, both in the barracks area and in the notorious Changi Jail a couple of miles distant.

In the post-war reorganization, Changi was earmarked as a transport base and a PSP runway was laid. This enabled the Station to open officially on 8 April 1946 and begin accepting four-engined aircraft. At the same time the first permanent squadron, No 48 with Dakotas, transferred from temporary accommodation at Kallang. Changi's attractive environment also caught the eye of HQ Air Command South East Asia (HQACSEA) which moved in from Singapore city. During May the 439 aircraft which used the airfield included Lancastrians, Liberators, Skymasters, Catalinas, Dakotas, Mitchells, Expediters, Harvards, Spitfires and Mosquitoes. In addition to visiting aircraft from Qantas, the US Air Transport Command, the US Navy and the French armed forces, RAF Yorks of 511 Sqn made

Field Marshall Montgomery disembarks from a Transport Command Avro York at Changi in May 1947. (F Brown)

a daily night stop, departing the following morning. By the end of the year HQACSEA had been renamed HQ Air Command Far East (HQACFE), sharing accommodation at Changi with a subsidiary formation, Air HQ Malaya. In June 1949 HQACFE would become the more familiar HQ Far East Air Force (HQFEAF).

During the first two months of 1947, four Lancasters of 7 Sqn were detached from the UK to carry out a series of Red Lion exercises, involving practice bombing sorties on targets in Malaya. No 48 Sqn's VIP task was taken over by the Far East Communications Flight (later expanded to a full squadron and known as 'FECS') which formed with five aircraft in January. Four other squadrons were taken on strength throughout the year: 52 and 110 (Dakotas), 84 (Beaufighters) and 81 (Mosquitoes), while 1914 Flight's AOP Austers were also based here until January 1948, when Sembawang became their new home.

At the declaration of the Malayan Emergency in mid-1948, 81 and 84 Sqns had moved on but the transport squadrons (starting with 110) began providing detachments to the Task Force formed at Kuala Lumpur for Operation Firedog. Reinforcements in the shape of a detachment from 41 Sqn, RNZAF,

operating Bristol Freighters arrived in September 1949 and the following month a de Havilland Devon arrived for FECS, which was now carrying VIPs as far afield as Saigon, Hong Kong and Aden. In August, after a reorganization of the AOP Austers, the HQ of 656 Sqn returned from Sembawang. Finally, the new permanent runway, begun in February 1949, was completed in early 1950 enabling the airfield to become an RAF Transport Command terminal in March.

Because the ground operations of the Malayan Emergency were carried out in a jungle environment, casualty evacuation by helicopter was essential and the use of helicopters in FEAF began at Changi (the location of the RAF hospital) with the formation, on 1 April 1950, of the Casualty Air Evacuation Flight. Initial equipment consisted of three Westland Dragonflies. In 1953 the Flight was expanded into 194 Sqn and relocated to Kuala Lumpur. September 1950 marked another inaugural air evacuation when the first Handley Page Hastings air ambulance left Changi for the UK. It was during this month that communist leaflets bearing the exhortation: 'Destroy the Imperialist Running Dogs...' were found on the Station.

By October 1950 a detachment of 38 Sqn, RAAF, with Dakotas had arrived, for Changi's Dakotas generally were very busy at this period. In addition to their normal work they were conducting experiments with paper parachutes, and even being employed for fire bomb attacks on a bandit garden in Malaya. Similarly, the role of the Dragonflies was widened when, in December, they flew airborne street patrols during the worst riots in Singapore for many years.

Through the 1950s Changi's role continued to be that of FEAF's main transport airfield, the terminus for Transport Command's Far East schedules, and a route stop for flights to Hong Kong and even Austrialia when the Woomera range was active. Two previous tenants which both returned from Kuala Lumpur for extended stays were 52 Sqn (July 1951–September 1959) and 110 Sqn (October 1951–December 1957). Both units had by now replaced their Dakotas with Valettas. In 1957 48 Sqn gained a bit more muscle when it exchanged its Vickers Valettas for Hastings. The Squadrons later formed a Flight of Blackburn Beverleys, which then moved to Seletar as the basis of 34 Sqn. In addition to Valettas, FECS was flying the Hastings C4 on VIP tasks.

Some months after forming at Changi in May 1958 with Shackleton MR1s, 205 Sqn featured in one of aviation's stranger accidents. One of the unit's aircraft, VP254 'B', disappeared over the sea while on a routine anti-piracy patrol in December. Despite an extensive search nothing was found, until the sixth day when the crew of

another Shackleton spotted the symbols 'B205' marked out in coral on an island. There the crew of a New Zealand frigate later found the grave of one of the missing Shackleton's crew members, who had been buried by Chinese fishermen who had witnessed the crash and anticipated a search.

As with the other Singapore bases, Changi's main preoccupation in the 1960s was the Indonesian Confrontation. The Station was involved in the opening rounds of this campaign when Hastings of 48 Sqn helped to fly troops to Borneo to quell the Brunei rebellion of December 1962. A Transport Command Britannia which happened to be at Changi was also requisitioned. So strong was Indonesian feeling against the emergence of the new nation of Malaysia that it was decided to evacuate British personnel from Djakarta. The airlift duly took place in September 1963 and was carried out by 48 Sqn, supplemented by three Armstrong Whitworth Argosys from 215 Sqn which had fortuitously moved out to Changi from the UK in July/August.

Throughout 1963 Changi was at full stretch supporting operations in the North Borneo territories, and in February 1964 Nos 48 and 215 Sqns completed their thousandth supply sortie to Labuan and Kuching. No 41 Sqn, RNZAF, also played a significant part in the transport operations. Faced with a threat of Indonesian saboteur landings, 205 Sqn flew

Hastings C1A TG532 of 48 Sqn banks to starboard after overflying Changi airfield, which can be seen beneath the tail of the aircraft — c. 1960. (Capt B Priest)

Avro Shackleton MR2c of 205 Sqn at Changi, summer 1964. (T Fairbairn)

anti-invasion patrols while 26 Light Anti-Aircraft Sqn, RAF Regiment, took care of airfield defence. The Station also temporarily took on all commerical traffic after a BOAC Comet crash-landed at Singapore's Paya Lebar airport in March 1964. In fact the workload was now such that, to enable 205 Sqn to participate in a large SEATO exercise in Manila, a reinforcement detachment of three Shackletons of 204 Sqn was sent out from the UK in May.

The declaration of a state of emergency in Malaysia in September 1964 following Indonesian para drops resulted in all leave being cancelled. In preparation for possible air attacks, slit trenches were dug and aircraft dispersed around the airfield, and in November a Hastings flying near the Indonesian border was hit by machine-gun fire. During the same month Argosys and Hastings flew a leaflet raid over Indonesian bases on the islands near Singapore. More reinforcement Shackletons, this time from 203 Sqn in Northern Ireland, arrived to help out 205 with its nightly patrols of the waters around Borneo and with search and rescue commitments at Changi and Gan. The air power available was further boosted by the arrival of Sabres from 77 Sqn, RAAF, which were immediately placed at operational readiness, together with the Fleet Air Arm Buccaneers of 801 Sqn which disembarked from HMS *Victorious*. Tragically 801 lost two of its aircraft in November, one of these crashing

into the sea just after take off from Changi, flown by the squadron commander. The year closed with armed Shackletons being scrambled on Christmas Eve to reconnoitre Indonesian sampans in the Straits of Malacca.

The new year opened with further detachments of RN Buccaneers (800 Sqn from HMS *Eagle*) and RAAF Sabres (3 Sqn). As part of HRH Prince Philip's 1965 visit to the Far East, a representative of every FEAF aircraft type was assembled at Changi for his inspection on 27 February. Other diverse visitors during the year included the Historic Aircraft Preservation Society's Lancaster *en route* from Australia to the UK, and USAF HC–97 Stratofreighters detached here in June and October for the Gemini space capsule returns. From July onwards the Station's many Hastings presented a forlorn sight, grounded and minus their rudders and elevators as a result of a fatal crash in the UK. The VC10, on the other hand, would soon become a familiar sight following the arrival of XR808 in August on its route-proving flight. During the same month 120 Sqn replaced 201 Sqn in the continuing series of Antler Shackleton reinforcement detachments from the UK, and the Confrontation officially ended.

The task of providing realistic training for front-line units, both air and naval, in the Far East was met by Changi-based 1574 Flight which had been flying Meteor T7s, F8s and TT20s in the target facilities role

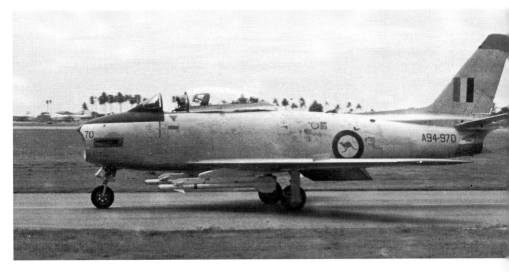

Sidewinder-armed RAAF Sabre at Changi in September 1964. (T Fairbairn)

since December 1959. Prior to the Confrontation the Flight had formed a FEAF aerobatic team but now, in response to Indonesian landings in Johore, its ageing F8s were put on a high alert state alongside the other FEAF fighters. Throughout the Confrontation the Station had handled a steady and sometimes motley stream of freight aircraft, ranging from Hercules of the Pakistan, Australian and New Zealand air forces, to weary Constellations, DC-4s and -6s, and Carvairs operated by many now defunct companies such as Ace Freighters, Transmeridian and British Eagle.

The move here from Tengah of the Naval Aircraft Support Unit (NASU) in 1965 resulted in a dramatic increase in the number of visiting RN aircraft disembarked from the great aircraft carriers of

Buccaneer S1 XN954 of 801 Sqn at Changi in late 1964. (T Fairbairn)

Above *Flt Lt Chris Preston taxies his 1574 Flight Meteor TT20 back to its parking area at Changi on 27 February 1965.* (T Fairbairn)

Below *Hastings C4 of Far East Communications Sqn at Changi — March 1965.* (T Fairbairn)

Above *Boeing HC-97G Stratofreighters detached to Changi in May 1965 during one of the Gemini space missions.* (T Fairbairn)

Below *Argosy XP446 of 215 Sqn taxiing at Changi with VIPs for Labuan, Borneo on 23 August 1965. The captain is Flt Lt Doug Fairbairn, the author's father.* (T Fairbairn)

the day. Until its closure on 1 May 1969, NASU's trade included Sea Vixens, Scimitars, Buccaneers and Gannets.

The British withdrawal from the Far East wrought many changes at Changi: the first unit to be axed was 215 Sqn which relinquished its first Argosy in November 1967, at about the same time that 48 Sqn began to re-equip with the Hercules. Several 215 Sqn aircraft and crews went direct to 70 Sqn in Cyprus. The last RAF Shackleton MR2 Phase 2, WL759 (ex-205 Sqn), and Hastings C4s WJ336 and '337 (ex-FECS) were all scrapped in January 1960. FECS then became a VIP Flight of 52 Sqn which brought its Hawker Siddeley Andovers to Changi from Seletar in February. The following month 103 and 110 Sqns (Whirlwind HAR10s) together with the de Havilland Beavers of 130 Flight, Royal Corps of Transport also transferred from Seletar. Changi's aircraft now took part in numerous exercises and the Station hosted detachments of Lockheed P-3 Orions from the US Navy, RNZAF and RAAF. In December 1959 52 Sqn disbanded after more than 25 continuous years' service in the Far East. The Squadron Andover CC1s were ferried back to the UK, its two C2s remaining behind as the Far East Communications Flight, attached to 48 Sqn. The re-inforcement exercise Bersatu Padu gave Changi a brief respite from the running down process and resulted in a flurry of visiting transport aircraft in April 1970.

The remaining units which disbanded at Changi throughout 1971 included the FEAF Survival and Parachute School at which FEAF aircrew had learned their jungle survival theory, 110 Sqn (in February) and 205 Sqn (in October), while 103 Sqn transferred to Tengah in September. With the demise of HQFEAF on 31 October 1971, Changi came under the auspices of Air Support Command in November and a farewell parade to mark the Station's closure was held at the Changi Creek transit hotel on 9 December 1971. Having been returned to the Singapore government the airfield gained a new lease of life as Singapore International Airport, a role it took over from Paya Lebar airport.

China Bay/Trincomalee, Ceylon

Like its sister airfield at Ratmalana, China Bay was developed early in the Second World War for the defence of Ceylon. In this capacity it hosted not only RAF units but also a succession of Fleet Air Arm

squadrons from visiting aircraft carriers, and in Royal Navy service the Station was often referred to as Trincomalee, the name of the nearby naval base and harbour.

On the same date that the Station opened (1 August 1939) 273 Sqn reformed here with six Vickers Vildebeests and three Fairey Seals to provide a fighter defence for Ceylon. With these types No 273 flew coastal patrols, but the Fairey Fulmars which were taken on strength in June 1940 gave the Squadron a bit more punch. China Bay's naval strains were reflected in 273's establishment, which was 50 per cent RAF and 50 per cent Fleet Air Arm at this point. The Squadron moved on in July 1942 but returned for a six-month spell in February 1943, by which time it was equipped with Hurricanes.

During 1940 and 1941 work proceeded steadily to provide more permanent accommodation on the grass airfield sufficient for one RAF squadron (with buildings and two 'C' type hangars) and one FAA squadron (a hutted camp). A small refuelling base and slipway for flying boats was added in June 1941.

Royal Navy units had begun using the lodger facilities as early as January 1940 when the Swordfish of 824 Sqn disembarked from HMS *Eagle*, which arrived in the Indian Ocean to look for enemy shipping. More Swordfish visited in March 1941, this time off HMS *Hermes* which was again in the area, on ship search duties. A more permanent Fleet Air Arm presence began with the formation at China Bay on 16 February 1942 of No 788 Sqn as the Torpedo Reconnaissance Pool for the Far Eastern Fleet. The unit's initial equipment comprised six Swordfish, but these were all shot down in the course of Japanese raids on Ceylon on 5 April. The remains of No 788 were shipped to East Africa abroad HM Ships *Athene* and *Cornwall*.

The Hurricanes of 261 Sqn which arrived in March 1942 fared rather better. Embarking on HMS *Illustrious* earlier in the year, 261 had sailed to reinforce the Far East. The fall of Singapore had made the journey pointless and the Squadron was offloaded, instead, at Ceylon. Here it was soon in action against some 60 Japanese bombers escorted by a similar number of fighters which made for China Bay at a height of 15,000 feet on 9 April. During the heavy raid that ensued 261 Sqn shot down seven enemy aircraft, probably destroyed one, and damaged three, for the loss of three of their own pilots. A good deal of damage was caused to Station buildings during the raid. The remainder of 261's stay prior to transfer to India in January 1943 was comparatively uneventful. Between March 1942 and February 1943 258 Sqn also used China Bay for detached operations with its Hurricanes from their main base at Colombo. Yet another Hurricane squadron to take its turn here in the air defence of Ceylon was 17 Sqn which was deployed from India in August 1943. After No 17 had relocated elsewhere in Ceylon early in 1944 and re-equipped with Spitfire VIIIs it sent back detachments of its fighters to operate from China Bay.

Air defence, however, was not the only war role for this particular base, for it was also a centre for the anti-submarine operations flown by the Catalinas of 321 (Dutch) Sqn. The crews from this unit had escaped when Java and Sumatra were overrun by the Japanese, and the Squadron was reformed a Koggala (Ceylon) in August 1942, moving to China Bay in October. In addition to patrols over the Indian Ocean, detachments were mounted to Capetown, Durban Ratmalana, Masirah, Socotra and the Cocos Islands, the Squadron finally moving on to Java in October 1945.

In 1943, after some uncertainty as to the precise future role of the Station, it was decided to complete China Bay to take two flying boat and six FAA squadrons or, alternatively, two flying boat and four RAF land-based squadrons, both with appropriate headquarters. The necessary construction work was set in train and the completion of a runway enabled the heaviest of aircraft to begin using the airfield. The largest of these were the B-29 Superfortresses of the USAAF's 20th AF in India, which used China Bay as a forward operating base to attack the Pladjoe oil refinery at Palembang in Sumatra in August 1944. Fifty-four B-29s took off on 10 August for the 3,600 mile trip to Palembang to bomb the refinery, which was estimated to be producing as much as three quarters of Japan's aviation gasoline and a fifth of its fuel oil. Eight of the B-29s laid mines in the Moesi river to the north of Pladjoe. The final year of the war saw detachments of 357 Sqn (based in India and tasked mainly with delivering and supplying insurgent groups), 684 Sqn with North American Mitchells for survey work, and 159 Sqn's Liberators.

On the RN side the years 1944–7 saw intense activity, principally as a result of carriers sailing to and from the Far East. In fact such was the volume of military shipping generally that a Fleet Requirements Unit was established here. This was 733 Sqn which transferred from Minneriya in March 1944. Equipped with Martinets, Wildcats and Avengers, the Squadron provided a wide range of services for the Eastern Fleet, including radar

Miles Martinet target tug at Trincomalee in 1946. (J Lindop)

A Royal Navy Swordfish II LS454 in SEAC markings at Trincomalee in 1946. (J Lindop)

calibration. In this latter role one aircraft flew halfway to Singapore at a steady speed and height of 30,000 feet. Additional types operated later on included the Defiant, Stinson Reliant, Corsair, Mosquito, Vengeance and Seafire, and 733 remained at China Bay until disbandment in December 1947. More than a score of disembarked visiting squadrons took advantage of the Station's servicing facilities during this period, including Nos 800, 806, 807, 808, 809, 810, 812, 828, 832, 834, 837, 845, 847, 851, 854, 879, 888, 896, 898, 1700, 1830, 1831, 1833, 1839, 1844 and 1851. The range of aircraft handled was almost as long, and embraced practically every type in the Fleet Air Arm inventory. The airfield was actually handed over to the RN on 15 November 1944, at which time it became known as RNAS Trincomalee. The small RAF element which remained formed the RAF Detachment, China Bay, and was finally disbanded in May 1946.

The RAF regained ownership in October 1950, placing the airfield under Care and Maintenance and planning to use the flying boat facilities which had been constructed earlier for periodic squadron attachments, as well as for transitting flying boats. The first flying boats to use the harbour had been the Sunderlands of 230 Sqn which had been based here between October 1939 and May 1940. These were followed later in the war by detachments of 240 Sqn's Catalinas, and then from September 1949 onwards by detachments of 205 Sqn which was flying Sunderlands in Singapore. The airfield and its associated installations were handed over to the Royal Ceylon Air Force on 30 November 1957.

Christmas Island, Pacific Ocean

'Join the "Sunrise" industry and win a better life-style!' was an apt catch-phrase for personnel posted to this short-lived but historically significant base, which will forever be associated with nuclear weapon testing during the 1950s. When, in 1955, Britain decided to carry out a series of tests to prove it could produce a megaton thermonuclear H-bomb, the threat of a ban on such tests meant that a deadline of June 1957 had to be set. Christmas Island, the largest coral island in the world, was selected as the operational base from which to conduct the tests codenamed Operational Grapple.

Basically the plan was to use Vickers Valiants to drop the test weapons, the drops actually taking place over Malden Island some four hundred miles south-east of Christmas. Thus Christmas had to be equipped to a high standard for the Valiants and other supporting aircraft, while Malden would need an airstrip to enable test equip and instrumentation to be flown in by Dakota. The Atomic Weapons Research Establishment at Aldermaston would provide the necessary civilian scientific staff, while the Royal Navy would contribute an aircraft carrier – HMS *Warrior* – equipped with an aircraft direction room to communicate with and track the Valiant during its bomb run, plus other guard and monitoring vessels.

Set in the South Pacific some 3,500 miles from the USA and 4,000 miles from Australia, facilities at Christmas were practically nil. There was a small jetty, and the Americans had constructed a long-disused coral airstrip known as Cassidy Field during the Second World War, for aircraft being ferried to the south-west Pacific. The task of constructing a Class I standard airfield on the island was given to the Royal Engineers, and their task was a formidable one due to the extremely tight schedule that had been imposed.

The whole operation was thus very much a joint-Service affair and hence a Task Force was formed which was given the formal instruction to proceed in February 1956. The first Army unit to arrive was 55 Sqn, Royal Engineers, in June, their task being to establish a camp in the port area to facilitate the arrival by sea of the main force and its equipment, which would be engaged on the construction of the airfield facilities. These facilities included a runway of at least 2,000 yards, together with supporting technical and domestic accommodation, for in addition to the Valiants the airfield would be used by a variety of other aircraft throughout the operation. Shackletons would carry out low and medium level meteorological flights in addition to their more normal maritime reconnaissance role, Hastings would undertake a regular freight schedule, Dakotas would be used on a shuttle service to Malden, Canberra PR7s would take on the higher level weather flights plus high speed trips back to the UK with cloud samples, while Canberra B6s would mount cloud-sampling sorties. In addition, RN Avengers would provide an air link with HMS *Warrior* stationed off Malden.

It was on 19 June that the first two Shackletons (WG836 and '529 of 206 Sqn) landed on Christmas Island, which still consisted simply of a coral airstrip. The 'Shacks' carried personnel tasked with establishing initial staging post facilities on the island. One of the earliest problems encountered, the enormous number of flies, was solved by importing an Auster which, swiftly dubbed 'Captain Flit', was soon in action spraying the offending bugs with DDT. Another milestone was reached on 9 July with the arrival of the first Hastings, with additional personnel and freight.

By 13 September the final Army units had arrived and that Service was up to its full strength of over 1,200 souls housed in a tented camp. The task of constructing a runway and hardstands by November, plus working areas, involved the clearance of vast areas of scrub and bush. The runway was duly finished on schedule to enable the first of many civil charter aircraft to land on 4 November. The completion of most of the base's technical, domestic and operational facilities by January 1957 enabled the RAF flying units to begin arriving, the first of which (on 17 January) were two Dakotas of 1325 Flight which had been formed with three aircraft especially for the task of providing a service between Christmas Island and Malden. 1325 was beaten into second place for the inaugural landing at Malden, however, by a Hastings

Avro Shackletons on Christmas Island, with Canberras in the background. (AWE Aldermaston)

Canberra B6 of 76 Sqn being washed down on Christmas Island. (AWE Aldermaston)

which put down on 16 January; but the Dakotas, nicknamed 'Christmas Airways', began regular flights to the small island on the 20th. The first 70 RAF technical and administrative personnel arrived on 1 February aboard a Qantas Constellation, and RAF Station Christmas Island took on the standard three wing system. When HMS *Warrior* anchored off Christmas Island early in March she brought not only her own Whirlwinds and Avengers, but also two RAF Whirlwind HAR2s of 22 Sqn for search and rescue duties. More Shackletons, this time from 240 Sqn in Northern Ireland, arrived to augment those of 206 Sqn on 12 March, and the Canberra B6s of 76 Sqn also began to filter in during the month, initially providing a fast courier service between Christmas and Honolulu.

But perhaps the most important arrival in March was that of the first Valiant of 49 Sqn, XD818 flown in by Wing Commander K. G. Hubbard and crew on the 12th. Three more Valiants (XD822, '823 and '824) joined the Air Task Group, which had been established as 160 Wing, over the next few days. The aircraft parking area, adjacent to the weapon Assembly Building, where the Valiant would be loaded with its bomb, would eventually be fenced in from prying eyes. In April the Valiants began a series of 'Inert Drops' at Malden, while a few days

later Sunderlands of the RNZAF's No 5 Sqn started fortnightly supply runs with fresh food. Canberra PR7s, of 100 Sqn plus B6s from 76 Sqn arrived throughout the month, and on 9 May components of the first bomb to be tested arrived aboard Valiants XD825 and '827. No 58 Sqn, normally based at Wyton alongside 100 Sqn, was also tasked at about this time with providing a courier service over the Christmas-Hickham AFB-Travis AFB route with its Canberra PR7s.

The first 'live' drop was made on 15 May from Valiant XD818 flown by the Hubbard crew after Shackletons had swept the danger area. Following the nuclear explosion, Canberra B6s sampled the cloud and radiation levels. High level photographs were taken by Canberra PR7s and at the lower level by Shackletons. Back at Christmas Island, Canberra PR7s were standing by to whisk samples to the UK. A second and larger weapon was dropped by XD822 on 31 May, watched by the world's press, with a third, and it was thought final drop, from XD823 on 19 June.

Following the completion of this series of tests and the dispersal of the various participating units, the Air Ministry issued instructions that Christmas Island was to be reduced to a Care and Maintenance basis for six months. Two Hastings were to be

One of 49 Sqn's Valiants on Christmas Island. (AWE Aldermaston)

retained to fly in fresh food from Honolulu. But rumours of a new series of tests were already circulating, and in the event they proved correct. Known as Grapple X, these tests were held in November 1957. The following year two further series of tests were carried out, comprising Grapple Y (in April) and Grapple Z (in August and September). Finally, the Americans carried out a series of their own tests here in 1960.

Christmas Island ceased to be part of the British Crown Colony of the Gilbert and Ellice Islands in 1979 and is now named Kiritimati. The former Officers' 'B' Mess has been turned into a motel which caters for a steadily increasing flow of tourists who arrive and depart by air, using the runway constructed for Operation Grapple.

Cocos Islands, Indian Ocean

Long before the outbreak of the Second World War, responsibility for the Cocos Islands had been vested in the government of the Straits Settlements (Singapore and Malaya) some 885 miles away to the north east. By February 1942, however, invading Japanese forces had reached as far south as Singapore and responsibility for the Islands was passed to Ceylon. Japanese ships and

aircraft now roamed the Indian Ocean and had all but severed communications between India/Ceylon and Australia. Catalinas of 205 Sqn based at Koggala in Ceylon began a 3,000 mile mail service to Australia in July 1943, but the distance was such that only a limited payload could be carried. For reasons best known to themselves the Japanese never occupied the Cocos Islands, although they did make some air attacks in the autumn of 1944. By the spring of 1945 attention was already turning from Europe to the Far East, and plans were being made to reinforce the theatre with the Bomber Command Lancasters of 'Tiger Force'. The necessary deployment airfields were under development in Ceylon and Australia, but there was no refuelling base in between. The choice of an Indian Ocean staging post fell on Cocos and the airfield, to be completed by 1 June 1945, would be capable of handling 500 aircraft per month.

Manpower, stores and equipment (including spares back-up for the 'Tiger Force' Lancasters) needed for the development of Cocos were assembled in and around the Indian port of Bombay, from where they were shipped to the Islands, the first vessel arriving on 20 March 1945. The airfield had been sited on the broadest part of West Island, the largest

136 Sqn's Spitfire VIIIs at Cocos — summer 1945. (B Robertson Colln)

island of the group, and despite changes in the planning requirements Cocos was, by mid-1945, becoming a vast base with fuel storage tanks, a narrow-gauge railway, servicing facilities and large storage dumps. Much jungle had been cleared and a PSP runway laid, enabling the first heavy bomber to land on 28 May. The plan for the airfield had always included an air defence squadron, and 136 Sqn with Spitfire VIIIs had duly been shipped in from its previous base in Ceylon in April, but one significant change was the decision to base operational units here. With increasing Allied success in Burma, the idea of an attack on Singapore was mooted; Cocos was to have been used for the air side of this operation and notification came from the Air Ministry that four Heavy Bomber squadrons, one Long-Range Reconnaissance squadron, one PRU Flight, one Flying Boat squadron, and one Air/Sea Rescue unit of both air and sea craft would be based here.

The new squadrons began arriving in July 1945, the first being No 356 with Liberator VIs, following in August by 99 Sqn also on Liberators. Detachments of 684 Sqn's Mosquitoes from India carried out recce flights over Malaya and the East Indies, and the British units were augumented by detachments of Dutch Liberators from 321 Sqn in Ceylon. Meanwhile, the stockpiling of bombs and ammunition proceeded apace in preparation for large-scale operations against the Japanese.

The last offensive sortie by the Cocos Liberators took place on 7 August when 99 Sqn bombed and strafed Benkoelen airfield in Sumatra. Crews were being briefed for a shipping strike on Singapore harbour on 9 August when news of the dropping of the second atomic bomb on Japan filtered through, and operations were suspended.

Following the end of the Pacific war on 14 August it was the crew of a Cocos-based Mosquito of 684 Sqn who became, purely by chance, the first British servicemen to return to Singapore. The aircraft took off on the morning of 31 August to photograph southern Malaya but after developing a fault in one engine the pilot decided to land at the nearest airfield, which proved to be Kallang, Singapore. The Naval Task Force destined to relieve Singapore was still several days away. The two Liberator squadrons remained on Cocos after the end of hostilities, for they were still needed in the Far East to repatriate POWs from the East Indies and for supply dropping. 99 Sqn even dropped supplies to ex-POWs in Singapore's notorious Changi jail, but the commitment as a whole ended in November when both squadrons were disbanded here. Their last task before flying their aircraft to Maintenance Units in India for disposal was to evacuate the majority of the Cocos Islands personnel to India and Ceylon. No 136's Spitfires had, the previous month, embarked on HMS *Smiter* for shipment to Singapore.

Using the facilities of 129 Staging Post which was established here, a limited number of aircraft had staged through on their way to Australia but with Changi (Singapore) opening in April 1946 for four-

Liberator B VI KN745 'F' of 356 Sqn taking off from Cocos in July 1945. (via P Green)

engined Transport Command aircraft on the UK-Australasia schedules, there was little use for this coral atoll airfield, which was now closed. The latter part of 1945 and 1946 was spent dismantling many of the facilities, whilst stores and transport which were uneconomical to recover from the Island were dumped at sea. The effort that had gone into the Station was by no means wasted, however, and those who had been involved in its brief but energetic existence could perhaps take some comfort from the message sent by the Allied Air Commander-in-Chief, South East Asia, Sir Keith Park: 'You and your team have created the best organized base I have seen in any overseas theatre in this war.'

Drigh Road, India

'New, stone-built and spacious' with no hot water but 'excellent' food. Thus was Drigh Road described by one Aircraftman 2 T. E. Shaw, alias T. E. Lawrence – 'Lawrence of Arabia', in a letter home to his mother in 1927. Lawrence had re-enlisted in the RAF in 1925 under an assumed name and had been drafted out to India. Posted to Drigh Road, he was assigned to the Engine Repair Shop, where the discovery that he was Colonel Lawrence caused some embarrassment.

The Repair Shop where Lawrence found himself working was part of the Aircraft Depot which had been established in India back in 1920. Formed with resources drawn from the existing Aircraft Park at Lahore, the new independent Aircraft Depot moved

to Karachi in early 1921. The task of the Karachi Depot (it became known as Drigh Road later on) was the assembly and overhaul of RAF aircraft in India, and it would remain in this role throughout its entire career. Situated some seven miles from Karachi itself, the Depot's location was a convenient one for the delivery by sea of stores and crated aircraft. Thus, throughout the inter-war years, the various stalwarts of the North West Frontier operations, such as Westland Wapitis, de Havilland DH9As and Bristol F2Bs, were a familiar sight at the base.

Few resident units were based at Karachi, but one exception was No 31 Sqn and even this arrived more by default, after a severe earthquake caused much damage and loss of life at its previous base of Quetta in May 1935. Following this disaster No 31 was moved to Drigh Road where it operated from a tented encampment on the edge of the airfield. From here it detached Flights of its Vickers Valentias to other locations in India for operations against hostile tribesmen. The Squadron remained until 1938, returning for a spell in 1941.

Records of activity before 1942 are scant, but in that year the Depot was redesignated No 1 (India) Maintenance Unit with a Group Captain as CO. Now that war had come to the Far East, the support that Drigh Road provided was extended to cover Burma and Malaya, and during early 1942 large numbers of Hurricanes and Mohawks were prepared for service. Later in the year two Maintenance Units were established, No 320 which was an aircraft

DH9A at Drigh Road in 1929. Part of a wartime order, E878 is an ex-60 Sqn machine. (B Robertson Colln)

storage unit, and No 301 – and equipment supply depot. Throughout 1942 Harvards, Hurricanes, Vengeances, Mohawks, Battles and Ansons were assembled, tested and delivered, while quantities of Wright Cyclone and Pratt and Whitney Twin Wasp engines were overhauled. To facilitate the transportation of equipment and fuel a rail siding was constructed into the Station in 1943, and this enabled a total of 236 aircraft contained in 436 crates to be delivered by rail in September.

Newer, faster types of aircraft began to appear and August 1943 saw the arrival of the first Spitfires, whilst by the end of the year No 320 MU was also handling Defiants, Blenheims, Liberators, Wellingtons, Moths and Dakotas. The following February the first two Republic Thunderbolts arrived by sea and the FL731 was airtested on the 21st. In March 1944 night shifts were begun to increase the output of Spitfire VIIIs for use against the Japanese in Burma, while in May Thunderbolt assembly was moved to Madras. During June 111 aircraft were accepted, with 109 being despatched after 426 test flights. Hurricane IVs were added to Nos 320 MU's production target, together with Beechcraft Expediters which arrived by crate, and the overhaul of Mercury XV and Cheetah IX engines was taken on. The arrival of 'E' Flight, 292 Sqn with Sea Otters for air sea rescue duties in August increased the already considerable variety of types.

By the beginning of 1945 No 320 MU had a detachment at St Thomas Mount (Madras) preparing Thunderbolts, and the MU was also responsible for Beaufighter servicing. A small consignment of Mustangs and Spitfire XIVs arrived for attention in March, the Mustangs being referred to as 'experimental'. In June a new east/west runway was opened enabling all reinforcement aircraft being flown into India to begin using the airfield, and to help with this new task No 202 Staging Post moved in from Mauripur Road. The assembly of the first example of yet another new type was completed in March. This was the Hawker Tempest II. Intended for use with the Tiger Force against the Japanese, the war in the Far East came to an end before it reached the squadrons. Similarly, the end of hostilities brought an end to Harvard and Mustang production by No 320 MU, though output of Spitfire FR XIVes continued.

Flying activity at Drigh Road was now much reduced and in April 1946, for example, consisted mainly of Tempest II sorties. The following month all work on Mosquitoes stopped and in September all Mosquitoes were struck off charge. Work on Spitfires, particularly Mk XVIIIs, went on until 1947. On 30 October, however, the airfield was handed over to the Pakistan Air Force, having been an RAF station for 25 years.

Eastleigh, Kenya

Undoubtedly one of the more desirable overseas airfields (it was situated on the outskirts of Nairobi), Eastleigh became operational on 1 August 1940. Prior to that date a detachment administered by RAF Station Nairobi had been operating here. The detachment consisted of personnel from Station Workshops, Nairobi, and No 2 (Training) Flight of the Kenya Auxiliary Air Unit equipped with de Havilland Moths. No 6 Aircraft Repair Depot, SAAF, together with a detachment of No 237 (Rhodesia) Sqn, flying Audaxes, Harts and Hardys from Nairobi were also based here at this point. Originally intended for a single squadron, construction of the Station had begun before the war, but extra accommodation had been added for the Repair Depot.

A period of reorganization followed during which certain repair sections on the Station were rationalized into a Combined Repair Depot responsible not only for the repair of various aircraft types but also the assembly of Hurricanes and Tiger Moths. The KAAU Flight, on the other hand, was successively titled an Elementary Flying School and finally (in November 1940) No 30 FTS, by which time it boasted Tiger Moths. Although 30 FTS disbanded in March 1941, the Combined Repair Depot remained busy and was responsible for salvaging an extrordinary range of aircraft including Italian-built Savoias, Audaxes, Hartebeests, Tutors and Marylands. Crated Curtiss Mohawks arrived for assembly and delivery to the SAAF and in August 1941 one of these, flown by the Station Commander, crashed into the nearby railway workshops. Even a Junkers 86 was overhauled for the SAAF. During the year several operational units of the SAAF taking part in the Abyssinian Campaign were based here and large quantities of captured Italian equipment were sifted. The SAAF's No 6 Depot finally ceased to exist in October 1941, its resources being absorbed by the Station.

By mid–1942 most of the South Africans had left, but in their place had come Fleet Air Arm personnel whose task was to service visiting naval aircraft. Two Walruses in April are the first types mentioned, but 805 Sqn with Grumman Martlets was based here permanently over the latter half of 1942. The sailors represented about a quarter of the Station strength at this period, and their numbers warranted the commissioning of the RN

elements of Eastleigh at HMS *Korongo* in September, an arrangement which lasted until October 1944. Other fresh units to appear during 1942 were 1414 Meteorological Flight with Gladiators (in July), and No 133 MU which remained here for four years carrying out airframe, electrical, engine and armament work on Blenheims, Battles, Ansons, Baltimores, Wellingtons, Rapides, Gladiators and Leopard Moths. A regular and convenient air link with such destinations as Madagascar was completed by the establishment of a Communications Flight using Hudsons donated by 163 Sqn.

No 25 Anti-Aircraft Cooperation Unit was formed here in early June 1943. Almost immediately its Fairey Battles were grounded, but they were cleared again towards the end of the month. In November No 133 MU modified Defiant TT1 DS122 for 1414 Met Flight (the Station Commander was killed in one the following February), and received its first Dakota for a 300 hours inspection. On the civil front BOAC aircraft were, by January 1944, routeing through to Khartoum, Salisbury and Cairo, and in its role as a formal Staging Post the Station glimpsed many transitting VIPs. March witnessed the assembly of the Anti-Locust Flight (Middle East) which, with its five Ansons specially adapted with spraying gear, then moved off to its permanent base at Nakuru. The first South Africa-bound Avro York passed through in May, and the month saw the emergence of the East African Communications Flight operating Ansons, Hudsons and probably other types as well.

In the immediate post-war years, communications flying remained the primary activity and the EACF added Dakotas to its books. But in the midst of this No 500 Sqn put in an appearance in October 1945. Equipped with Baltimores in the bomber role it had, before the month was out, been renumbered No 249 Sqn and given responsibility for all photographic tasks in East Africa. In March 1946 it began to re-equip with Mosquito FB26s before moving on to Iraq in June. Due to evacuation commitments in Somaliland in 1950, EACF was assisted by detachments of Dakotas from both 216 and 78 Sqns.

Meanwhile, Transport Command aircraft movements (including the new Hastings) continued apace, but in March 1951 a Lancaster PR1 of 82 Sqn (Benson) arrived to carry out a photographic survey of Kenya. Another four-engined 'heavy' to visit was French Air Force Halifax RG560

*Mosquito FB26 KA370 'Q' of 249 Sqn at Eastleigh in 1946. The Hudsons behind are
probably those of the East African Communications Flight.* (via P Green)

on a scheduled flight to Djibouti in French
Somaliland. In September 1951 AHQ East
Africa was disbanded and the Station was
transferred to the control of AOC British
Forces Aden. EACF was by now operating
Ansons, Valettas and Proctors.

The Mau Mau Campaign which began in
1952 involved the Station in a particularly
hectic period of offensive activity, and
Eastleigh's first reinforcements for the
emergency, four Harvards of the specially-
formed No 1340 Flight, flew in on 23
March 1953. Modified to drop 20 lb
fragmentation bombs and to fire a fixed
.303 Browning machine gun, the Harvards
began operations against Mau Mau gangs
in May, KF420 crashing on the ninth of
that month. Two Meteors of 13 Sqn
(Egypt) arrived in October to begin a
photographic survey of Kenya's Abadare
Mountains, and the following month 49
Sqn started a series of Bomber Command
Lincoln detachments, which would include
aircraft from Nos 100, 61 and 214 Sqns.
Using 1,000 lb bombs the Lincolns
pounded suspected Mau Mau positions,
though sadly RF335 crashed in the
Abadares in January 1954 with the loss of
all on board. At the other end of the scale

Vampires from 8 Sqn in Aden were
detached during April and May for rocket
and cannon sorties. So successful were
'Skyshouting' trials with Austers that the
system of aerial broadcasting to terrorists
on the ground was used regularly, and the
Pembroke was also modified to carry the
necessary equipment. A Sycamore
helicopter arrived in October 1954 for trials
in evacuating casualties from forest areas,
and performed its first 'live' evacuation in
December. The less glamorous but
nevertheless vital, and certainly greatly
accelerated, air transport role that
Eastleigh was required to play in the
campaign should not be forgotten, a
succession of RAF Hastings, together with
civil Yorks, Tudors, Argonauts and
Hermes airlifting in the troops needed for
the emergency. All the strike aircraft had
gone their separate ways by October 1955
leaving only the Pembrokes, and the
Sycamores which scanned wheatfields for
terrorists foraging for food. The
operational phase of the emergency ended
in December 1956.

British military expansion plans in the
Middle East generally, including the
presence of 24 Brigade in Kenya

Avro Tudor 2 G-AGRY of Air Charter at Eastleigh. Air Charter used this aircraft on trooping flights during the period 1953-4. (Fairbairn Colln)

specifically, led to the arrival of several units throughout 1959. First in was No 142 Sqn which, with Venom FB4s for the fighter/ground attack role plus a pair of Vampire T11s for training, soon took over a more famous Middle East numberplate, that of 208 Sqn. Formed primarily to work with 24 Brigade, No 21 Sqn on Twin Pioneers followed in September. Finally, No 30 Sqn flew out to Eastleigh from the United Kingdom in November, its Beverleys ideally suited to the job of airlifting the Brigade's heavy equipment and vehicles. Converting to the Hunter FGA9 at Stradishall in March 1960, No 208 flew its new aircraft to Eastleigh, and alongside No 30 Sqn, took part in the Kuwait crisis of 1961. Later that year 208 moved to Aden to help form the 'Khormaksar Wing'.

Beverley of 30 Sqn over Mount Kenya. (MoD Crown Copyright)

The Beverleys and Twin Pioneers lingered on at Eastleigh, 30 Sqn moving to Muharraq in October 1964, and 21 Sqn disbanding in June 1965 (only to reform immediately in Aden). A detachment of two Beverleys from 84 Sqn, Aden, took over No 30's remaining tasks but these were finally withdrawn in 1965. With the departure of all its squadrons the airfield became a Staging Post maintained by a detachment, and had closed by July 1967.

Ein Shemer, Palestine

On the night of 28 March 1947 a Lancaster was being refuelled at Ein Shemer when a fire broke out in the bowser, which soon engulfed the vehicle and spread to the front part of the Lancaster. The nose and cockpit of the aircraft were destroyed before the fire could be extinguished. More than twenty other aircraft were parked close by, the damage would have been far more widespread had it not been for the bravery of the refuelling SNCO, Sergeant J. A. Beckett, who, in spite of severe burns to his head, face and body, climbed into the blazing bowser and drove it clear of the aircraft park. Beckett was rushed to hospital but died from his burns. His courage was later recognized by the posthumous award of the George Cross.

Built in 1943, Ein Shemer opened on 11 November of that year to control 78 OTU, whose task was to train Wellington General Reconnaissance crews. 78 OTU had itself been formed from 3 (Coastal) OTU which had used Wellingtons at Cranwell and then Haverfordwest in the UK. The 78 OTU advance party sailed from Gourock, Scotland in October 1943 aboard HM Transport *Almanzore*, which was attacked by German aircraft as it steamed through the Mediterranean. In addition to general reconnaissance work, Leigh Light Wellington crews were to be trained and the first aircraft for the OTU, consisting of Ansons and Wellingtons Mks III, VIII, X, XII, and XIII, began arriving in February 1944.

Basically the OTU consisted of 'A' and 'B' Flights, which were based at Ein Shemer's satellite airfield of Megiddo converting crews to the Wellington; 'O' Flight (Ansons); 'Z' Flight for *ab initio* radar training (Ansons and Wellingtons); and 'X' and 'Y' Flights for crew training. The Leigh Light training was complicated, since it required a special sea target upon which aircraft could home by means of their ASV radar equipment, and which could be illuminated for practice attacks.

The target had to be positioned at least five miles away from land responses to the ASV equipment. This requirement posed a problem, due to the very strong tidal currents in the local Palestine waters. Boulton Paul Defiants were used for target towing, and by the time 78 OTU closed on 1 July 1945 some 343 crews, including Greeks, Canadians, South Africans, New Zealanders, Free French and Australians, had been trained.

In March 1945 the Staff Navigation School (Middle East) arrived from Gianaclis. Using Wellington XIVs the School offered the highest form of training for navigators, and its students were often, for example, involved in the administration of navigation back at their units. When the School closed on 30 November 1945, 102 Staff Navigators had been trained and the Wellingtons had performed countless air-sea rescue and ferry flights.

In addition to the training units the Station also housed a number of operational squadrons, and the first of these (from July 1945) was a detachment of two Austers from 651 Sqn which, in addition to spotting for artillery ranges, also flew exercises with the Army and ferried VIPs.

Next to arrive, in August 1945, were 178 and 214 Sqns flying Liberator VIs and VIIIs respectively, which together made up 240 Wing. Basically a bomber organization, 240 Wing was heavily involved in trooping at this point, in particular the repatriation of South Africans from Italy. The Wing moved on to Egypt in November.

From 10 December 1945 until mid-1946 the Station was under Care and Maintenance and during this period the 6th Airborne Division Training School was based here (January to May), together with 'C' Flight of 651 Sqn and several minor administrative and logistics units.

On 1 June 1946 the Station reopened and once again became the scene of operational flying. The month saw the arrival of 6 Sqn on Spitfire LF9s, 208 Sqn with Spitfire VIIIs (which were replaced by FR18s in August), and 621 Sqn flying Lancasters and Vickers Warwicks. Under Operation Sunburn, 621's aircraft flew sea searches for illegal immigrant ships. In July, 680 Sqn completed the move of its Mosquito PR34s here from Egypt, while 38 Sqn sent in a detachment of its Lancaster GR3s from Malta. The two Spitfire squadrons were meanwhile flying fighter affiliation sorties with local Lancaster squadrons.

September 1946 marked a number of

Lancaster GR3s of 38 Sqn at Ein Shemer in April 1947. (MoD Crown Copyright)

organizational changes: right at the beginning of the month 621 relinquished its Warwicks and was renumbered 18 Sqn. This arrangement, however, lasted only two weeks for on the fifteenth No 18 was absorbed into Ein Shemer's 38 Sqn detachment, becoming 'B' Flight of that Squadron. Finally, 680 Sqn, which was already flying PR sorties, was renumbered as 13 Sqn.

No 6 Sqn left for Cyprus in October, but the same month 32 Sqn with its Spitfire IXs was taken on strength, joining 208 Sqn in exercises with the Army and in patrols of oil pipelines. There were similar unit moves in December, when 13 Sqn left for Egypt and 38 Sqn moved in *in toto* from Malta. By now the sea search for illegal immigrant shipping over an area bordered by the Palestine coast, the Nile Delta and Cyprus, were known as Bobcat operations. On 1 February 1947 285 Mobile Fighter Wing was established here to control 32 and 208 fighter squadrons and to form a fully mobile tactical force capable of deployment anywhere in the Middle East. Two months later No 32 exchanged its Mk IX Spitfires for FR18s, making that the standard version in the Wing.

With the end of British rule in Palestine planned for May 1948 prior to the establishment of the new State of Israel,

Ein Shemer's squadrons were withdrawn, 32 and 208 moving to Cyprus on 25/26 March 1948, and 37 and 38 returning to Malta on the last day of the month. There was no activity of any significane after that.

El Adem, Libya

After Britain went to war with Italy in June 1940, El Adem, some fifteen miles south of Tobruk and the main Italian air base in Cyrenaica, was one of the first targets to be attacked by RAF aircraft. When the airfield was captured in early 1941 during the first British advance into North Africa, the wreckage of scores of Italian aircraft clearly indicated its previous use. In the opening months of 1941 detachments of Nos 73 Sqn (Hurricanes) and 70 Sqn (Wellingtons) spent short periods here, but with the arrival of the Germans in Africa and the loss of Cyrenaica it was not until December that RAF units returned, and then only temporarily in the shape of No 112 changing its Tomahawks for Kittyhawks. 112 Sqn was back again in February 1942, alongside a Hurricane unit, No 274 Sqn. Now, in 1942, Cyrenaica was lost for a second time and the airfield again came under Axis control. At the Battle of El Alamein in October, however, the picture changed dramatically and the

British units swept in, this time for good. No less than five Hurricane squadrons (Nos 33, 73, 80, 213 and 238) passed through, together with a pair of Hudson squadrons (117 and 267) which remained until January 1943.

The RAF's planned permanence here was reflected in the formation of the Station on 12 December 1942, its primary role being to provide servicing and refuelling facilities on the North African reinforcement route. BOAC began operations in February 1943, and throughout the first three months of the year over 1,400 battle casualties were processed. The nature of this air traffic led to the disbandment of the Station and its redesignation, on 1 April 1943, as No 12 Staging Post. In spite of this, it played a brief role as a bomber airfield (January/February 1944), hosting Nos 178 and 462 Sqn with Liberators and Halifaxes respectively. Two fighter squadrons were also based here in the last three years of the war, No 94 with many Yugoslav pilots, and No 336, a Greek-manned unit carrying out bombing training on Spitfires.

On 1 August 1945 the airfield once again became RAF Station El Adem, although it was still handling a vast amount of through traffic both in terms of types and numbers. This resulted in some unusual visitors and tasks. In May 1947 Mosquito PR34 RG238

was turned round in 29 minutes, on its way to setting a new London to Cape Town record, while in a more leisurely exercise later in the year the station sent out a team to repair and refuel Airspeed Consul G–AIOU which had force-landed on a main road. The team constructed a runway which enabled the Consul to make a safe take-off. BOAC schedules ceased in November 1948, but there were always new commitments such as visting de Havilland Hornets on long range navigational training flights from England. The Station Anson (VM310) joined Lancasters from Malta, and Middle East-based Dakotas and Valettas to search for a Vampire of 73 Sqn which crashed in the desert in February 1950 on its way to El Adem. The Vampire was on one of many similar squadron visits which included Shackletons (37 and 38 Sqns) based here in October 1955 to carry out anti-arms smuggling patrols in the Cyprus area. The constant need to provide search and rescue facilities prompted the attachment, in 1960, of a Flight of Bristol Sycamores from 103 Sqn in Cyprus. In July 1963 this became 1564 Flight, re-equipping with Whirlwinds.

From the 1960s, detachments of units based in the United Kingdom and elsewhere began to make much greater use of the fine weather at El Adem to carry out training. Foremost among these was 242 OCU at

RAF Mustang IV KH810 being ferried through El Adem in August 1945. (J Keward)

Above *G-AGJI — the first Lancaster to be civilianized. Here it is, in BOAC markings with Merlin 102s, visiting El Adem in August 1945.* (J Keward)

Below *Egyptian Air Force Spitfire F22s being refuelled at El Adem in 1950.* (P Cook)

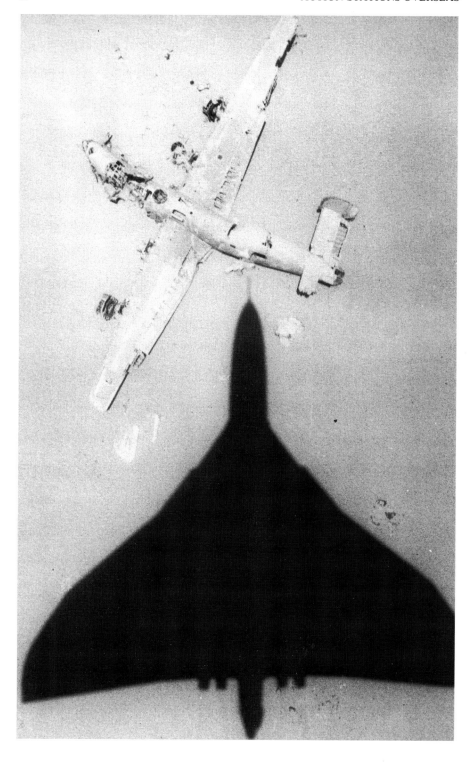

Left *Cast a giant shadow! The camera of a Vulcan B2 operating out of El Adem captures the aircraft's shadow alongside the wreck of the celebrated B-24 Liberator 'Lady Be Good' of the US 376th Bomb Group which went down in the Libyan desert in 1943.* (Fairbairn Colln)

Thorney Island which regularly sent out Argosys and Beverleys, together with their student crews, to escape the vagaries of the English winter. In addition, the Air Weapons Range was much in demand by NEAF Canberra squadrons and the Hunter ground attack units on Armament Practice Camps. A well-known navigation point for all El Adem-based aircraft was the 'Lady Be Good', a USAAF B-24 Liberator which had come down in the desert in April 1943. For communications duties, the Station boasted a single Pembroke (WV706), which also took on casualty evacuation. Although off the strategic trunk route to the Far East, the airfield was used by Britannias during the Zambian airlift and continued to attract light aircraft working for the oil companies.

By the mid-1960s Vulcan Lone Ranger fights were in full swing, the aircraft remaining for four or five days. Similar visits were made by Hastings from the Bomber Command Bombing School at Lindholme. In August 1966 Kingdom of Libya Airlines began a twice-weekly schedule using Fokker Friendships for the benefit of local residents and the oil companies. Four months later the weapons range was used for trials on the AS–30 missile. One of the highlights of El Adem's calender in the late 1960s was the annual competition for the Lord Trophy, when RAF transport crews from all commands would converge on the Station to fly air support sorties and sit a written exam. The competition normally followed one of the many 38 Group air transport exercises, and it was during one of these exercises that Argosy XR133 crashed, killing all on board in May 1968.

One of the more unusual visitors was an Egyptian Air Force L 29 Delfin which made a dead stick landing in June 1969. An Egyptian servicing team arrived in an IL–14 to rectify the trainer, which later flew safely back to its base at Mersah Matruh. Next month, following a sabotage threat, two Wessexes of 72 Sqn arrived as air freight aboard Short Belfasts. The helicopters were used to patrol the airfield perimeter; in the event, the threat did not materialize.

By August 1967 El Adem was the last remaining British base in Libya, and Army units, including four Sioux helicopters, arrived for the defence of the Station. An opportunity to test the newly-installed airfield Rotary Hydraulic Arrester Gear was provided by the arrival, in February 1968, of the first Lightnings to visit El Adem. These were four aircraft of 23 Sqn which had flown non-stop from their base at Leuchars. A need to provide desert search and rescue facilities was fulfilled, in April 1969, by the re-emergence of the previously-disbanded 1564 Flight with two Whirlwind HAR10s.

Events were now overshadowed by the Libyan *coup d'état* and Colonel Gadaffi's announcement that all British bases must go. Following talks that agreed on a British withdrawal from Libya by 31 March 1970, No 1564 Flight was disbanded in December 1969 and the Army Sioux (No 12 Aviation Flight) followed suit a month later. The Station Pembroke was despatched to Cyprus for 70 Sqn and the final handover parade was held on 28 March.

Fayid, Egypt

Overlooking Egypt's Bitter Lakes, little is known about Fayid's early history except that a landing ground existed there before the Second World War. It sidles into the history books in February 1937 when 'A' Flight of 208 Sqn was detached in from its main base at Heliopolis, for exercises in cooperation with the Canal Infantry Brigade. The next significant milestone was the formation of a Station Headquarters on 1 December 1940 to administer a bomber wing within No 202 Group. The bomber wing, comprising No 37 and 38 Sqns, both with Wellingtons, duly arrived but on the eighteenth of the month the whole Station, aircraft and all, moved to Shallufa.

The airfield was commissioned as an RN air station in May 1941, under which guise it was known as HMS *Phoenix*. Remaining in this role until February 1946, it was used as an Aircraft Repair Yard and provided storage for up to 130 aircraft.

In the meantime the Station reopened as an RAF unit on 6 June 1941. No 112 Sqn was already in residence after a brief spell in Crete, and began to rearm with Curtiss Tomahawks alongside the similarly equipped No 2 Sqn, South African AF. This latter unit left for the Western Desert in July, followed by No 112 in September. Two days after 112's departure, Fayid once again assumed the mantle of a bomber station with the arrival of No 108 Sqn's Wellingtons. The 'Wimpys' flew bombing missions against targets in North Africa and Greece, and in December were joined by the first Liberator Mk II for No 108. The plan was for the Squadron to re-equip entirely with Liberators, but this was never completed, 108 moving on in May 1942. The main party of another Liberator unit, No 159 Sqn, spent a very brief period here in April and May before continuing onto its intended destination in India.

It was Liberators, though those of the USAAF, that would link Fayid with one of the most infamous targets of the war, that of Ploesti in Romania. These were the B-24Ds of the so-called 'Halverson Detachment', named after their commander Colonel Harry Halverson. The B-24s had actually set off from Florida with the eventual aim of bombing Japan from China, but they were diverted instead to attack the Ploesti oil refineries from Egypt. Thirteen of the 'Libs' set off from Fayid late on 11 June 1942, arriving over the target at dawn on the twelfth to carry out the USAAF's first heavy bomber raid on Europe of the Second World War. Three days later they joined RAF Liberators of No 160 Sqn for a raid on the Italian fleet east of Malta.

More four-engined aircraft, this time a detachment of Halifaxes of 76 Sqn, arrived

in August 1942 for attacks on Tobruk. The amalgamation of this detachment with a similar one known as 10/227 Sqn resulted in the formation at Fayid of a new No 462 Sqn, RAAF, whose Halifaxes first raided Tobruk in early September before transferring to Kilo 40 in November. September also brought the RAF's first operational Martin Marauder squadron, No 14, from LG 224 where the new aircraft had been delivered the previous month. Although the Marauder had a reputation for being difficult to handle, the Squadron completed its conversion with relatively few incidents and went on to complete its first operational mission, a reconnaissance sortie, in October.

No 5 (Middle East) Aircraft Repair Unit formed in August 1942 for the repair and overhaul of multi-engine aircraft. After a spell as No 161 MU it moved to Kabrit in March 1944, by which time it had been renamed No 2 Transport Aircraft Repair Unit. In the interim, between November 1942 and February 1943, B-24 Liberators of the US 98th Bombardment Group were stationed here. A Care and Maintenance Party arrived in March 1944 and began to prepare the Station for occupation by No 73 OTU, which moved in from Abu Sueir in June. This was a fighter OTU equipped with Spitfires, Hurricanes, Kittyhawks, Tomahawks and other support aircraft.

Hawker Audax K7525 at Fayid. (R C B Ashworth)

Harvard T2b of 73 OTU Fayid in 1945. (via S Bond)

The last OTU course passed out in September 1945 and two months later Fayhid changed its role to that of a heavy bomber unit when two Liberator squadrons, Nos 178 and 214, flew in. The two squadrons formed No 240 Wing, immediately re-equipped with Lancasters which were used for trooping and freighting, and then, in April 1946, renumbered as Nos 70 and 37 Sqns which transferred to Kabrit in August. The following month the Dakotas of No 216 Sqn began a five-month stay as part of the Middle East Transport Wing.

In addition to the Mediterranean/Middle East Communications Squadron flying a variety of types, 1947 saw the arrival of No 13 Sqn. A reconnaissance unit, No 13 was intially equipped with Mosquito PR34s, but had gained Meteor PR10s by the time it moved on to Abu Sueir in early 1955. A fighter squadron in the shape of No 6 was taken on strength in May 1948 and its Tempest F6s mounted many widespread detachments before making way the following year for No 39 Sqn's Mosquito NF36s. Yet another fighter squadron, No 208, took up post in November 1948 and its Spitfire FR18es soon found themselves embroiled in the friction between Jews and Arabs. During one reconnaissance sortie in

January 1949 to verify Israeli incursions into Egypt, four of 208's Spitfires were shot down by Israeli Spitfires, resulting in the death of one pilot.

Throughout the early 1950s, no less than five medium range transport squadrons were based for varying periods at Fayid, comprising Nos 70, 78, 114, and 204 which was renumbered 84, with Valettas replacing Dakotas. In addition, the Station was home for No 683 Sqn when it reformed here in November 1950 with Lancaster PR1s for mapping and survey duties in the Middle East. There was no operational activity after January 1956.

Gan, Indian Ocean

Fringed with palm trees and coral and located in the Indian Ocean, it is hard to imagine a more idyllic setting for an RAF station than Gan, one of the Maldive Islands. The most southerly of a string of islands forming Addu Atoll, Britain's military connections with Gan go back to 1941 when, in anticipation of war in the Far East, a highly secret Safe Fleet Anchorage known as 'Port T' was built here. Later in the war a short airstrip was laid out and this was used by detachments from 160 Sqn flying Liberator Vs on coastal photo-reconnaissance, air/sea rescue and meteorological sorties. In addition, the lagoon was used by flying boats patrolling the Indian Ocean. At the end of the war the military installations were dismantled and all Service personnel were withdrawn.

Gan's postwar development began in 1957 following the realization that Britain's vital route to the Far East depended on the continued assurance of overflying rights from countries in Asia. This vulnerability of the empire reinforcement route led to the Chiefs of Staff's quest for a staging post in the Indian Ocean between the Middle East bases and Singapore. The choice of location was virtually limited to Gan.

Plans were drawn up for a single runway spanning the full length of the island, together with technical facilities and domestic accommodation for around 500 personnel. The contract for this work was let to Messrs Richard Costain, and an advance party of 5001 Airfield Construction Sqn led by Flight Lieutenant George McNeil arrived off Gan abroad HMS *Modeste* at the end of January 1957. The advance party's tasks were to refurbish the wartime landing strip, survey the nearby island of Hittadu, which would later house a Signals Unit, and to build a power station and living quarters for the contractor's workforce. Nearly 11,000 trees needed to be cleared and the most effective method of achieving this was found to be pushing them over with bulldozers. In addition, a 400 ft jetty had to be constructed for the landing of plant and heavy machinery. Initially the advanced party was supported twice-weekly by Sunderlands of 205/209 Sqn from Singapore, which landed on the lagoon with food, mail and personnel. Moorings, together with refuelling and basic servicing facilities, were established off Hittadu for the flying boats. By the end of August 1957 the refurbished landing strip was ready to receive its first aircraft, a Bristol Freighter of the RNZAF. A regular service from Ceylon using Vickers Valettas began the following month.

Within two years the majority of the construction work had been completed at a cost of £4,000,000 by a labour force of over 2,000 men including Pakistanis, Maldivians and Europeans. In order to avoid creating a hazard to flying, the radio transmitting station was constructed on the wartime radar site on Hittadu, adjacent to the flying boat anchorage. A coral causeway was built to link Hittadu with Gan, and this also enbled locally employed islanders to commute to Gan on foot rather than by the more customary boat.

The peace and tranquility of this tropical island were rudely interrupted in January 1959 when, to everyone's surprise, the Adduans rebelled against their own Maldivian Government. A new Government had recently taken office and wished to negotiate a fresh Agreement with Britain. This would have involved a temporary halt to development work on the station. The Adduans, however, were quite happy with the existing arrangements. This put Britain, which had promised to defend the Maldives but not to interfere in internal affairs, in an awkward position. Eventually the two governments endorsed a slightly revised Protection Agreement, the islanders were placated and harmony was restored.

Throughout the late 1950s and early 1960s the development of Gan as a staging post continued. Much of the Station's traffic was comprised of transport aircraft flying the Far East route schedules, and the number of passengers handled built up to a peak of between 6,000 and 7,000 per month. The vast majority of these were Service personnel and their families moving to and from the Far East on posting, and hence transit facilities for both passengers and aircraft had to be provided.

In addition to the steady flow of transport aircraft a wide variety of frontline types staged through, including Vulcans, Canberras and Shackletons reinforcing FEAF in times of crisis, such as the Indonesian Confrontation, or simply participating in Far East exercises. Later on, Gan was one of several route stations from which Victor tankers took off to refuel Lightnings and Phantoms transitting to Singapore from the UK. The airfield's diversity of visitors, together with its isolated location, required the presence of an efficient rescue service and this was achieved by a combination of 1125 Marine Craft Unit and detachments of Shackletons of 205 Sqn from Changi, Singapore. Equipped with launches, vehicles and liferafts, the MCU was instantly ready to answer calls in local waters, and in addition maintained a ferry service to local islands. The Shackletons, on the other hand, were able to cover the whole of the Central Indian Ocean area in the search and rescue role. Control of these air and sea resources was vested in a Rescue Coordination Centre established on Gan.

Fortunately no major accident ever occurred on the airfield itself, but more distant incidents occasionally demanded a rapid response. For example, on 21 March

10 Sqn VC 10 during a night-stop at Gan. (10 Sqn)

1964 an SOS was received from a ship, the *Chinglong Yik*, which had caught fire in mid-ocean. One of 205 Sqn's Shackletons took off from Gan and eventually located the burning vessel after a three hour search. Dinghies and a set of Lindholme rescue gear were dropped, and the crew of the doomed vessel all managed to scramble to safety. In another incident at sea the following year, a 201 Sqn Shackleton took off from Gan *en route* to Singapore. During the flight the No 4 engine caught fire after overspeeding. The fire then spread to the starboard wing, which folded up. The two pilots controlled the aircraft superbly until it hit the sea, but sadly were amongst the eight people killed in the crash. The survivors were later picked up by HMS *Ajax*.

Living quarters at Gan consisted of prefabricated bungalow-type accommodation. The tropical oceanic climate, hot and humid but relieved by sea breezes, meant that air conditioning was required only in specialist technical areas. There were no hangars, and all aircraft servicing was carried out in the open, often in extreme temperatures.

In the final years of its existence the number of aircraft movements sometimes edged towards 350 per month, many of which were larger types such as VC10s and Belfasts. However, once the British defence policy of the late 1960s referred to a withdrawal from the Far East, a question mark inevitably hung over the future of Gan. This uncertainty was clarified in the 1975 Defence White Paper, which announced the planned closure of the base by 1 April 1976. Although the pull-out of British forces from Singapore temporarily increased the flow of traffic, the Station became much quieter once this was complete and it began its own run-down in 1975. The first three months of 1976 were spent in preparing air and sea freight for return to the UK and in handing over installations to the Maldivian Government. The ensign was lowered for the last time on 29 March 1976, and only a small monument erected by the Department of the Environment and bearing the inscription 'Royal Air Force Gan 1956-76' remained as a tangible reminder of this erstwhile stepping stone to the Far East.

Gatow (Berlin), Germany

In April 1963 Hughie Green, the television personality, had agreed to travel to Berlin for ITV to record two editions of his famous show 'Double Your Money', for subsequent transmission in the UK. A qualified pilot, he set off in a Cessna 310 chartered from British Executive Air

Services, London, bound for Gatow, the airfield serving the British sector of Berlin. Flying from Stuttgart, Green entered the appropriate air 'corridor' but was immediately warned by Air Traffic Control that an unidentified aircraft was approaching him from behind. A MiG fighter then passed to the right of the Cessna, followed seconds later by a twin-engined fighter on the left side. Both fighters bore Soviet markings and both then made several more close passes, lowering their wheels to indicate that they wanted Green to land. Well inside his authorized airspace Green maintained height and heading, whereupon one of the fighters fired in front of, although not at, the Cessna. A shaken but undeterred Green eventually descended towards, and landed safely at, Gatow but the incident highlighted the precarious position of Berlin – 'the divided city' – in general, and Gatow in particular.

Built by the Germans in 1934 as a 'Forestry and Agricultural Flying Experimental Institute' (a ploy to sidestep the limitations of the Teaty of Versailles), the newly-formed Luftwaffe came clean in 1935 and admitted that the facilities at Gatow in fact comprised the Air Force Academy, School of Air Warfare, Aeronautical Technical Institute, and a Flying Training School. Something of a showpiece, the project embraced ten hangars and six miles of perimeter. Training was well under way by 1939 and continued throughout the Second World War, and it is known that at least two FW 200 Condors were based here in connection with radio/radar training. The last frantic days of the war saw Gatow's involvement in some desperate missions. For example, after Hitler decided, on 22 April 1945, to hand over control of the Reich to Goering, news of the abortive plan was relayed by a messenger who took off in a Heinkel 111 the following day, flew to Berchtesgaden in Bavaria and then drove to nearby Obersalzberg to deliver the information personally to the Reichsmarschall. In another incident (described in her autobiography, *The Sky my Kingdom*), test pilot Hanna Reitsch claims she was one of two people crammed into the rear space of a two-seat FW 190 which was flown into Gatow from Rechlin by a Luftwaffe pilot on 26 April. At Gatow, Reitsch and her colleague then clambered aboard a Fieseler Storch and completed their errand to the Reich Chancellery in Berlin, landing near the Brandenburg Gate.

The airfield fell to the Russians late on 26 April, but their occupation lasted only until the summer, the RAF taking over and forming 19 Staging Post, which made its first report on 2 July 1945. By the end of July over 1,400 aircraft had transitted through, and at the end of August the units listed here also included the British Air Command Berlin Communications Flight. The first colour hoisting was held on 14 September, and throughout the latter half of the year the Station handled many notable VIPs travelling to Potsdam, Warsaw and other destinations. Aircraft types seen included the Spitfire, Lancaster, Hurricane, Mosquito, Expediter, Grumman Goose, Martinet, Dominie, Savoia, Ju 52, Yak and Ilyushin 2 Shturmovik.

Regular RAF squadrons also began to operate from the airfield for brief periods, the last three months of 1945 bringing in 451 and 453 Squadrons (Spitfire XIVs) and 174 (Tempest Vs). Over the 1946–8 period, constant redeployments in Germany as a whole saw Nos, 2, 16, 26, 33, 56 and 80 (all Tempests – 2s and 5s), 14, 69 and 98 (all Mosquito XVIs), and 107 (Mosquito VIs) all serving here, some of them on multiple occasions. When 80 Sqn returned for the third time in June 1948 it had exchanged its Tempest Vs for Spitfire F24s.

Gatow's role as a fighter/bomber station ended in mid-1948, when it was earmarked as the British terminal for the Berlin Airlift. Thus, in June of that year when the Airlift began, it was decided to develop the airfield for the largest intensity of traffic that it could handle. Based on the estimated tonnage that would be required to break the siege, and an estimate that 480 aircraft could be landed in any 24-hour period, major improvements were initiated on the runway, unloading apron and other facilities. Operation Knicker (later changed to Plainfare) was called on 28 June, and at 0600 hours on that day the first Dakota left Wunstorf in Germany's British Zone for Gatow. As the intensity of the Operation increased, American as well as British aircraft began to use the airfield, and the military types involved ranged from the Dakota to the C-74 Globemaster. Avro Yorks began Airlift flying into Gatow on 3 July, Hastings following suit in November. Civil types varied from the Bristol Wayfarer to the Avro Tudor, the largest of the liquid fuel tankers. The Station's first Airlift fatality was Skyways York G-AHFI, which crashed on 15 March 1949. By the time the last official Airlift aircraft, a Hastings, landed at Gatow on 6

Gatow during the Berlin Airlift. Avro York MW105 (the first pure freighter York built) in 241 OCU markings trundles down the taxiway, followed by Airflight's Avro Tudor 2 G-AGRY. Airflight operated the Tudor on the Airlift between September 1948 and May 1949. (RAF Gatow)

October 1949, more than 110,000 landings had been made on the airfield.

With the ending of the biggest air support operation ever mounted by the RAF in peacetime, the Station returned to its normal routine, handling such military communications aircraft as Dakotas and Devons. A somewhat unexpected military visitor in October 1952 was a two-seat MiG which landed by mistake and taxied past the hangars, before the pilot realized his error. Various individuals vainly tried to block the progress of the fighter with road vehicles, but it took to the grass and eventually got airborne. Shutting down temporarily in 1953 the airfield was officially reopened on 1 December 1954.

The period 8–14 February 1962 saw the Soviets trying to reserve air space in the Berlin Corridors, a move which resulted in the Allies instituting a system of counter-flights using transport and training aircraft. The Station Prentice was used to exercise Britain's right to fly in the Berlin Control Zone and in December 1966 this task was taken over by two Chipmunks established especially for the task. The two-seat trainers (which were still here in mid-1989, although individual aircraft have rotated over the years) also provided useful continuation training for pilots posted to RAF Gatow. The inaugural flight of a BEA Viscount in April 1964 marked the start of air trooping to Berlin from the UK, BAC 111s taking over the schedule in July 1965.

Military types being handled at the beginning of 1966 included Pembrokes, Comets and Valettas, The most dramatic event of the year was the crash of a Yak 28 Firebar in the River Havel, some four miles from Gatow, on 6 April. The Station was closely involved in the recovery of the wreckage, which was of considerable interest from an intelligence point of view. Priority was given to extricating the dead aircrew, and then the salvage work began, a task made more difficult by the state of the ejector seats, one of which was still live. The last of the various pieces of the Yak had been handed back to the Soviets by 2 May.

Infantry activity in Berlin continually generated a need for air support of one type or another, and when the Argyle and Sutherland Highlanders replaced the Light Infantry in April 1969, the battalion exchange was made by air using both RAF and civil chartered Britannias. RAF Argosys brought in more troops from the Anglian Regiment for an exercise later in

Gatow Station Flight's Chipmunk WG486 'formates' with Soviet Mi 8 'Hip' during a routine Berlin Wall patrol. (7 Flight AAC)

the month. Then, in 1970, 7 Aviation Flight of the AAC was established at Gatow to carry out routine border patrols for the Berlin infantry, becoming operational with four Sioux helicopters on 1 April. They were joined later in the month by a detachment of 131 Flight, Royal Corps of Transport, whose two Westland Scouts were flown in by Argosy. The Flight had already mounted similar detachments to Gatow in previous years. Later on (in April 1974, for example) 669 Sqn, AAC, would mount similar detachments, the Squadron's Scouts being airlifted from Wildenrath by Belfast transport aircraft.

The last flight of an RAF Valetta occurred on 10 April 1972 when WJ491 flew in from Boscombe Down, to be retained for crash/rescue training. Another, more appropriate, veteran aircraft to end its days here was Hastings TG503, delivered from Scampton on 29 June 1977 as the result of a request by the Station for an aircraft of this type to be sited as a static memorial to the Berlin Airlift. Before landing for the last time the pilot, Squadron Leader K. Jackson, made a

farewell 30-minute flight over West Berlin carrying representatives of BFBS, the German press and TV, and five German civilians who had worked at Gatow during the Airlift.

In May 1977 7 Flight re-equipped with three Gazelles, and in 1989 continued to operate under the control of the Berlin Brigade HQ. The Flight's main roles are surveillance of the Berlin Wall, movement of VIPs and other personnel, law enforcement in support of the Berlin Police, and providing assistance to the fire and customs services. In addition to the regular RAF Chipmunk sorties the Station continues to handle a variety of transport and communications flights.

Geilenkirchen, Germany

The name of Geilenkirchen today (1991) immediately brings to mind the Boeing E-3A Sentry AWACS aircraft in NATO markings whose home base this is, but throughout the 1950s and 1960s the RAF ensign flew here, for it was the fourth and most southerly of the 'Clutch' stations. The base was built by 5357 Airfield Construction Wing who began handing over newly-completed facilities in April 1953. The Station became a self-accounting unit on 15 May, by which time 25 Wing RAF Regiment was established here, having arrived at the beginning of the month.

But it was as a fighter airfield that Geilenkirchen had been created, and the first operational unit arrived in July 1953. This was 3 Sqn flying the North American Sabre. No 3's busy training activities at this point included low-level dog fights, and tactical recce missions to give the pilots practice in map reading, while aircraft were detached to Sylt for armament practice camp. Early in January 1954 234 Sqn arrived from Oldenburg to become the Station's second Sabre squadron.

Amongst the facilities that had been built on the Station were dispersal pans proctected by concrete revetments. In October 1954 three Venoms from 16 Sqn at Celle were detached here to carry out RP attacks on the revetments to test their effectiveness. Concrete warheads were used first, followed by HE warheads in a series of trials which were nothing if not realistic! The resident Sabres on the other hand continued with their programme of high-level battle formation training, cine work, low-level cross countries and air-to-ground firing, deploying temporarily to another airfield in June 1955 to operate under canvas. The following month the two squadrons were detached to Cyprus for air-to-air firing training, and in their absence roads and hardstandings at Geilenkirchen were 'toned down' for camouflage purposes.

No 2 Sqn, a unit specializing in reconnaissance, arrived from Wahn with its Meteor PR10s in October 1955, but began re-equipping with the Swift FR5 in April 1956. Nos 3 and 234 Sqn both re-equipped with Hunters in May, the last Sabre leaving the Station on 21 June. After taking part in simulated bomber attacks on targets in the UK, 3 Sqn disbanded in June 1957, followed in July by 234 Sqn. This left behind the Station Flight's Vampire and Chipmunk, and 2 Sqn whose activities included an exchange with Danish AF RF–84F Thunderflashes at Karup.

As part of the annual SHAPE atomic exercise in September 1957, 141 Sqn's Javelins were detached here from Coltishall, freight and personnel being airlifted in by Beverley and civil Hermes. Exercise flying was controlled from an Operations Wing bunker for the first time. Other exercises were held before the year was out, and taking part in these was 59 Sqn which arrived in November. Ground attack was 59's role, for which it operated Canberra B(I)8s.

January 1958 saw the departure to Jever of 2 Sqn, which was replaced the following month by Nos 96 and 256 Sqns, both night fighter units with Meteor NF11s. Now back up to three squadrons, Geilenkirchen mounted its first major off-base dispersal exercise (Exercise Trek) in April 1958, for which the Canberras flew offensive and recce sorties. An exercise in September of that year saw 256's Meteors operating in the ground attack role against armoured units of the Coldstream Guards, at the same time as 96 Sqn began re-equipping with Javelin 4s.

As part of a renumbering exercise, 96 and 256 Sqns became 3 and 11 Sqns

11 Sqn's Javelin FAW9s at Geilenkirchen in June 1965. (P Russell-Smith Colln)

respectively in January 1959, although their role in the many exercises of the period remained unchanged. 59 Sqn normally flew pre-planned offensive sorties in such exercises, but in September the unit was exempted from participating due to the need to concentrate on training for Low Altitude Bombing Strike (LABS) sorties. In November, 11 Sqn began converting to Javelins, which were soon featuring in the monthly AMLED Danish air defence exercises.

The 1960s opened with the Station meeting SACEUR's requirement for one aircraft to be kept armed at fifteen minutes' readiness, round-the-clock, for QRA, and by now the Station Flight had accumulated such diverse types as the Meteor 7, Chipmunk, Canberra and Varsity. In January 1961 3 Sqn disbanded with its Javelins, at the same time as 59 Sqn (still on Canberra B(I)8s) renumbered as 3 Sqn. Visiting Javelins of 29 Sqn arrived for an eight-week detachment from Leuchars in December, while twelve months later, in December 1962, the Station gained another permanent Javelin unit, 5 Sqn, which moved over from Laarbruch, bringing with it the Mk 9 aircraft it had taken over from 33 Sqn which had disbanded in the UK. Nos 5 and 11 Sqns now took it in turn to provide the Battle Flight of two aircraft, which were at immediate readiness 24 hours a day, seven days a week, the Javelins always flying with loaded guns and live Firestreak missiles to enable them to respond instantly to any call.

The Javelin, however, was nearing the end of its career and was due to be replaced in the RAF by the Lightning. No 5 Sqn returned to the UK in October 1965, while 11 Sqn disbanded here in January 1966, the last unit in Germany to fly the aircraft. The two squadrons were replaced at Geilenkirchen by 92 Sqn which deployed from Leconfield, UK with its Lightning F2s in December 1965. The Lightnings performed much the same role as their predecessors, providing a constant battle-readiness flight to intercept suspicious radar contacts and taking part in numerous air defence exercises, but at Geilenkirchen 92 Sqn was not ideally located to make its presence felt, particularly in the Berlin corridors. A sister Lightning squadron was already operational at Gütersloh, where it was decided to centralize Germany's interceptor units, and 92 Sqn moved there in January 1968.

Earlier the same month 3 Sqn had moved with its Canberras to Laarbruch, for the RAF was soon to vacate Geilenkirchen. Flying formally ceased on 26 January, and the Station was handed over to the German Air Force on 31 March 1968.

Gibraltar

Tacked incongruously on to the southern end of Spain, a dozen or so miles opposite the African coast, Gibraltar's strategic position at the western entrance to the Mediterranean has led to its use as a military base of long standing. Moreover, surrounded on three sides by water 'the Rock' was a natural site for both land- and seaplane operations, a feature not missed by the Royal Navy when it began what was probably the earliest military flying here in 1915.

This initial activity consisted of ten assorted aircraft which were shipped to Gibraltar to be used for spotting submarines after the first German U-boat to enter the Mediterranean (U–21) had passed through the Straits in May of that year. The consignment comprised three marine types (a Short seaplane – probably a 184, and two Curtiss H4 flying boats), and seven landplanes (three Caudrons plus four BE2cs). The seaplanes operated out of the harbour from an area later designed New Camp, while the landplanes were flown from the racecourse situated under the north face of the Rock. It was the racecourse area which, much later on, was developed as an airfield proper, and which was known as RAF North Front from 1942 until 1966. The problems of maintaining the assortment of machines, combined with the notorious wind turbulence around the Rock, made these early operations fairly hazardous.

This pioneering naval activity spawned Gibraltar's first RAF squadron, No 265, which formed here in August 1918 from Nos 265, 266 and 364 Flights, RNAS. Equipment consisted of Short 184s and Felixstowe F3s which flew anti-submarine patrols from the harbour area, until the unit's disbandment in 1919

The only military flying units to use the racecourse area on a formal basis during the inter-war years were those of the Royal Navy, and even these were brief disembarkations from visiting ships. 820 Sqn, operating Fairey IIIFs and Seals, called in January 1934; another Fairey IIIF unit, 822 Sqn visited in February 1936; and in January 1937 the Blackburn Sharks of 821 Sqn were here. The harbour area, on

Saro London K6932 'TQ-B' of 202 Sqn at its New Camp mooring in Gibraltar harbour in 1939. (via D Skinner)

the other hand, began drawing RAF units: 210 Sqn was based here with its Short Rangoons and Singapores from September 1935 to August 1936 while 228 Sqn's Stranraers passed through in September 1938 on their way east for a Mediterranean cruise. Early in 1939 Saro Londons from 202 Sqn, based at Kalafrana, Malta, visited with a view to using Gibraltar as a wartime base, and a week after the outbreak of the Second World War the Squadron moved here on a permanent basis. At the same time a detachment of 3 Anti-Aircraft Cooperation Unit was established here with Swordfish to provide the Army with sound location and searchlight practice, and to control the activities of these two flying units 200 Group was formed on 25 September.

Throughout 1940, 202 Sqn patrolled the Straits of Gibraltar, adding Swordfish floatplanes to its complement in October for shorter range work. Whilst 202 Sqn's Swordfish operated from the harbour, the RN's 810 flew the land-based version from the airfield in the course of a detachment which began in April 1940 and lasted until early 1942. June and July 1940 saw detachments of Sunderlands, from 228 Sqn based in Egypt, sent in to assist 202 Sqn with its western Mediterranean patrols.

In May 1941 202 Sqn began converting from Londons to Catalinas, which in June attacked three U-boats. Two squadrons paused here briefly *en route* to Gambia

during the summer months and carried out useful work: No 200, whose Hudsons escorted a batch of 48 Hurricanes to Malta; and No 204 which, with Sunderlands, flew convoy escorts. More Hudsons, a detachment from 233 Sqn in the UK, appeared in August, and by 1942 the Sqn was flying the majority of its operations from Gibraltar. This awkward arrangement was regularized when the Squadron was formally posted here in June 1942 – remaining until February 1944. On its way to Egypt 89 Sqn spent the autumn months of 1941 here with Beaufighters. Throughout the last three months of 1941 the emphasis was on RN activity. October saw the formation of 779 Sqn as a Fleet Requirements Unit, equipped initially with Blackburn Skuas for drogue-towing and coastal defence duties. (Swordfish, Fulmars and Sea Hurricanes were used later, and in April 1943 Defiants replaced the Skuas in the target-towing role. Beaufighter IIs arrived in mid–1943, while Martinets replaced the Defiants in mid–1944, 779 Sqn disbanding in August 1945.) In November, 700 (Gib) Sqn took on the task of daily patrols from the Rock with Walruses, and then the following month an ASV radar-equipped Swordfish from 812 Sqn (disembarked for three months) carried out the first-ever night sinking of a U-boat by an aircraft.

But it was in 1942 that flying from the Rock reached a peak, for that year saw Operation Torch – the Allied invasion of

North Africa, in which Gibraltar would play a vital springboard role. In preparation for this, Royal Engineers transformed the existing landing strip into a fully tarmacked runway 1,400 yards long – with the last 400 yards protruding into the sea – and 100 yards wide, while dispersal areas were increased to facilitate the parking of 600 aircraft. At the same time, air activity increased, beginning in February with detachments of 95 Sqn Sunderlands from Freetown for convoy escort work. In April 24 Sqn began regular communications flights from Hendon using Hudsons, followed in September by a detachment of Whitleys from Tempsford-based 161 Sqn for undercover work in North Africa. Gibraltar's rise to prominence now required a new organization and accordingly on 1 May AHQ Gibraltar was formed to administer RAF North Front (controlling the operation of land-based aircraft) and RAF New Camp (responsible for the resident and transit flying boat activity).

Meanwhile, the Royal Navy's 813 Sqn disembarked its Sea Hurricanes from HMS *Eagle* for extended periods during 1942; its four aircraft were all lost when *Eagle* was sunk in August, although the Squadron itself was ashore at the time. A large detachment of Catalinas from 210 Sqn arrived in October, and on the 24th of the month a 202 Sqn 'Cat' picked up Brigadier General Mark Clark (deputy to General Eisenhower, who was to command the North African landings) from a submarine following his covert meeting with resistance leaders in Algiers. The means to gather the vital photographic intelligence for the landings was provided by a detachment of 540 Sqn (Mosquito IV) plus 544 Sqn 'B' Flight (Spitfire IV). Two Hudson squadrons, 500 and 608, were taken on strength in November to cover the convoys bringing in the invasion forces, together with 179 Sqn operating Leigh Light Wellington VIIIs. In addition, 511 Sqn (based at Lyneham) set up a Liberator detachment to fly a shuttle service to Malta. General Eisenhower himself arrived on 5 November in a B–17 Flying Fortress flown by Major Paul Tibbets of the US 97th Bomb Group.

Operation Torch began on 8 November, and the first air unit to depart from the airfield at Gibraltar for North Africa was 43 Sqn (Hurricanes), followed by 81 and 242 with Spitfires. Other squadrons to be launched to North American bases over the succeeding days including 72, 93, 111, and

152 (all Spitfires), 225 (Hurricanes), 255 and 600 (Beaufighters) and 13 (Blenheim Vs), together with the Spitfires of the US 31st and 52nd Fighter Groups. The hectic air activity continued into December, 48 Sqn arrived to escort the North African convoys with its Hudsons, and later on using rockets in attacks on U-boats. The last weeks of the year also saw detachments of special duties Halifaxes from 161 Sqn and of 87 Sqn Hurricanes from their North African base for shipping patrols.

In the aftermath of Torch, 1943 saw much coming and going. Firstly there was the formation of 1676 Gibraltar Defence Flight, formed on 12 April with eight Spitfire Vcs for the air defence of the Rock. (Prior to this a fighter capability had been provided from the resources of the so-called Spitfire Erection Party, formed the previous year to assemble Spitfires for Torch. No 1676 Flight became 'C' Flight of 253 Sqn, and then 256 Sqn based elsewhere, before fading out of the picture by May 1944.) Then there were detachments of 59 Sqn Liberators from Northern Ireland for anti-submarine duties, of photo-reconnaissance Sptifires from 541 Sqn for sorties over North Africa, and of 248 Sqn Beaufighters from Cornwall, which tangled with the FW 200 Condors that were threatening Allied convoys. During April and May Hurricanes of the Merchant Ship Fighter Unit disembarked to the Rock while attached to an Algiers convoys, one of the machines crashing fatally on take-off from the airfield, due to treacherous weather. In August 179 Sqn re-equipped with Wellington XIVs, and U-boat activity increased markedly, prompting a detachment of Wellington XIVs from 172 Sqn in the UK in October. During this period 272 Sqn Beaufighters were detached here, taking part in shipping strikes, while throughout the year visits were made by disembarked RN Martlet, Swordfish and Seafire squadrons.

On a more permanent basis, 520 Sqn formed in September 1943 from the Gibraltar detachment of 1403 Meteorological Flight, which had been flying Gladiators. (1403 Flight itself grew out of what was known simply as the 'Met Flight'.) No 520 Sqn spent its entire existence here until disbandment in 1946, during which time it was equipped with the Hudson, Halifax, Spitfire, Hurricane and Warwick, together with a small Flight of Martinets for target-towing from September 1944 onwards. (Prior to September the TT task had been performed

Above *Dakota at Gibraltar during a searchlight practice in the Second World War.* (T Fairbairn Colln)

Below *Shackleton MR1s and MR2s of 224 Sqn at Gibraltar. Nearest camera is MR2 WL753 'B-Q'.* (via D Skinner)

by No 1500 Target Towing Flight, which had begun work with Lysanders and Martinets back in mid-1943.) The most notorious event of the year, however, was the mysterious crash immediately after take-off on the night of 4 July of 511 Sqn Liberator AL523 carrying the Polish Prime Minister, General Sikorski, and his party.

The first quarter of 1944 saw both 48 and 233 Sqns returning to the UK with their Hudsons, and the arrival of 52 Sqn, whose Baltimores flew a limited number of anti-submarine patrols before the unit disbanded in March. No 179 left for home in April, followed by 202 in September, leaving detachments of Liberators from US Navy Squadrons VB–112 and 114 to take up the anti-submarine commitment. In February 775 Sqn, a Fleet Requirements Unit, moved in from Egypt and during its stay (which lasted until August 1945) it flew the usual miscellany of types, including the Martlet, Beaufighter II, Hurricane, Seafire IIc and Blenheim IV. Another invasion, that of Southern France in August (Operation Dragoon), resulted in another burst of air transport activity in the summer, when the airfield was crammed with Dakotas. The only other fresh units to serve here before war's end were 458 Sqn which, arriving in January 1945 with Leigh Light Wellington XIVs, flew regular if fairly fruitless patrols before disbanding in

June, and 22 SAAF Sqn on Venturas.

Post-war Gibraltar consolidated its role as a maritime station, hosting detachments of Lancasters from Malta and the UK throughout the late 1940s. In addition, 520 Sqn was still here in the specialist meteorological reconnaissance role, and when it disbanded in April 1946 its duties were taken over by a detachment of 518 Sqn Halifax VIs from Northern Ireland. This detachment was maintained after 518 Sqn was renumbered 202. In May 1948 224 Sqn was reformed for meteorological reconnaissance in Northern Ireland and also began sending detachments of Halifaxes to Gibraltar, before moving *in toto* to the Rock in October 1948. Its role soon widened into more general maritime reconnaissance, and during 1949 it took on a curious dual identity, that of 224/269 Sqn. Shackleton MR1s were received in July 1951, and then in January 1952 269 Sqn formed as an independent unit alongside 224, before moving out to Northern Ireland the following March, the same month in which 224 finally relinquished the last of its Halifax GR6s. No 224 maintained a particular watch on shipping passing through the Straits, re-equipping with Shackleton MR2s in May 1953 and disbanding here in October 1966.

Between February and April 1951, 737 Sqn 'X' Flight (formed at Lee-on-Solent

Sea Hornet F20 VZ708 '456/C' of 801 Sqn flies over the southern tip of Gibraltar c. *1950.* (Charles Brown)

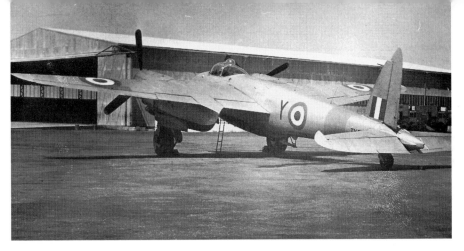

Mosquito TT35 TK610 'Y' of the Gibraltar Station Flight c. 1953. (D Snow)

for special trials with search receivers to detect submarine radar) was based here with a Firefly and an Anson. The 1950s generally set the pattern for future military air activity on the Rock – as a venue for detachments of units engaged in maritime exercises and operations. Coastal Command Lancaster and Shackleton squadrons were frequent visitors, and Royal Auxiliary Air Force fighter squadron summer camps were hosted. As a result of tension with Spain (which went on to close its border with Gibraltar in 1969) Britain saw fit to maintain a detachment of Hunters from the operational training units in the UK.

Beginning in mid-1966 with aircraft provided by 229 OCU Chivenor, the arrangement lasted unit August 1978 when the last two Hunters were flown back to 2 TWU at Brawdy.

The annual programme throughout the 1980s remained fairly constant, revolving primarily around two major exercises each year, one national and the other NATO. As well as RAF units, the national exercise (e.g. Spring Train) usually starred the Hunters and Canberras of the RN's Fleet Requirements and Air Direction Unit (FRADU), while the NATO exerices (e.g. Open Gate) also drew aircraft from the

Canadair Argus 10732 of VP-415, Summerside, at Gibraltar for Exercise Test Gate — February 1981. (T Fairbairn)

Top *Jaguars of 20 Sqn visiting Gibraltar on 27 March 1981. Behind is a visiting Nimrod.* (T Fairbairn)

Above *FRADU pilot Tommy Thompson climbs out of Hunter GA11 XE689 '864' after a sortie with the Royal Navy on 11 April 1981 during exercise Spring Train at Gibraltar.* (T Fairbairn)

Dutch and West German navies and the Canadian Armed Forces. In addition to weekend navigational exercise visits from UK-based Dominies, there were periodic appearances from Jaguars, Harriers and Buccaneers taking part in Armament Practice Camps in Sardinia. Literally every type of RN helicopter disembarked at one time or another during this period, and in October 1980 the first Sea Harriers to visit, those of 800 Sqn, flew in off HMS *Invincible*. Tornadoes (from 9 Sqn at Brüggen, Germany) made their first appearance as part of a visit in June 1987. The US Navy was also a regular caller, routeing in Sigonella-based Sabreliners, Hercules and Greyhounds of VR–24 Sqn, together with Orions from other US Navy patrol squadrons detached to Sigonella. Since the Second World War, Gibraltar airfield had also functioned as the Rock's civil airport.

Goose Bay, Canada

Known to the locals as 'Grand Old Goose', this particular base, although not an RAF Station as such, unquestionably merits inclusion by virtue of its long and very active association with the RAF. Canadian Forces Station Goose Bay is located on the 53rd parallel, the same latitude as Liverpool, at the head of a tidal waterway known as Lake Melville, some 200 miles inland from Canada's Labrador coast. There are no road links with the base, and air transport provides the only access once the waterway freezes during the winter months. There are no climatic similarities to Liverpool, summer temperatures reaching 38 degrees and those in winter plummeting to − 36.

Military interest in the area began in March 1941 when Canadian and American authorities met to discuss the need for airfield facilities to augment those of Newfoundland Airport. The meeting tasked the two nations with carrying out surveys, and the US survey party was led by Captain Elliott Roosevelt from the Army Air Corps' 21st Recon Sqn. Much use was made of material from an earlier civilian survey carried out in August 1935 by a three-man team using a Fairchild 71 floatplane, G-CAIW. Of the various sites examined, Roosevelt's report favoured that at Goose Bay, and in August 1941 a recommendation was made to the Canadian Government for the construction of an airfield with runways and technical and domestic facilities –

In order to facilitate the ferrying of long and medium range aircraft across the Atlantic, to enhance the effectiveness of plans for hemisphere defence, to prevent congestion at the Newfoundland Airport and to provide greater security for crews and equipment....

Preparation for the construction of the airfield began virtually straight away and the epic engineering task, with the awesome logistics problems posed by its isolated location, is worthy of its own book. Suffice to say, all major work was completed by the end of 1943. One of the first tasks had been to carve landing strips out of the forest, enabling the first aircraft to land at Goose Bay on 3 December 1941 (a ski-equipped, twin-engined machine of Quebec Airways). The first military type (from the RCAF) arrived six days later. The RCAF

ensign was hoisted for the first time on 29 March 1942, and on 1 April the various facilities which had been built became known collectively as RCAF Station Goose Bay.

Located some 850 miles north of Gander, Newfoundland, Goose Bay was designed primarily for the medium-range aircraft being ferried to the UK via Iceland, and RAF Ferry Command established a unit here in April. This unit immediately began despatching Catalinas, Hudsons and Liberators across the Atlantic. The Americans arrived in June, received permission to built their own facilities in July, and became an independent organization in August. During 1943, when it handled 1,799 tactical aircraft, Goose was second only to Presque Isle, Maine, in terms of transatlantic traffic, and in the year ending 30 September 1945 the airfield turned round 25,000 aircraft.

Military activity dwindled after the war and the RCAF alone maintained the base for air sea rescue and anti-submarine patrols. However, the Cold War and the formation of the North Atlantic Alliance in 1949 generated a new period of expansion, with the RAF re-establishing a small detachment and the USAF setting up a Strategic Air Command (SAC) presence (which would last until 1 October 1976). Another milestone that year was the arrival in July of six Vampires of 54 Sqn, which, after refuelling at Iceland and Greenland, had become the first RAF jet aircraft to cross the Atlantic. Between December 1952 and December 1953 the airfield became a key location in Operation Bechers Brook, the ferrying of Canadair-built North American Sabres across the Atlantic to equip RAF squadrons in the UK and Germany.

The annual Anglo-American Strategic Bombing Competition, beginning in 1957 when SAC first invited RAF Bomber Command to enter the competition at Pinecastle AFB Florida, resulted in a further expansion of the RAF detachment, now mounted by Bomber Command. Goose also began handling regular Western Ranger flights consisting of RAF 'V' bombers transitting to and from Offutt AFB Nebraska. Bomber Command activity here intensified even more when, in 1964, RAF Vulcans began flying low-level training sorties from the airfield after the 'V'-Force had been assigned the low-level penetration role. The eight-day detachments from the UK, during which each crew flew three or four special low-level routes, were known as Goose Rangers. In addition to Vulcans staging through to Hawaii and Guam in the course of Pacific Rangers, practically every type of RAF transport aircraft called in throughout the late 1960s on resupply or trials support duties.

A detachment of six Victor tankers from Marham arrived in May 1969 to support RAF Harriers and Phantoms participating in the Daily Mail Transatlantic Race, while in October traffic included Vulcans returning to Waddington after the Giant Voice competition at Fairchild AFB. Back on 4 October 1965, RN Buccaneer S2 XN974 had flown non-stop, without in-flight refuelling, from Goose to Lossiemouth to become the first Fleet Air Arm aircraft ever to make the Atlantic crossing non-stop. In November 1970 another Buccaneer staged through in the opposite direction, this one on its way to cold weather trials at Churchill, Manitoba, supported by two Hastings from Boscombe Down. The Nimrod made its first appearance in June 1971 at the start of a world tour, and in June of the following year the Red Arrows practised their display from the airfield in prepartion for a show at EXPO '72.

Victor tanker detachments continued throughout the 1970s, in February 1975, for example, to support Jaguars returning to the UK after cold weather trials at Cold Lake, Alberta, and Buccaneers making for Cecil NAS, Florida. Prince Philip passed through in his Queen's Flight Andover in March, while two months later a Canberra PR9 of 39 Sqn arrived to photograph the

low-level routes. The categories of visiting Vulcans also included Midway Rangers, flying between the UK and McClellan AFB, California. In July 1978 Flying Officer Warren-Wilson spent a weekend here while piloting his Piper Cherokee on an eastabout round-the-world flight, and by now there was a steady flow of Jaguars and Buccaneers taking part in either Red Flag competitions or Pirate Trail training detachments.

Due to be superseded by the Tornado, the Vulcan's days at Goose were numbered. In June 1982 XL361 was handed over to the town of Happy Valley, Goose Bay, and on the fifteenth of the month the hangar roof was crowded with spectators witnessing the departure of the last Vulcan detachment for the UK. (The last individual visiting Vulcan was probably the aircraft taking part in the Winnipeg air display in September 1984.) In June 1983 the prototype Tornado F2 staged through on its way to Luke AFB for hot weather trials, Marham Tornadoes transitted in August making for the Toronto air display, and then in October came the first Tornado squadron detachment when 9 Sqn arrived for Exercise Western Vortex.

Between the months of April and October, Goose Bay is rarely without a Tornado squadron either operating from the airfield or passing through to and from the Flag series of exercises (which also attract the UK-based Jaguar squadrons) in Canada and the USA, or indeed participating in bombing competitions. The Tornado programme is punctuated by the occasional unusual visitor; in February

Tornado GR1s of, left to right, 16, 17 and 20 Sqns at Goose Bay in September 1988. (MoD Crown Copyright)

1984, for example, there was the British Aerospace 146 heading for cold weather trials at Calgary; when F-4J Phantoms were delivered to 74 Sqn in the UK in November/December 1984 they refuelled here; and perhaps most exotic of all, Mosquito RS712 called en route from the UK to its new home at the Weeks Air Museum in Florida. At the time of writing (December 1988) several other air forces are active at Goose Bay: the Canadian Air Force (which coordinates all military flying here) operates CH-135s for search and rescue and uses the airfield as a dispersed base for CF-18 Hornet operations; C-5s, C-141s and C-130s of the USAF visit in the transport role; and low-level flying training is carried out by the Dutch Air Force with F-16s and the German Air Force using Tornadoes, Phantoms and Alpha Jets.

Gütersloh, Germany

The only former Luftwaffe station still in RAF hands in 1990, Gütersloh's origins go back to 1933 when military installations were first planned here and construction work began. The Luftwaffe formally took over the base on 24 April 1937 and the first aircraft to be based here were Ju 86s of III/KG 154. Gütersloh's combat group was mobilized during the Sudetenland crisis of 1938, when it moved to Silesia, and the following year the Station took part in exercises involving simulated RAF bomber raids. By the outbreak of the Second World War the resident unit here had become KG 28 operating He 111Ps. During the fighting in Poland the base provided refuelling and servicing facilities for Luftwaffe units moving to and from that country.

In May 1940 Ju 52s took off from the airfield to drop paratroops in support of a ground attack on Holland, and the same month He 111s of KG 4, using Gütersloh as well as other bases, mounted the first air raid on Rotterdam. Later in the year the station became an important night fighter base for such Me 110-equipped units as I/NJG 1 and II/NJG 1, while in June a fighter wing, III/JG 51 with Me 109s, was taken on strength for eight months or so. Between 1941 and 1944 Gütersloh's main function was as a servicing and modification centre for aircraft, although it was also an area HQ with responsibility for a number of subordinate airfields, a maintenance unit at Paderborn, a flying school at Detmold, a radio centre north east of Paderborn, and a bombing range at Augustdorf. A return to the night fighter role came in late 1943 with the arrival of radar-equipped Ju 88s, and by June 1944 the Bf 110s of II/NJG 5 were based here. Gütersloh-based FW 190s of IV/JG 3 took part in the Bodenplatte attack on Allied airfields in Belgium and Holland on 1 January 1945. More day fighters, from III/JG 27, arrived in March and Me 262 jets operated from the airfield during the closing months of the war. With the Allies pressing ever closer, the base was bombed several times during March by the US 9th Air Force, and at the end of the month all remaining Luftwaffe fighter aircraft were withdrawn. The US 651st Mechanized Cavalry Group arrived in the area on the evening of 1 April and accepted the surrender of the airfield the next day.

American engineers immediately began clearing the airfield of debris, which included the remains of Ju 88s, He 111s, Bf 109s, Me 410s and a FW 200, to enable two US units, the 363rd Reconnaissance Group (P-38 Lightnings) and the 370th Fighter Group (P-51 Mustangs) to fly from here for a short period. From 14–22 April the US XXIXth Tactical Air Command was also headquartered here.

Gütersloh, however, was apparently surplus to American requirements and was already being eyed for future use by the British. The first British personnel to move in (during June 1945) were from the RAF Regiment, who described the state of the airfield – known at this time as 'Y-99' – as 'a shambles'. It was to be November 1945 before the first British operational unit was deployed here. This was 140 Wing, comprising Nos 4, 21 and 107 Sqns, all flying the Mosquito FB6 and commanded by the famous Group Captain R. N. Bateson, who in effect became Gütersloh's first station commander. Specializing in night interdiction, 140 Wing's Mosquitoes also exercised with the Army, and during the period of the Nuremberg trials they provided a courier service between nearby Fürth airfield and Blackbushe in the UK. Meanwhile, the RAF's No 2 Group HQ had been located in the town and the Group's Communications Flight was based on the airfield, equipment consisting of Ansons and other utility types.

When 140 Wing disbanded in November 1947 the Mosquitoes were replaced by three Tempest squadrons, Nos 16, 26 and 33. They were joined the following summer by two more fighter squadrons, Nos 3 (with Vampires) and 80 (still with the Spitfire F24), deployed here because of the requirements of the Berlin Airlift at other

A visiting dignitary talks to 26 Sqn, whose Tempest F2s can be seen behind, at Gütersloh in late 1947. (via C Jefford)

stations. Although not playing a leading part in the airlift Gütersloh nevertheless acted as a diversion airfield throughout the operation, the Tempests maintaining standing patrols in Allied airspace, and detachments of Spitfire PR19s from 2 Sqn at Wahn flying photo reconnaissance sorties while the latter's runways were being repaired. By April 1949 16 and 26 Sqns had joined 3 Sqn in operating Vampire FB5s, while in July of that year 33 and 80 Sqns both got their marching orders for the Far East. Two other Vampire FB5 squadrons, 67 and 71, reformed here in September 1950, but by April 1952 all such units had either moved on or had disbanded, for Gütersloh was now to have a new role – that of reconnaissance.

A change of role meant fresh units and different aircraft, and accordingly 79 Sqn reformed here in November 1951 on the Meteor FR9. No 541 Sqn moved in during April 1952 with Meteor PR10s, and 2 Sqn followed a month later with more FR9s. Exercises were the staple diet at this point, but the 'Cold War' occasionally made its presence felt, with at least one Meteor pilot finding himself flying alongside a MiG 15, and a Yak 11 making a low-level photo pass over the airfield during 1954.

Gütersloh's roles were nothing if not varied, and as the last two Meteor squadrons transferred to Laarbruch in October 1954, the Station turned its attention to bomber operations, becoming the home base for 551 Wing comprised initially of Nos 149, 102 and 103 Sqns, all on the Canberra B2. Under a somewhat unusual arrangement these Squadrons were all controlled by Bomber Command in the UK. The exercises in which the Wing participated now had a NATO flavour and the Canberras also played the attacking role in UK air defence exercises. A fourth Canberra unit (104 Sqn) reformed here in March 1955, all five disbanding in August 1956. However, from 102 Sqn was reformed 59 Sqn which, after re-equipping with Canberra B(I)8s, moved on to Geilenkirchen in November 1957. The Gütersloh Canberra story would not be complete without mention of the Junior Technician who, having incurred the wrath of the local police, decided he would return prematurely to the UK in a stolen B2. Having been successfully started and taxied, the aircraft fortunately became bogged down in soft ground before it could be taken off, and the would-be pilot was apprehended!

With the arrival of 79 Sqn's Swift FR5s in the tactical reconnaissance role in

September 1956, the emphasis switched to fighter activity. The Swift, however, was not a success and the extent of its unreliability is illustrated by the fact that during some months nearly half of 79 Sqn's flying hours were achieved on a borrowed Vampire T11 and Meteors. It speaks volumes for the quality of the aircrew who secured first place flying the aircraft in a NATO reconnaissance competition in 1959. A sigh of relief no doubt accompanied the delivery of Hunter FR10s to 79 Sqn in December 1960, at which time the Squadron also renumbered as 4 Sqn, remaining at Gütersloh until disbandment in May 1970. A sister Hunter FR10 squadron, No 2, was also based here from September 1961 until it disbanded in March 1971.

The FR10s were not the only Hunters here, for in September 1958 an entire Wing of F6s made up of 20, 26 and 14 Sqns were posted in from Alhorn. Responsible for maintaining a Battle Flight, the Hunters were scrambled many times a month, occasionally to look at Warsaw Pact aircraft making incursions into Western airspace. With the disbandment of 20 and 26 Sqns in December 1960, 14 Sqn became RAFG's last interceptor unit, operating Hunters until it too disbanded two years later. In January 1961 the Station received two Westland Dragonfly HC4s to form a

Communications Flight for the use of the 1 BR Corps Commander and his staff. Located as it is in the centre of the 1 BR Corps area, Gütersloh was a natural choice as an airhead, and to enable it to handle the full range of transport aircraft the runway was lengthened during 1961. Thereafter the Station was responsible for processing the airlift of troops and other personnel to and from all parts of the world.

More helicopters were taken on strength in January 1963 when 230 Sqn arrived from the UK with Whirlwind HC10s to provide front-line support for BAOR. No 230, which also provided a detachment of aircraft at Nicosia, was replaced two years later by 18 Sqn equipped with Wessex HC2s. Not only was the beefier Wessex much better suited to the Army's needs, it was also used by the RAF for a variety of purposes, flying standing intruder patrols during exercises and being trialled in the fire-supression role with a weapons fit. During its three-year tour here 18 Sqn also mounted a Nicosia detachment in support of the UN peace-keeping force. (No 18 would return for a second – but not last – tour of duty here, still with the Wessex, running from August 1970 to November 1980 when it disbanded to work up in the UK as the RAF's first Chinook squadron.)

Gütersloh once more became a principal air defence base when, in September 1965,

14 Sqn Hunter F6 XJ691 'M' at Gütersloh in September 1959. (via P Russell-Smith)

19 Sqn was deployed here from the UK with Lightning F2s, arguably the most successful version of the fighter. A purpose-built Battle Flight hangar was constructed adjacent to the runway and this, with its accommodation for two Lightnings, enabled aircraft to be scrambled at the required five minutes' notice, day or night, all year round. No 19 Sqn was supplemented by a second Lightning unit, 92 Sqn, in January 1968. Although a superb interceptor, the Lightning was perhaps not in its ideal environment in NATO's Central Region, and after a career in Germany spanning almost twelve years it was decided that the type should be replaced in the command by the more versatile Phantom. Thus, 19 Sqn was disbanded at the tail end of 1975, followed by 92 Sqn in March 1977.

The only RAF Germany airfield east of the Rhine, and located approximately 80 miles, or ten minutes' flying time, from the border with East Germany, Gütersloh was selected as the base for the RAF's remaining Harrier squadrons – Nos 4 and 3 – which decamped here from Wildenrath in January and April 1977 respectively. The primary role of the Harriers is close air support (ground attack and reconnaissance) for NATO ground forces, and to achieve this the aircraft deploy to preselected sites in the countryside where 'hides' are constructed complete with fuel, weapons and spares support.

Also operating in support of 1 BR Corps are the Pumas of 230 Sqn which deployed from Odiham in December 1980. During a battle their tasks would include movement of stores, redeployment of troops (including anti-tank teams), and casualty evacuation. Finally, in April 1983, 18 Sqn

returned once again to provide the Army with its main airborne heavy lift capacity. At the time of writing (August 1990) the Station is established with an RAF Regiment Rapier Sqn (No 63, which was located here in July 1974 as the first such Regiment unit), 3 Sqn has re-equipped with the Harrier GR5, while 4 Sqn is preparing to receive the GR7.

Habbaniya, Iraq

Designed from the outset as the permanent Headquarters of the RAF in Iraq, it is difficult to avoid superlatives when describing this, possibly the grandest of all RAF stations. Work on Habbaniya, which in Arabic means 'of the Oleander Tree', began in 1934 under a clause of the Anglo-Iraqi Treaty permitting a British base west of the River Euphrates. First formed as a station in March 1937, it was originally named Dhibban, changing to the more familiar 'Habbaniya' on 1 May 1938. Its airfield career began in October 1936 with the arrival of No 30 Sqn, which had been based in Iraq since 1920 on policing duties and which was now flying Hawker Hardys. Other units on strength for similar duties during the 1937–9 period were 55 Sqn with Vickers Vincents followed by Blenheims, and 70 Sqn on Vickers Valentias. These operational units all moved on in August 1939, making way for 4 FTS from Egypt with its Airspeed Oxfords, Hawker Audaxes and Harts, Fairey Gordons and an Avro Anson. In addition to a Marine Craft Section, there were mooring facilities on nearby Lake Habbaniya for flying boats, both Service and civilian (e.g. BOAC).

At the outbreak of war, Habbaniya encompassed within its seven mile perimeter

Lightning F2A XN728 'F' of 92 Sqn — Gütersloh, June 1970. (via P Russell-Smith)

Hawker Hardys of 30 Sqn drawn up at Dhibban (Habbaniya) for AOC's inspection in April 1937. (MoD Crown Copyright)

not only the customary buildings and facilities of a large flying station, but also an Aircraft Depot with two large repair shops, together with Air Headquarters Iraq. The early war years were quiet, with detachments of 224 Sqn's Vincents from Shaibah for communications duties, and of 216 Sqn from Egypt. At the end of 1940 this latter detachment took over the Valentias of 'C' Flight, 70 Sqn, which had remained as a detachment at Habbaniya after 70's departure the previous year.

On 3 April 1941, a pro-Axis Iraqi politician, Rashid Ali, seized power in Baghdad, setting in train events which culminated in the siege of Habbaniya (the Regent Abdulla Illah having earlier fled from Baghdad to the sanctuary of RAF Habbaniya). Concerned at this change of regime, Britain reinforced Iraq with troops by both sea and air, and Habbaniya itself was beefed up with detachments of the King's Own Royal Regiment flown in by No 31 Sqn. This move heightened tension between the two countries, and on the morning of 30 April the Station awoke to find itself surrounded by Iraqi artillery. The only local flying unit available for the defence of the base was No 4 FTS which could muster approximately 80 aircraft, together with three tired Gloster Gladiators of the Station Flight. Throughout April many of these aircraft were modified to carry small bombs, and intensive courses were begun in bomb-aiming and air-gunnery. The entire fleet was then formed into four bombing 'squadrons' plus a Gladiator Flight, collectively designated the

Habbaniya Air Striking Force and commanded by the OC 4 FTS. The besieging Iraqi force continued to grow, and 4 FTS went into action on 2 May, alongside Shaibah-based Wellingtons. Reinforcements from Egypt arrived the following day in the shape of Blenheims of 203 Sqn, and the enemy withdrew on the night of 5/6 May. During the siege the Station was shelled and more than twenty aircraft were lost or damaged.

Whilst the local threat from Iraq had receded, that from Germany now became manifest with air attacks on the Station by Heinkel 111s. Bomber (84 Sqn Blenheims) and fighter (94 Sqn Hurricanes and Gladiators) reinforcements were again despatched from Egypt. Meanwhile, in mid-May 1941, Valentias from the Station's Iraq Communications Flight helped ferry troops for the British advance on Baghdad. Once the Iraq Revolt had been quelled, attention turned to Syria, still sympathetic to Germany. For Habbaniya this meant the formation of 127 Sqn from 'F' Flight of 4 SFTS with four Gladiators, two long-range and four standard Hurricanes, and a detachment of 31 Sqn with Valentias and DC-2s, both units operating in the Syrian theatre. In July 127 Sqn was renumbered 261 Sqn, which then moved to Shaibah for Operation 'Y' – the campaign against Persia (Iran). Following this campaign, which lasted for only a few days in August, several of the participating Blenheim squadrons (Nos 11, 14, 45 and 84) moved to Habbaniya for short periods.

Meanwhile, there had been other

Tempest F6 NX143 'GN-H' of 249 Sqn at Habbaniya in 1948. (via A Thomas)

changes during 1941. No 4 SFTS had been disbanded back in June, while August had seen No 52 Sqn reformed with Audaxes which were used for occasional recce work. It was in the crash of Audax K7544 that the CO of Habbaniya's RAF Hospital was killed in August 1942. The Aircraft Depot moved to Shaibah in September, and a month later No 123 Sqn put in some hours on Gladiators while awaiting delivery of

Hurricanes. By November the Iraq Communication Flight was operating Blenheims and Hudsons and one of the latter crashed in mountains south-west of Tehran in January 1943. Wellington BK143, used to ferry personnel to Palestine for leave, was burnt out in September 1944 and had to be replaced by a Hudson.

Habbaniya's establishment had burgeoned during the last three years of the

6 Sqn's Vampires being marshalled onto the tarmac at Habbaniya in the early 1950s. (6 Sqn)

war and units on strength in mid-1945 included the following: Iraq and Persia Communications Flight; No 1415 Met Flight (which operated Gladiators and Hurricanes); Nos 115 and 134 MUs; No 6 RAF Hospital; HQ RAF Levies, Nos 1 and 2 Battalions; Aircraft Safety Centre (Iraq and Persia); No 156 Repair and Salvage Unit; and No 1 Armoured Car Company HQ plus three Sections. The Station was the location for Air Headquarters Iraq and Persia, and there was a detachment of No 680 (PR) Sqn, from which Mosquito FBVI RF771 crashed fatally in September. Finally, No 40 Staging Post was here to handle the brisk flow of air transport traffic. No 40 SP was controlled by HQ 151 Wing, itself located at Habbaniya and responsible for other SPs at Shaibah, Bahrein and Sharjah.

February 1946 saw a burst of activity by transport aircraft, with an air drop by 6th Airborne Division from six Halifaxes of 644 Sqn, followed in March by an exercise in quick landing and dispersal by nineteen Halifaxes of 620 Sqn. No 249 Sqn took up post in June, but its Mosquito FB26s were suffering from terminal wood shrinkage and were superseded by Tempest VIs. A second front-line squadron, No 84, arrived towards the end of the 1948 and began receiving Bristol Brigands. The New Year opened on a depressing note with the destruction of one of the Tempests by Israeli Spitfires over Egypt and the crash of

Comms Flight Proctor HM406 into the Euphrates. Unusual visitors in May 1949 were twelve USAF Thunderbolts from Germany on delivery to Persia, with an escort of two Fortresses and a Dakota.

The distinctive whistle of the de Havilland Vampire now became a familiar sound, and Habbaniya was home for three squadrons of the diminutive jets throughout the early 1950s. These were No 6 (1951-6), No 185 (1952 until disbandment in 1953) and finally No 73 (1953-6). Venoms replaced the Vampires in 1954, and No 73 Sqn lost a complete section of four aircraft in December when their pilots, unable to land due to the cloudbase and visibility, all had to bale out. Two others force-landed. At the other end of the scale were the Lancaster PR1s of 683 Sqn which arrived in May 1952 for mapping duties over the Persian Gulf and remained until disbandment here in November 1953.

A new government in Iraq, with the expressed intention of terminating the Anglo-Iraqi Treaty, meant the withdrawal of British forces from its bases there. One of the first steps was the handover of Habbaniya to the Royal Iraq Air Force, and this took the form of an impressive parade on 2 May 1955, attended by HM King Feisal of Iraq. The Station now became simply 'RAF Unit, Habbaniya'. At the same time AHQ Iraq became AHQ Levant, moving *in toto* to Nicosia in December for amalgamation with AHQ

Valiant WP209 basking in glory at Habbaniya on 31 July 1955 after breaking the London-Baghdad record. (Fairbairn Colln)

Cyprus. Equipped with the Pembroke (e.g. WV700) and Valetta (e.g. VL269), the Iraq Comms Flight underwent a similar change of title. Withdrawal also resulted in the disbandment of the RAF Levies (Iraq). Other notable events in 1955 were the visit of four Canberras of 76 Sqn from Wittering for trials with the T2 bombsight, and the visit in July of Valiant WP209 from RAE Farnborough after breaking the London-Baghdad record (532.482 mph). Habbaniya's Aircraft Servicing Flight worked all night on the Valiant to cure a fuel leak, before it took off for Karachi the next morning.

After the departure of 6 Sqn's Venoms in 1956 the Station was relegated to a transit base and was used extensively by RAF Transport Command and ferry aircraft on the trunk and reinforcement routes to the Far East. But Iraq's withdrawal from the Baghdad Pact in 1959 made even this difficult, and a final and complete withdrawal took place on 31 May 1959. The size and appearance of Habbaniya, with its tree-lined boulevards, air-conditioned buildings, stock farm, irrigation system and almost infinite recreational facilities, became legendary, and at its height the station was a showcase for British design and engineering.

Hal Far, Malta

The first airfield to be built in Malta, Hal Far was opened by the Governor and C-in-C, Field-Marshal Lord Plumer, on 16 January 1923, control of the new Station being exercised by RAF Base Calafrana. Its origins stemmed from the need for an airfield on the island at which to disembark the Fleet Air Arm carrier-based, wheel-fitted aircraft, which were replacing floatplanes at this point. In January 1924 the first Fairey Flycatcher was sent to Malta, erected and the following month made the first flight by a Service aircraft from the new aerodrome.

That year marked the beginning of carrier operations in the Mediterranean, and during the summer HMS *Eagle* visited Malta, disembarking four Flights: No 402 (Flycatchers), No 422 (Blackburn Is), No 440 (Supermarine Seagull III amphibians), and No 460 (Balckburn Darts). This set the pattern for future disembarkation, with visiting aircraft participating in a wide range of exercises and trials.

Fairey Flycatcher of Malta Station Flight — Hal Far — 1928. (MoD Crown Copyright)

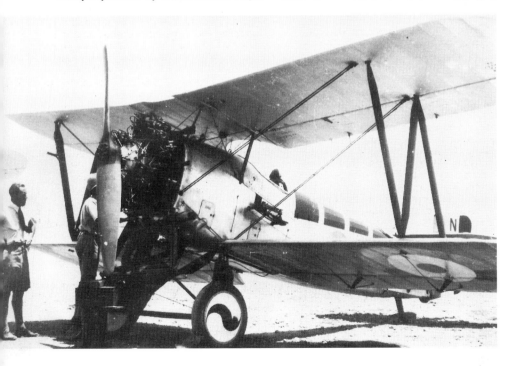

RAF Station Hal Far was officially formed on 31 March 1929, with personnel being drafted in over the next few days and the first CO, Wing Commander C. W. Nutting, taking up post in May. A Station Flight was formed during the year and was equipped initially with Fairey IIIFs. The majority of the flying at this point was by FAA aircraft, and three squadrons in particular made regular use of the airfield as a disembarkation base during 1933-4. These were 802 with Hawker Nimrods and Ospreys, 812 flying Blackburn Ripons and Baffins, and 823 on Fairey IIIFs and Seals. A spectacular display of illuminated night formation was put on by 812 Sqn in May 1935 together with illuminated aerobatics by two Avro Tutors.

In September 1935 twelve Hawker Demons arrived to form 74 Sqn, in response to the Abyssinian Crisis. The period of tension also resulted in the deployment of 22 Sqn, whose Vickers Vildebeests were placed on readiness to attack the Italian Fleet if necessary. The two RAF units returned to the UK in July and September 1936 respectively and Hal Far returned to its predominantly Fleet Air Arm role. In October HMS *Glorious* disembarked Nos 802, 825, 812 and 823 Sqn, and by Christmas the latter two units had both re-equipped with Fairey Swordfish.

Like certain other overseas bases, Hal Far was established with its own Anti-Aircraft Cooperation Unit, No 3, which formed on 1 March 1937 with de Havilland Queen Bees. Later in the year the Unit sent detachments to Alexandria and Gibraltar, while in October 812 Sqn disembarked four of its aircraft for anti-piracy patrols. A Spotter Detachment for coastal defence cooperation was formed in July 1938 and, equipped with one Fairey Seal, was attached to the Station Flight. October saw transitting Avro Ansons on delivery to 4 FTS in Egypt, and later in the month Vickers Wellesleys of the RAF's Long Range Development Unit on their way out to Ismailia for an attempt on the world distance record.

Prior to the outbreak of hostilities, 3 AACU was, in August 1939, designated an operational unit, temporarily absorbing the Station Flight in the process. Anti-submarine and close recce patrols were flown throughout this 'precautionary crisis period' by the Unit's Swordfish. Exercises, including practice low-flying attacks on Army units now became the staple diet of Hal Far's aircraft which, in the opening months of 1940, also numbered the Sea Gladiators of 802 Sqn and 812's Swordfish. On 19 April four Sea Gladiators were sent across from storage at Kalafrana and issued to the Station Flight which became the Station Fighter Flight with six pilots. After only a short period of R/T and armament training, however, the Gladiators were dismantled and returned to Kalafrana. Three of them (the celebrated 'Faith', 'Hope' and 'Charity') then reappeared in May, and on the twentieth, together with a Swordfish of 3 AACU, were placed at readiness.

Immediately following Italy's declaration of war, Har Far was raided on 11 June, during the course of which one of the Gladiators was credited (incorrectly) with shooting down a Macchi C.200. During the month the Station was reinforced by an FAA Swordfish squadron, No 767, which began searching for enemy subs and ships. In July, after 767 had been renumbered 830, the Swordfish went on to bomb the Augusta oil refinery and Catania airfield. Later, a submarine was successfully attacked, but in August three of the Swordfish failed to return from a torpedo attack on ships in Augusta harbour, while other aircraft were destroyed in raids on Hal Far during the month.

Throughout early 1941 Hal Far was reinforced by a variety of types: 806 Sqn operated from here, losing two of its Fairey Fulmars to enemy aircraft in mid-January. The action was not too one-sided though, for a raiding Ju 87 was shot down a few days later, its crew being killed when it crashed near the married quarters. Eight Hurricanes arrived from Luqa for operations in February, followed in April by ten Hurricanes plus two Skuas from Gibraltar. The airfield was under frequent attack at this period and one of two Bombay transports was attacked as it approached to land. When 261 Sqn disbanded at Ta Kali in May, the unit's Hurricanes were used to reform 185 Sqn at Hal Far. The Hurricanes, together with Fulmars from HMS *Formidable*, were soon involved in dogfights and deaths with Me 109s. Deliveries of Hurricanes from Gibraltar continued in May and June, and 185 Sqn tangled with Macchi 200s in July, shooting down two of the Italian machines on the fourth. RN Swordfish and Fulmars were operating practically every day, the former attacking convoys and the latter (from 800X Sqn, which had arrived in May for a six-month spell) putting up night patrols.

The vigorous offensive by Hal Far's squadrons continued throughout 1941, No 822 Sqn's Albacores arriving in October to join the raids on Italian-held railway junctions, airfields and harbours. In February 1942 the attacking Ju 88s faced the Hurricanes of 605 Sqn which were based here briefly, followed in March by 229 Sqn (also Hurricanes), which flew in from North Africa only to disband at the end of April. By June 185 Sqn had re-equipped with Spitfire Vcs, which were scrambled several times a day, and which began sweeps over Sicily in September. In May 1943 185's escort activity covered Liberators bombing Catania and Beau-fighters seeking out shipping. There was much movement in June with, first, the departure of 821 Sqn (whose Albacores had been here since December 1942 for torpedo and bombing attacks on shipping), and then the arrival of 324 Wing comprising Nos 43, 72, 93, and 243 Sqns. The Wing, with its Spitfire squadrons, was here for the invasion of Sicily and carried out its first sweep over the island on the fifteenth. July saw the Wing escorting bomber formations of USAAF Marauders, Mitchells and Flying Fortresses, and maintaining a dawn-to-dusk patrol over the landing beaches in south-east Sicily, which resulted in numerous combats. Kittyhawks of 250 Sqn also used the airfield for bombing attacks in the campaign.

When 324 Wing moved on to Sicily in July its place was taken by 3 SAAF Wing with 12 and 24 Sqn (Bostons), and 21 Sqn (Baltimores). Operating in support of the 8th Army, by August the wing was making daily raids on targets in the toe of Italy. During the month, an ASR Flight of 284 Sqn which had arrived in June equipped with Beaufort, Wellington and Walrus aircraft, left for Ta Kali. No 185 Sqn had moved to Krendi in June, but in September it returned, together with two other Spitfire squadrons, 229 and 249, the former putting up daily meteorological flights and the latter transferring to Taranto in October. Now that the pressure on Malta had eased somewhat, the rebuilding of Hal Far's blitzed buildings began in November, and the Station carried out modification work (the fitment of bomb racks etc.) on SAAF (2 and 4 Sqns) and USAAF (52nd Fighter Group) aircraft.

There was little action for 185 and 229 Sqns in the opening months of 1944 and, fitted with bombs, the Spitfires flew fruitless sorties down the Albanian coast. March, however, saw the formation of the

Malta Communications Flight to provide a service to Sicily using an Anson. The inaugural flight took place on the fourth, and later two Wellingtons were delivered. No 283 Sqn arrived for air-sea rescue duties in April and the unit's Warwick later provided anti-submarine escorts for Malta convoys. No 185 Sqn moved on in July, its place being taken by a detachment of 1435 Sqn (based in Italy) known as the Malta Defence Flight. Equipped with Spitfire IXs the Flight got off to a good start, destroying a Ju 88 on the 26th. The month also saw a brief stay by 108 Sqn's intruder Mosquito NFXIIIs, followed in August by a detachment of 27 (SAAF) Sqn's Venturas for convoy patrols and anti-submarine searches.

While the Yalta Conference was in progress in January 1945, Hal Far was reinforced with detachments of Mosquitoes from 256 and Spitfires from 1435 Sqn, but in March HMSs *Venerable* and *Vengeance* disgorged a much larger contingent of FAA squadrons, comprising 812 and 814 (Barracudas), 1850 and 1851 (Corsairs) and 736B (Seafires). RAF aircrew were impressed with the speed and efficiency of deck operations, but declined offers of flights off the carriers!

The presence of RN ships at Malta in May drew detachments of Mosquitoes of 614 Sqn and Spitfires of 682 Sqn to assist with Fleet calibration work, although the latter proved unsuitable for the work. No 1831 Sqn's Corsairs operated briefly out of the airfield in May, having disembarked from HMS *Glory*. A detachment of 624 Sqn Walruses, described as 'showing their age', arrived in June to assist with minesweeping, while the following month the Spitfire IXs of 73 Sqn took up post for island defence duties. Although 283 Sqn and the Walrus detachment moved on in September, the Station gained a detachment of Mosquito NF30s from 255 Sqn, together with 1702 FAA Sqn whose Sea Otters were needed for minespotting sorties. While using the Kaura Point range for air-to-ground firing in November, one of 255's Mosquitoes was hit in the radiator by one of its own bullets, setting fire to the engine. The Mosquito made a down-wind crash landing and overshot, badly shaking the crew. In order to transport troops back from various Mediterranean locations to Malta for embarkation back to the UK, No 765 FAA Sqn flew out to Hal Far in October, its Wellingtons specially fitted with bench seats.

Soon to be handed back to the RN, Hal Far was being used with increasing regular-

Above *Sea Otter II JH183 of Hal Far Station Flight 1948.* (P Cook)

Below *Tiger Moth 'K28', 'New Life', Hal Far 1949, maybe from 728 Sqn.* (P Cook)

ity by FAA squadrons; in January 1946 it was 892 Sqn's Hellcats together with Firefly nightfighters of 1792 Sqn, off HMS *Ocean*. The RAF ensign was hauled down for the last time on 14 April 1946 and the following day the base was commissioned as HMS *Falcon*. The RAF's 255 Sqn had moved on in January, but 73 Sqn would remain for a short time as a lodger unit. No 728 Sqn, an RN Fleet Requirements Unit, began a long association with Hal Far in May and during its time here, which lasted until disbandment in May 1967, the unit flew a most exotic selection of types including the Wellington XIV, Beaufighter TT10, Expediter, Gannet, Harvard, Heron, Meteor, Mosquito, Sea Devon, Sea Hornet, Sea Vampire and Short Sturgeon. A helicopter element was added in 1952 initially with Dragonflies and later (June 1957) with Whirlwinds. Main customer was the Mediterranean Fleet, but the Army and the RAF Regiment also used 728's target-towing facilities.

Another navy, that of the US, began a presence in late-1950, consisting initially of detachments of VP-20's Privateers, normally based at Port Lyautey. The USN moved in on a more permanent basis in late 1953 and the airfield was referred to as Fleet Aircraft Service Squadron (FASRON) base 201. Not only were there detachments of VP-20s Privateers, squadrons VP-11, VP-21, VP-23 and VP-24 etc.) but the base also hosted numerous squadrons of US carrier-based

types. Two squadrons were permanently based here, VW-2 with Lockheed WV-2 Warning Stars in the airborne early-warning role, and VR-35 equipped with Fairchild Packets for logistic support duties. The US tenure finally came to an end in September 1959 when VP-24's Neptunes left for Sicily.

Meanwhile, the early 1950s saw the annual visits of Royal Naval Volunteer Reserve Air Divisions to Hal Far for intensive flying unfettered by British weather. The RAFs No 208 Sqn served here from January to March 1956 with Meteor FR9s, and the year also saw the busiest flying period to date with up to ten front-line squadrons operating from the base. Later still in the year, the Station even played a part in the Suez crisis, when it received detachments of Canberras from 9 and 12 Sqns.

For several periods during 1958 No 728C Sqn served here. Formed in the UK with the task of developing the airlift of Royal Marine Commandos from ship to shore for large-scale beachhead assaults, the Squadron's four Whirlwind HAS22s were shipped to Malta in February 1958. In October the unit was renumbered No 848, and became the first Royal Marine Commando Squadron before returning to the UK in November. No 750 Sqn, based at Culdrose for observer training, reverted to the title of Observer School in May 1959, and then flew its Sea Princes out to their new home at Hal Far in October to

Meteor TT20 VM147 of 728 Sqn at Hal Far in 1964. (R C B Ashworth)

Sea Venom FAW22 XG721 of 750 Sqn at Hal Far in 1965. (R C B Ashworth)

continue the training task in a kinder climate. Sea Venoms were added in July 1960 for high-level navigation and FRU work. This idyllic arrangement lasted until June 1965 when the Squadron/School returned home to Lossiemouth. In addition to observer training, the airfield acted as a shore base for squadrons embarked on carriers operating in the Mediterranean throughout the early 1960s.

After HMS *Falcon* paid off at the end of August 1965, Hal Far once more reverted to RAF control on 1 September, though the only permanent RAF squadron to be based here was No 38 which moved in from Luqa later in the month with Shackleton MR2s, disbanding *in situ* in March 1967. RAF Hal Far itself disbanded on 15 September 1967, but was put on a Care and Maintenance basis as a satellite for Luqa for occasional use by visiting Canberras, Meteors and Javelins. Bloodhound missiles of 41 Sqn were deployed here from the UK for a Maltese air defence exercise in April 1969.

Over the following years the airfield saw sporadic use, both military and civilian: for example up until 1978 it was used by the Malta International Aviation Company (MIACO) for the overhaul of DC-3s and DC-6s, while later in 1978 it became a temporary base for the Helicopter Flight of the Armed Forces of Malta. Hal Far was handed over to the Maltese government in January 1979, and has since seen some development as an industrial site.

Heliopolis, Egypt

Located close to, and to the north-east of Cairo, flying activity at Heliopolis goes right back to the Army days of December 1915, when No 17 Sqn with BE 2cs set up its HQ prior to mounting detachments at a number of other locations. The following year No 1 Sqn of the Australian Flying Corps sailed from Melbourne with its BE 2s to take up post at Heliopolis as No 67 Sqn, Royal Flying Corps. A general purpose squadron, its role was defence of the Suez Canal. Also operating as part of the Canal defence force was No 14 Sqn, which mounted detachments of BE 2cs at Heliopolis from its home base of Ismailia during 1916. All these squadrons had left by the end of the year, but in 1919 two bomber squadrons arrived. The first of these was No 58 which, with Handley Page 0/400s, was immediately taken on strength by the Training Brigade, Middle East. When 58 Sqn was renumbered No 70 on 1 February 1920, Vickers Vimys were arriving to replace the Handley Pages, two of the latter being used to supply fuel and rations to the motor convoy which ploughed the furrow marking the desert airmail route between Cairo and Baghdad. No 70 moved on to Iraq in 1922, but the other squadron to appear on the books, albeit for only a week in June 1919, was No 206 with DH 9s. No 1 Armoured Car Company formed during 1921.

A more settled existence was to be enjoyed by No 216 Sqn, which began a twenty-year stay in April 1925. Initially equipped with DH 10s as a bomber unit, it later received Vickers Vimys. No 45 Sqn reformed at Heliopolis with DH 9As in April 1927, before moving elsewhere in Egypt six months later. During the same month (October 1927) No 208 Sqn flew in its Bristol Fighters operating in the Army Cooperation role. This included tactical bombing, message pick-up, smoke-screen laying and artillery spotting. The longevity of 208's association with Egypt is reflected in the squadron badge consisting of a sphinx.

Station Headquarters Heliopolis formed on 1 March 1928, and at the same time the Specialist Instructional Flight was renamed the Heliopolis Communications Flight. Support for machines aeronautical was not limited to aircraft, and in 1931 the Station provided a landing party for the airship *Graf Zeppelin* when it landed at nearby Almaza. Throughout its time in Egypt No 216 had been carrying passengers and mail, and in 1931 it was officially designated a Bomber-Transport squadron, by which time it was equipped with Vickers Victorias.

In the year leading up to the Second World War, visits were made by a number of Fleet Air Arm units, and several RAF squadrons were based here for varying periods. These latter included No 64 (March – April 1936) with Hawker Demons, No 208 again (April 1936 – September 1938) with Hawker Audaxes and Westland Lysanders, No 113 in May 1938, whose Hawker Hinds were exchanged for Blenheims in the summer of 1939, and No 33 in September/October 1938, flying Gladiators. By June 1939 the flow of Bristol Blenheims through the Station *en route* to India was such that a Blenheim Servicing Flight was established. Bristol Bombays began to appear for 216 Sqn in October, and in July 1940 these were used for night raids on Tobruk. One aircraft failed to return, another crashed on return killing three of the crew, while a third force-landed near Alexandria.

Hostilities brought in several fresh squadrons during the course of 1940, including No 70 whose Vickers Valentias were replaced by Wellingtons in the autumn, No 84 with Blenheims, and No 73, a Hurricane unit. In addition, the Heliopolis Communications Flight was expanded to form No 267 Sqn whose inventory included Ansons, Magisters,

Percival Q6s, Proctors and Hudsons. The duties of this new unit embraced a daily mail delivery to units in the Western Desert. The year ended with an attachment of seven Gladiators of 'K' Flight for 'special duties'.

Throughout the early part of 1941 No 216 Sqn was busy airlifting supplies to Crete, Greece and the Western Desert, and evacuating the wounded. The Blenheims and Martin Marylands of 39 Sqn began maritime recce operations in January, No 2 Photographic Reconnaissance Unit began forming in March with locally modified Hurricane PR1s (moving on to North Africa towards the end of the year), while the Engine Repair Section of No 102 Maintenance Unit set up shop in September, having been bombed out of Abu Sueir. Two Blenheim IV squadrons, Nos 14 and 55, were on strength for short periods during the first half of the year, as were the Marylands of No 60 Sqn SAAF.

The most significant event of 1942 was undoubtedly the formation of the British Airways Repair Unit (BARU). Tasked with the repair of damaged aircraft and the major modification of all types, this civilian unit increased in establishment and output (it had 351 aircraft on hand in February 1943), before becoming No 168 Maintenance Unit in March 1944. It formed a Boston Flight in June 1942 to maintain three Bostons for VIP flying, and a Salvage Unit in November to recover all manner of crashed types from the Western Desert. During the summer the Station was badly damaged in German bombing raids, which prompted the formation of the Heliopolis Defence Flight. This comprised two Spitfires which were soon pitted against low-flying Ju 88s and Me 109s, together with high altitude reconnaissance Ju 86s. Detachments of No 417 Sqn took over the air defence task in October. An increasing demand for communications flying was met by the formation of No 173 Sqn operating a wide range of types, including the Lockheed Lodestar, Proctor, Magister, Boston, Audax, Dakota and Hurricane. It was in one of 173's Lodestars that Lady Tedder (wife of the Air Officer Commanding) and ten others lost their lives when it crashed close to the airfield in January 1943.

Yet more units were spawned in 1943, principally the Air Supply Development Centre, tasked with developing the delivery of stores by air, and No 20 Air Despatch and Reception Unit, responsible for the air movement of passengers, mail and freight. By mid-1944 No 173 Sqn had become the

Above *Bristol Fighter of 208 Sqn flying over Heliopolis.* (MoD Crown Copyright)

Below *In late December 1932 Mk I Vickers Vildebeest S1714, converted to a Vincent, was sent on a tour of RAF stations in Africa and the Middle East. It is seen here at Heliopolis with its long-range tank.* (S Kingham)

Middle East Communications Sqn complementing No 216 Group Communications
Flight which had on charge Hurricanes,
Fairchild Arguses, Proctors and Ansons.
September saw Beaufighters of No 46 Sqn
operating against smugglers in the Western
Desert, and No 168 MU beginning a series
of interesting projects. The first of these
was the delivery of a Halifax for
development as a transport aircraft. Then,
in January 1945, the MU began converting
an Anson XII for the use of King Farouk.
Air tests on a Vickers Warwick V modified
for the carriage of a lifeboat were followed
by the conversion of Dakota KN814 to VIP
standard for the C-in-C Middle East. In
March 1946 the MU began preparing 42
Wellingtons Mk X and XIII for the French
Air Force, before disbanding in October.
The Station as a whole closed in May 1947.

Jever, Germany

Arriving in March 1951, Jever's first RAF
inhabitants (apart from 664 Sqn's Austers
which were based here during 1–12
September 1945) were a detachment of
5352 Airfield Construction Wing, led by
Squadron Leader F. Herbert, their task
being to convert what had been an
operational wartime Luftwaffe airfield into
a modern RAF station suitable for three
Vampire squadrons. In the interim the base
had been used as a displaced persons camp;
looking into its wartime history, the 5353
Wing personnel gained the impression that
it had been a favourite with Hermann
Goering. Certainly the Officers' Mess, with
its distinctive design, wood carvings, two
large oil paintings and small private rooms
with stained glass windows seemed to
confirm this impression.

Sufficient renovation work had been
completed for the Station to begin life as a
self-accounting unit under the control of
HQ 2nd TAF on 1 September 1951. The C-
in-C and his staff visited the new Station on
20 November, and their aircraft was the
first to land here, although the airfield itself
did not officially open until 4 December.
Even then, the lack of facilities meant that
aircraft could not night-stop, and it was not
until 11 February 1953, when the first
Vampire flown by Squadron Leader P. G.
K. Williamson, OC 4 Sqn, landed that the
Station really started to get into gear.

No 4 Sqn was one of the three Vampire
FB5 units to assemble here in March 1953
and form the Jever Wing, the other two
being 93 and 112 Sqns. Meteors were used
for training, and the squadrons took turns

to provide aircraft for the Battle Flight,
which was on permanent standby. Low-
and high-level navigation exercises were
flown, together with practice low-level
interceptions, and cannon and rocket firing
on the Fassberg range. Also during March,
HQ 4 Wing, RAF Regiment and its
constituent squadrons began arriving.

In addition to routine training, the
Vampire squadrons took part in a wide
range of other activities, and in April 1952
aircraft from 4 and 93 Sqns took part in a
2nd TAF flypast for General Eisenhower.
May saw the start of regular visits to the
Armament Practice School at Sylt for live
firing at targets towed by Tempests, while
in June the first of many future exercises
embraced attacks on the airfield by 'enemy'
F-84s, and practice interceptions on USAF
B-36s and B-50s. The system of unit
exchanges was initiated with 112 Sqn
temporarily swopping bases with the Dutch
Air Force Meteors of 326 Sqn at Twenthe,
and a general round of detachments was
mounted as far afield as Odiham and
Duxford in the UK. There was also a
considerable emphasis on display flying
during this period, with 93 Sqn's aerobatic
team making a modest start to an
entertaining career by coming third in a
Command competition held at Gütersloh,
while in July 1952 the Wing as a whole
participated in the first NATO air display,
held at Melsbroek in Belgium. Jever briefly
gained a fourth squadron during the
summer, but after reforming here on
Vampire FB9s in June 20 Sqn began
moving out to Oldenburg the following
month.

The mobility concept, under which the
flying squadrons packed up their essential
support equipment and operated under
canvas from deployment locations, was
given its first airing in August 1952, and the
following month Jever's Vampires deployed to RAF Bückeburg, with personnel
camped in woods adjacent to the aircraft,
for an exercise in which their role was
ground attack and interception in support
of the Army.

This remained the pattern of activity
until March 1954, when 4 and 93 Sqns
began re-equipping with the eagerly-
awaited Sabre, the Vampires being disposed of to Wunstorf. While Jever's
runway was being reinforced in preparation
for the new fighter, the squadrons were sent
to Alhorn and it was there that 93 Sqn
received its first Sabre, XB856, on 25
March. On return to Jever normal
operations resumed with a permanent

Pilots of 93 Sqn pose for a squadron photograph in front of Sabre F4 XB829 'D' at Jever. (via P Russell-Smith)

Battle Flight being mounted and regular APCs at Sylt.

A popular aircraft, the Sabre was intended to meet the requirement for an interceptor only until Hawker Hunters became available, and the first of these appeared at Jever in the markings of 98 Sqn, which moved over from Fassberg in April 1955, leaving behind its de Havilland Venoms. A second ex-Venom unit from Fassberg, 118 Sqn, followed suit in May, also re-equipping with Hunters in the process, and pronouncing the Hawker fighter pleasant and easy to fly. As far as Jever's longer serving squadrons were concerned, No 4 took delivery of Hunters in July 1955, but it would be January 1956 before 93 Sqn did so. It was the Hunter F4 which now equipped Jever's squadrons, and in comparative tests with visiting Canadair Sabre 6s (not the version flown by the RAF) the performance of both aircraft in terms of high-speed runs, climb and turns, was found to be almost identical. An interesting feature of Hunter servicing at Jever in 1956 was that all 93 Sqn's pilots were qualified to carry out limited flight-line maintenance and kept themselves in practice by 'turning round' their aircraft during the regular ground crews' lunch-break.

The early months of 1957 saw 4 and 93 Sqns re-equipping with the definitive Mk 6 version of the Hunter and formally assuming the day fighter/ground attack role. The latter Squadron was again selected as the 2nd TAF aerobatic team, while 118 Sqn's Flight Lieutenant K. J. Goodwin was chosen as the Command's solo display pilot. Nos 98 and 118 Sqn disbanded in July and August respectively, but this at least made room for the visit in September of 50 USAF C-119s and 1,500 US Army paratroops for an exercise drop.

A newcomer to the Station in January 1958 was 2 Sqn from Geilenkirchen with Supermarine Swift FR5s in the tactical reconnaissance role. In July, 2 Sqn sent two aircraft to Karup in Denmark in exchange for two RF-84Fs, and then joined Jever's Hunters in a Practice Alert called by HQ 2nd TAF, the Swifts flying fighter recce sorties on pre-planned targets while the Hunters flew defensive mission sweeps. The following month No 2 competed with the other Germany-based Swift unit, 79 Sqn, for a place in the 2nd TAF team for the annual NATO reconnaissance competition Exercise Royal Flush, going on to take the team prize in 1959.

Nos 4 and 93 Sqn, still on Hunters, both disbanded in December 1960, the former transferring its numberplate to 79 Sqn at Gütersloh. In February 1961 2 Sqn began replacing its Swifts with Hunter FR10s, to be joined the following month by 4 Sqn, now also flying Hunter FR10s, which returned from Gütersloh. Between March

93 Sqn's Hunter F4s airborne from Jever.
(via P Porter)

and September No 14 Sqn Hunter F6s were based here, carrying out fighter sweeps and practice interceptions, while the runways at the Squadron's regular base of Gütersloh were repaired.

By the middle of 1961, however, preparations were well in hand for the move of all flying squadrons to Gütersloh, for Jever was destined to be handed back to the Germans. The transfer took place in September, and included the Station Flight's 'Cloth Bomber' – Anson TX160, the airfield closing on the eighth of the month. RAF personnel remained behind to hand over facilities to the German Air Force, but finally left on 10 January 1962.

Kai Tak, Hong Kong

Flight Lieutenant H. B. Gray was one of a small group of prisoners of war in Hong Kong planning a general escape from their Japanese captors. The plan was discovered and he was arrested in July 1943. Despite torture during his interrogation, and ill health throughout his lengthy imprison-ment, he refused to implicate any of his colleagues, and following a Japanese court martial he was subsequently shot. His courage was recognized by the award of a posthumous George Cross.

Gray, later to become a pilot, joined the RAF as an apprentice in 1927, the same year that Kai Tak opened. On 10 March of that year the airfield, located on the fringe of Kowloon on the Chinese mainland, was formally taken over for use mainly by Fleet Air Arm aircraft. Hong Kong's first military flight, however, was that by Fairey IIIF N9634 which took off from Kowloon harbour on 4 November 1924 with Flight Lieutenant G. E. Livock at the controls after arriving in the Colony on board HMS *Pegasus*.

Although officially open, much construction work remained to be done on the Station, and one of the principal projects outstanding was a seawall and slipway for the seaplanes and flying boats, which were becoming a familiar sight in the Far East. By now Kai Tak had its own permanent aircraft consisting of the Fairey IIIFs of No 442 Flight, operating alongside the more transient Fairey IIIFs and Fairey Flycatchers of 440 and 403 Flights respectively. This Fleet Air Arm preserve was broken by the arrival in November 1928 of four Supermarine Southampton flying boats of the Far East Flight. Touching down in the harbour, the 'boats made a short stay in the colony before returning to Singapore.

In August 1930, 442 Fleet Reconnaissance Flight returned home to the UK on HMS *Hermes* to re-equip with Fairey IIIFs, leaving no permanent military aircraft on the Station, although Fleet Air Arm Flights continued to disembark from visiting ships of the Far East Fleet. Up until 1 April 1935 the airfield had been known as RAF Base Kai Tak, but on that date it was retitled RAF Station Kai Tak. A small Marine Craft Section was established at this point and, equipped with motor launches, its duties included support for visiting flying boats. Such visitors included three Southamptons of 205 Sqn from Singapore in early 1935 during the course of a Far East cruise. A more permanent RAF presence was established the following year, when three Hawker Horsleys, previously operated by 36 Sqn in Singapore, were flown up to form a Station Flight. These machines, together with two Tiger Moths, carried out target towing and other duties. Obsolete Vickers Vildebeests replaced the Horsleys in February 1937, and three months later

Fairey Seals of 824 Sqn disembarked at Kai Tak from HMS Hermes *in either 1935 or 1936.* (TAG Assn via R Sturtivant)

gave a flying display as part of the coronation celebrations for King George VI. By this time the Station was also responsible for a small number of naval Walruses and Swordfish, which later made reconnaissance flights over Japanese ships when the Emperor's forces were advancing into China.

The need to improve facilities at Kai Tak had already been appreciated, and plans were drawn up for the construction of a 500-yard tarmac runway. A contract for the work was awarded to a local firm, but before it could begin the Japanese intervened. No air forces as such had been allocated to the colony for defence against the Japanese, and instead a complete reliance was placed on the Army. In early December 1941 the Japanese began violating British airspace with reconnaissance flights, and Kai Tak's motley collection of land-based aircraft were dispersed, the Walruses remaining rather vulnerable at their moorings in Kowloon harbour. On the eighth of the month the expected attack came, with Japanese aircraft strafing

barrack blocks and other buildings on the camp. Vildebeests were set on fire and Walruses were sunk at their moorings. On the civil side of the airfield, which also served as Hong Kong Airport, three Junkers of China National Airways Corporation were destroyed, while in the Bay a Pan American Clipper suffered a similar fate to the Walruses. With the prospect of an invasion of Hong Kong, on 9 December General Maltby ordered the evacuation of Kai Tak. Hearing this, the station commander requested permission for the remaining two Vildebeests to bomb either of the two Japanese-held airfields of Nam Tan or Canton and to land at Chinese airfields, thus also perhaps saving crews and machines from capture. The request was refused and the machines simply had to be destroyed. The RAF evacuation began on 10 December, and throughout the day obstacles were laid on the runway and facilities were demolished in order to deny the airfield to the approaching Japanese. The Colony as a whole finally surrendered on Christmas Day 1941.

Life for POWs in Hong Kong, Flight Lieutenant Gray among them, was the usual mixture of working parties and privation. Many RAF personnel found themselves extracting hard core for the airfield which the Japanese planned to develop. This work began in 1942 and involved the construction of dispersals and runways. The tenement buildings which were demolished to make way for the runways also provided useful hard core, and eventually two well-defended runways, each 1,500 yards long, were completed. The United States military aircraft which began appearing over the Colony in December 1944 in search of Japanese shipping were met by enemy fighters from Kai Tak, as well as intense anti-aircraft fire, and there were losses on both sides.

By coincidence it was once again the Fleet Air Arm which was the first to fly into Kai Tak at the end of the Pacific war. After the Japanese commander in Hong Kong had agreed to the signing of a surrender document on board the Fleet Carrier HMS *Indomitable* which had arrived with the British Fleet off Hong Kong, a Grumman Avenger with an escort of Hellcats was despatched to the airfield on 29 August 1945 to collect a Japanese representative. The Navy then formally reoccupied the Station on 3 September. The RAF, however, took over a day or so later, and on 6 September Catalinas of 240 Sqn began flying key personnel into Hong Kong. The airfield itself was generally in an unkempt condition, littered with damaged Japanese

aircraft and other debris. The runways were intact, however, and were soon in use by 132 Sqn which, in a fairly hazardous operation, flew its Spitfire XIVes off HMS *Smiter* with half-full tanks as the small carrier steamed at full speed into a stiff breeze. Later the Squadron began anti-piracy patrols.

Arriving the same month, the Royal Navy's No 8 Mobile Naval Air Base (MONAB) was established as HMS *Nabcatcher* to handle visiting Fleet Air Arm aircraft, together with a number of stored Corsairs. A second Spitfire unit, 681 Sqn with Spitfire PR19s, was added in late September, but left for Malaya after three months. Sunderland flying boats from 209 Sqn and 1430 Flight, also began to reappear, one of these aircraft taking the opportunity of flying under Sydney Harbour Bridge while on a short visit to Australia. The captain, Flying Officer George, was married shortly after his return to Hong Kong, the first post-war RAF wedding in the Colony, and was flown by RN Sea Otter to Macau for his honeymoon.

The New Year saw a number of changes, including the departure of 132 and 209 Sqns, and the return of a civil governor, which Kai Tak helped celebrate by providing a flypast of two Beaufighters and three Corsairs. The following month (June 1946) the newly arrived 96 Sqn was renumbered 110 Sqn, and its Dakotas became a permanent feature which would last until July 1947. The unit performed

RAF Kai Tak in 1945. A Spitfire PR XI can be seen at Left. (D S Rees via C Bowyer)

three main tasks: route flying over an area stretching from India to Japan; special flights carrying VIPs; and typhoon relief work. A particularly severe typhoon caused widespread havoc in July 1946, damaging five Dakotas, one of which was blown twenty yards away, and two visiting Sunderlands. The Sunderland was proving so successful in the transport role that 1430 Flight was equipped with a specially modified transport version of the aircraft. Renumbered as 88 Sqn in September 1946, the unit flew a thrice-weekly service to Iwakuni in Japan in support of the RAF element of the occupation force.

Preparations were now made to make the airfield capable of accepting the larger transport aircraft, such as Lancastrians and Yorks, which were beginning to use Kai Tak. The east/west runway could not be extended due to the proximity of buildings at the western end and hills at the eastern end, and so efforts were concentrated on the other runway, running north/south.

One of the most celebrated incidents involving this particular Station was the 'Yangtze Incident' of April 1949. In this, Sunderland 'D' of 88 Sqn, flown by Flight Lieutenant A. H. Letford, landed next to HMS *Amethyst*, which was trapped up the Yangtze river by communist guns, to land medical supplies and a doctor. The guns soon had the range of the Sunderland, which then made a hazardous down-wind, down-tide take-off in failing light.

In order to provide an air defence capability which Hong Kong lacked, particularly in the face of the communist takeover in China, it was announced that fighter aircraft would be based in the Colony. Accordingly, 80 Sqn with Spitfire F24s was despatched from the UK aboard HMS *Ocean*, arriving off Hong Kong in August 1949. Here, 80 Sqn joined No 28 which had flown in with its Spitfire FR18s in May. Both units were tasked with patrolling the border after Chinese Nationalist aircraft had entered Hong Kong airspace on a number of occasions. Following the outbreak of the Korean War, 88 Sqn began patrolling the Korean coastline in June 1950 from Iwakuni in Japan, although the Sunderlands returned to Hong Kong for servicing. The flying boat Squadron returned to Singapore a year later. Of the two fighter squadrons, No 28 was the first to lose its ageing Spitfires, exchanging them for de Havilland Vampire FB5s and FR9s in January 1951. No 80, on the other hand, began receiving de Havilland Hornets in

December 1951. In September 1953, twelve armed Hornets provided the air escort for a token naval force which entered the Pearl River estuary in response to an earlier incident between a Royal Navy launch and a Chinese gunboat. The following year two Hornets and one of 88 Sqn's Sunderlands were scrambled to look for a Cathay Pacific Douglas DC-4 *en route* for Hong Kong from Bangkok, which had ditched after being attacked by Chinese Air Force fighters.

No 80 Sqn was disbanded in April 1955, and 28 Sqn moved to nearby Sek Kong while a new runway stretching out into the sea was built at Kai Tak to meet the demands of both civil and military traffic. Work on the runway continued unabated until 1958. In the interim, new Venom FB1s were delivered to 28 Sqn and by August 1956 the unit had sixteen on strength. Returning from a spell at Sek Kong in 1957, 28 Sqn began a period of shrinkage. By December its strength had reduced considerably; in addition to a handful of Venoms there was a Vampire T11 (lost in 1959 when it ditched in the sea), plus some Meteors and a Beaufighter of the Station Flight element (which were disposed of to Singapore in 1958). It was a Venom of 28 Sqn which was the first aircraft to use the newly completed runway in August 1957, just pipping to the post a Cathay Pacific DC-6. The runway opening ceremony ended with a flying display which included civil airliners and aerobatics by a formation of Venoms of 60 Sqn sent up from Singapore for the occasion.

Air trooping was now becoming the accepted method of moving personnel and families to and from the UK on posting, and to cope with the increase in long-range transport operating alongside the varied civil traffic of Hong Kong's International Airport, an Air Movements Section was established in 1959. By the early 1960s RAF Comets and Britannias were becoming regular visitors and in later years VC10s were handled (the first in August 1966 and a thrice-weekly service by 1972), together with Hercules and Belfasts.

In the meantime, 28 Sqn's Venoms were being replaced by Hunter FGA9s, the first being delivered along with a a two-seat T7 in May 1962. However, squadron strength was limited to three aircraft, just sufficient for its roles of flag-showing, maintaining a token presence, and helping the Army monitor the cross-border passage of illegal immigrants from China. Kai Tak's resident fighters could in any event be reinforced

Above *28 Sqn's Vampire 9 aerobatic team over Kai Tak in October 1955.* (via C Bowyer)

Below *Whirlwind HC10 XP301 of 28 Sqn at Kai Tak in 1970.* (P Russell-Smith Colln)

Right *Westland Widgeon VR-HFL. First registered as G-APBK, this aircraft was delivered to the Hong Kong Police Force in December 1957, and passed on to the Hong Kong Auxiliary Air Force in 1958. Seen here in HKAuxAF markings at Kai Tak, it later became 9M-AOP.* (E B Goldsmith)

quickly by the Singapore-based Javelin and Hunter squadrons supported by transport aircraft from the island, a measure that was exercised frequently. No 28's few remaining Hunters were withdrawn when the Squadron was disbanded in early 1966. Another unit to leave the scene was the Marine Craft Unit, which was disbanded in February 1967. Besides supporting the earlier flying boat activity, it later performed a search and rescue role, and one of its most notable mercy missions was to pick up thirteen survivors from a US Marine Corps C-130 Hercules which ditched in August 1965.

The Colony was not without a 28 Sqn for long though, for in March 1968 the unit reformed at Kai Tak with Westland Whirlwind HC10 helicopters which began operating in a variety of roles including search and rescue, support for the Army and police, emergency air evacuation and photo reconnaissance. When the Whirlwinds were replaced by Wessex HC2s in 1972, No 28 was able to exploit the larger helicopter's greater payload and endurance in performing a number of unusual tasks.

Typhoons are an annual hazard in this part of the world and when, in September 1962, a particularly bad one flattened nearby Sha Tin, home base for 20 Flight Army Air Corps in the Colony, the Flight

sought refuge with its AOP Austers at Kai Tak. Re-equipping with Bell Sioux helicopters in 1967 it served here until October 1969 when, following an amalgamation of AAC units in the Far East, it moved to Sek Kong under the 656 Sqn banner.

28 Sqn's Wessexes were not the only helicopters wearing military markings in Hong Kong, for Kai Tak was also home for the Royal Hong Kong Auxiliary Air Force. A department of the Hong Kong Government, the RHKAAF began life in early 1930 as the air arm of the Hong Kong Defence Corps. Equipped with four Austers, four Harvards and four Spitfires (two F24s and two PR19s) it became the HKAAF in 1949, adding the 'Royal' prefix in 1951. Westland Widgeon helicopters were delivered in 1958 and these were replaced in 1965 and 1970 by Sud Alouette IIIs. The Aérospatiale SA–365C Dauphins which superseded the Alouettes carried out a wide range of utility and policing duties around the Colony. Fixed-wing types operated by the RHKAAF included the Cessna 404 Titan and Britten-Norman Islander, while Scottish Aviation Bulldogs were delivered in 1977 to replace Beech Musketeers in the pilot training role. RAF-type roundels were deleted in 1978 and a more appropriate coast guard style colour scheme adopted.

Under the 1975 Defence Costs Agreement between the British and Hong Kong Governments it was decided that all RAF units at Kai Tak were to be relocated at Sek Kong, for the former was required for redevelopment. These plans finally came to fruition when, on 30 June 1978, a flypast of four Wessexes ended the handing over and closure of the RAF's first station in the Far East.

Kallang, Singapore

Although used for only two brief periods by the Services, Kallang will be remembered for the heroic defence which its obsolete fighter aircraft put up against superior Japanese forces during the Second World War.

Located at the edge of Singapore City on the island's southern coast, Kallang was developed in the 1930s as the first civil airport there. It was selected in preference to another site on the Choa Chu Kang road, some fourteen miles from the city centre, which later became RAF Tengah. The rather swampy area was transformed into a domed grass aerodrome which, when it was opened as an airport on 12 June 1937 by the Governor of the Straits Settlements, boasted a fine, modern-looking terminal building.

Two of the first RAF units to be based at the airport were 11 and 39 Sqns, both flying Blenheim Is, which were sent from India to reinforce the Far East Command in September 1939. The crews found conditions at Kallang comfortable and convenient. At this period both units were working up on their new aircraft and carrying out a programme of navigation, high- and low-level bombing and photography, together with dive-bombing training, which was undertaken at Seletar. Before they could perform their war role, however, which would have included strikes against Japanese shipping, in April 1940 the Blenheims were ordered back to India.

Some time after the departure of the two Blenheim squadrons, No 4 Anti-Aircraft Cooperation Unit and a Spotter Flight were reported as being based here. (The AACU transferred to Tengah in February 1941.) Detachments of Blenheim from 62 Sqn at Tengah were also on hand in late 1940.

Early the following year, Kallang became a fighter base when 67 and 243 Sqns both reformed here with Brewster Buffaloes in March. In May the two squadrons provided a welcoming escort for the first Pan American Boeing 314 Clipper flying boat

(named 'California') to call at Singapore. The undercarriage of the tubby little Buffalo caused problems initially, and it was not until June that 67 Sqn was able to fly its first operational patrol. When this unit moved to India in October 1941 it left behind its aircraft for an incoming New Zealand fighter squadron, No 488. The Kiwis now operated alongside No 243 in the air defence of Singapore. Even though 488 Sqn was not fully operational when the Japanese attacks began, the more experienced pilots flew patrols over Singapore and its sea approaches. On 10 December it contributed aircraft to the fighter force despatched to assist the warships Prince of Wales and Repulse, following reports that they were being attacked by Japanese bombers. By the time the Allied fighters arrived on the scene, both vessels had been sunk. Throughout December pairs of Buffaloes were ordered up from Kallang to intercept high-flying Japanese reconnaissance aircraft, but the slow-climbing fighters could not catch them. The severely depleted 243 Sqn was disbanded during December.

Kallang suffered its first air raid on 9 January 1942, when stores and offices were badly damaged. Three days later the New Zealanders tackled an incoming formation of Japanese aircraft, in which two Buffaloes were quickly shot down and five others were damaged. The obsolete Brewsters were no match for the Japanese raiders which were now over Singapore every day.

Meanwhile, reinforcement men and machines were on their way, for on 13 January 24 pilots, made up of six each from 17, 135, 136 and 232 Sqns, and diverted from their original Middle East destination, arrived in Singapore by sea. This composite squadron was designated No 232 and was equipped with 51 Hurricane IIBs. By 19 January, 232 was operating a detachment at Kallang from its main base at Seletar. No 488 Squadron was re-equipped with nine of the Hurricanes, pilots and groundcrews having to convert to this unfamiliar type as quickly as possible. The task was made no easier by a Japanese air raid on 27 January, in which several Hurricanes were destroyed and two Blenheims, probably of 27 Sqn which had sent in detachments from Butterworth, were burnt out. The remnants of 243 Sqn were decimated and several road vehicles were set on fire. In another attack a short time later, the airfield was cratered and eight pilots had a narrow escape when a bomb exploded close to a gun emplacement in which they were sheltering.

Strenuous efforts were made to repair the damage, and the clearance of a single strip enabled three Hurricanes to take off. However, the situation in Singapore was so critical that on 31 January it was announced that all Hurricanes were to be withdrawn to Sumatra. This decision was queried by Winston Churchill, with the result that Kallang, the only Singapore airfield out of range of Japanese artillery fire, continued to be used as the base for what was virtually a composite Hurricane squadron with pilots drawn from 232, 488 and 258 Sqns. The latter unit had arrived in Singapore on 28 January 1942, and numbered among its pilots flying from Kallang the American, Flying Officer Arthur Donahue, who described his experiences in his book *Last Flight from Singapore*.

On 5 February two Hudsons of 1 Sqn, RAAF, flew down to Kallang from Sumatra with instructions to collect the Air Officer Commanding, Air Vice-Marshal Pulford, and his senior staff officers. The Hudsons escaped damaged from a heavy air raid which took place on the airfield while they were on the ground, but Pulford decided not to leave Singapore at that stage. With herculean effort from air and

ground crews alike, Kallang still managed to put Hurricanes into the air, which even turned back three waves of enemy bombers on 8 February. But with Japanese forces on Singapore soil, the last remaining Kallang personnel withdrew to Sumatra on 10 February.

At the end of the Pacific war it was, purely by chance, at Kallang that the first returning British personnel set foot in Singapore. On the morning of 31 August 1945, some days before the actual signing of the Japanese surrender document, a PR Mosquito of 684 Sqn took off from the Cocos Islands to photograph Southern Malaya. During the course of the sortie the Mosquito developed an engine fault, and looking round for somewhere to land the pilot decided on Kallang as the most suitable airfield. The crew received a friendly reception from the Japanese, who produced RAF engineers to effect the necessary repairs. A second Mosquito landed next morning, and the RAF was thus the first Service to return to the island.

The first administrative body to move in formally after the war was 903 Wing (part of Headquarters 224 Group), which in effect formed RAF Kallang. No 31 Sqn arrived from Burma with its Dakotas in September 1945, followed in October by another Dakota unit, 215 Sqn. The

An RAF Liberator GR VI in front of Kallang's distinctive control tower in late 1945. *(Straits Times* via Bruce Robertson)

Spitfires of 155 Sqn used the airfield as a stepping stone between India and Tengah in September, as did 84 and 110 Sqns, on their way to Seletar with Mosquito FB6s. Like the other Singapore airfields, Kallang was at this stage in poor physical shape and did not stand up well to the pounding it received from the RAF Dakotas, Liberators and Yorks which used it as a main transport base prior to the reopening of Changi in 1946. The single, relatively short runway was approached from one end over a low harbour wall, and over a main road from the other. These factors, together with poor drainage, gave it limited potential for development. However, the RAF had an urgent if temporary use for it, and so PSP runway was laid. Both Dakota squadrons moved on early in 1946.

Kallang gained notoriety in 1946 when postwar disaffectation, stemming from the unavoidably protracted repatriation and demobilization, spread to the Station. An airman was caught red-handed inciting his colleagues to come out on strike in sympathy with agitators at Seletar, and was subsequently court martialled.

By now, Kallang's future was becoming clearer. Although situated conveniently close to the city centre, its runway was too short for post-war four engined aircraft, and the approach over the harbour wall was hazardous. Eventually a Lockheed Constellation hit the wall on landing and crashed, with much loss of life. This and numerous other incidents led the civil aviation authorities to abandon the airfield in 1955 and to construct a new civil airport at Paya Lebar. The RAF, for its part, decided to hand over its interests at Kallang to the Singapore Government and to concentrate its transport aircraft operations at Changi.

Khormaksar, Aden

In its heyday in the mid-1960s, Khormaksar could justifiably claim to be the busiest RAF station in the world, and the hub of British military flying in the Middle East. This is perhaps fitting for a station whose career can be traced back to late 1917, when No 31 Sqn detached some Henry Farman F27s from India to form the Aden Flight, for reconnaissance of Turkish forces operating against Aden and the surrounding states. The Flight was still there the following year, and 1918 also saw a detachment from 114 Sqn, whose main base was Quetta where it operated Farmans and BE2es.

There is little activity of any significance to record until early 1927, when No 8 Sqn arrived from Iraq with its de Havilland 9As to begin a long and colourful association with Aden. From 1928 onwards No 8 was one of the main instruments of the policy of Air Control, which had been identified as the best method of supporting the administration of Aden Colony and the surrounding Protectorates. Re-equipping with Fairey IIIFs in May 1928, a formation of eight of the Sqn's aircraft carried out a demonstration flight, in June, over the principal towns of the Yemen, as far north as Dhamar. In February 1929 No 8 was involved in bombing the villages of Atifi and Mansuri. Later, there was the added variety of inter-tribal disturbances and the security of trade routes, and No 8 was reinforced in these policing duties by the arrival, in October 1935, of No 12 Sqn with Hawker Harts, and No 41 Sqn on Hawker Demons. The latter unit absorbed a Flight of Demons from 8 Sqn and was soon in action dropping 20 lb bombs on dissident villages. Before they both left for the United Kingdom in August 1936, 12 and 41 Sqns were based at other airfields (Robat and Sheikh Othman) in the Aden Protectorate. Meanwhile, in October 1935, No 8 Sqn sent a detachment of Vickers Vincents to British Somaliland to cooperate with the Somaliland Camel Corps in patrolling the Italian and Ethiopian borders.

With the Second World War looming and the possibility of opposition from the Italians in Somaliland, Aden gained its own Protectorate Defence Force in the form of the Sea Gladiators of 94 Sqn, which began assembling at Khormaksar in March 1939 before moving to Sheikh Othman in May. At the same time 8 Sqn started to add Bristol Blenheims to its existing Vincents, this dual equipment lingering on until 1942. On the outbreak of war, dispersal of aircraft was ordered, the identity of all ships in the area was passed to the operational squadrons, and under the terms of a bilateral agreement the Station began storing bombs for the French Air Force. Punitive bombing raids against dissident villages, however, were still 8 Sqn's main preoccupation, and during one such operation in November 1939 the Squadron lost Blenheim L6647. Two Vincents were despatched to search for the missing Blenheim, which was found to have crashed and burnt out. The crew had been shot dead by tribesmen. The Vincents themselves ran the gauntlet of ground fire

Vickers Vincents of 8 Sqn at Khormaksar in 1937. (MoD Crown Copyright)

during the course of a subsequent leaflet drop over a nearby dissident village.

More reinforcements arrived throughout 1940, the first of which was 203 Sqn with Blenheim IVfs. This unit found itself at Khormaksar in May almost by default, due to the difficulties experienced in operating Blenheims from its previous base, nearby Sheikh Othman. In essence a 'maritime fighter' squadron, 203 performed a number of tasks, including patrols over Red Sea convoys, anti-submarine work, and photo-reconnaissance of East Africa and Abyssinia. In an encounter with three Savoia-Marchetti SM.79s over Berbera harbour the Blenheims managed to shoot down one of the Italian bombers. The other resources to arrive (in July) were two French Air Force Martin Marylands from Egypt, which formed into No 1 French (Bomber) Flight. Finally, in September, the Station suffered an enemy air attack, one bomb hitting the oxygen plant and three others falling on the airfield itself.

Following 203 Sqn's departure in April 1941, the Command Training Flight moved to Khormaksar from Sheikh Othman, some five miles away, to form a Station Flight. Sheikh Othman was then placed under Care and Maintenance, to be administered by Khormaksar. In May, two of 8 Sqn's Vincents, which had been detached to Somaliland, flew to Bandar Kassim in Italian Somaliland, landed and called on the town to surrender. Thereafter, the Vincents cooperated with ground forces in forcing the surrender of other groups of Italians in the country. Routine reconnaissance flights over Djibouti, the Vichy-controlled French Somaliland coast, and dhows at sea were the norm for the remainder of 1941, which also brought Blenheim IVs to replace 8 Sqn's Mk Is.

The presence of HMS *Indomitable* in the area produced no less than four visiting FAA squadrons in January 1942. These were Nos 827, 830 and 831 (Fairey Albacores) together with No 800 on Fulmars. In addition to shadowing enemy vessels in the Gulf of Aden, the RN aircraft dropped leaflets over Djibouti, receiving a brisk welcome of anti-aircraft fire. Later in the year, in September, personnel from Nos 240 and 413 Sqns were drafted in to form an indigenous Catalina Flight, and during the same month an Aden Defence Flight was formed, initially with one Hurricane I. The following month yet more personnel, from 459 Sqn, arrived to form a Hudson Flight, which soon joined the Catalinas and Vincents on daily patrols. The Blenheim Vs with which 8 Sqn re-equipped in late 1942 saw action against French Somaliland.

There is reference at this point to a resident Communications Flight operating the Fairchild Argus, and later Ansons and

Expediters. Aircraft from the Flight dropped supplies to the survivors of the SS *Ramani*, torpedoed 50 miles out to sea in July 1943. In October the Flight took delivery of two Wellington Ics specially converted for transport duties. Operating alongside the British units during the year were the Hurricanes of No 3 SAAF Sqn. From June BOAC began weekly calls in the course of their new mail service between Asmara and Karachi, while in October there were extended visits by 834 Sqn with Seafires and Swordfish from HMS *Battler*, and 321 Sqn's Catalinas from Socotra.

Maritime patrol activity was boosted by the arrival, in December 1943, of 621 Sqn with Wellington XIIIs (replaced in November 1945 by Mk XIVs). More Wellington XIIIs arrived in March, this time from 244 Sqn, because of lack of space and facilities at their home base, Masirah. The Comms Flight had, meanwhile, inaugurated its new 'Baron' service to Riyan – Salalah – Masirah, later extending to Ras el Hadd and Sharjah, and the servicing of the various types of aircraft on the station was being carried out by 131 MU. The range of types on hand was increased by the arrival in September of 1566 Meteorological Flight with Hurricanes and Defiants.

In early 1945 a plan to use the Station as the base for a Liberator Conversion Unit, self-contained and under canvas, reached only brief fruition. Three Liberators actually arrived in April for the conversion of crews from 8 Sqn (244 Sqn crews would have followed) but flying was discontinued

towards the end of the month. Other changes to be effected by mid-year were the disbandment of 8 Sqn and the departure of 621 Sqn. The Comms Flight, on the other hand, was thriving and its inventory now also included the Ventura.

The gap created by 621 Sqn's departure was filled in September 1945 by 114 Sqn whose Bostons searched, in December, for a missing Mosquito which had ditched while on delivery to 114, for the Squadron was now re-equipping with the type. No 114's existence was brief, as in September 1946 it was renumbered 8 Sqn. In addition to Expediters and Wellingtons the Comms Flight (or 'Unit' as it had now become) was also equipped with Venturas, Baltimores, Albacores and Wellingtons. The Baltimores were gradually replaced by more Wellingtons, while in October Anson C19 TX170 was accepted for trials as a replacement for the Albacores. A second Anson, VL293, arrived a month later. In April 1946 1566 Meteorological Flight was disbanded, at which point it was flying Spitfires. The end of 1946 saw a detachment of 13 Sqn's Mosquitoes for recce duties over Somaliland, and 8 Sqn reconnoitring dissident tribesmen in cooperation with armoured cars.

Operations against warring tribes were now to preoccupy 8 Sqn, and the Tempests with which the unit re-equipped in May 1947 were used with deadly effect, carrying out 60 lb rocket and 1,000 lb bomb attacks on villages and other targets. The Comms Unit Albacores dropped leaflets on target areas and supplies to friendly forces. No 8

Wellington XIVs (NC828 nearest) of 621 Sqn at Khormaksar in 1945. (E Woodhouse via C Jefford)

began converting to the less manoeuvrable Bristol Brigand in mid-1949, and these were swiftly targetted against a Yemeni fort which had been put up illegally on the Aden side of the frontier. Buckmasters RP209 and '197 were used for training. In 1950 the Comms Unit became the Aden Comms Sqn and started to receive Vickers Valettas, but so widespread were the commitments for this and the other RAF units in Aden that it was decided to equip 'B' Flight of 8 Sqn with Ansons and Austers, and to title it the Aden Protectorate Support Flight. On the administrative front, control of Riyan, Salalah and Masirah, the three route stations round the periphery of the 'Empty Quarter', passed to Khormaksar in 1951, while right at the end of the year No 683 Sqn's Lancaster PR1s flew in to begin a survey of Aden Protectorate and Somaliland.

Re-equipping with the Vampire FB9 in December 1952, No 8 Sqn had reverted to the fighter ground-attack role. In January 1953 four Vampires of 32 Sqn (Egypt) flew in to reinforce No 8 in support of No 2 Wing Aden Protectorate Levies operating in the internal security role against dissident tribes. After the Ansons had dropped leaflets giving 24 hours' notice of attack, the Vampires followed up with 500 lb bombs. In a rather less agressive role the Station briefly hosted the Tropical Experimental Unit from Khartoum in July 1953 for trials with the Meteor and Venom. However, attacks on forts and Government Guard posts, together with the need to respond to raids from across the Yemeni border, resulted in 8 Sqn putting up the biggest operational efforts in its history in 1954. After a brief lull, intensive rocket, bomb and cannon attacks continued on into 1955, by which time No 8 had started to receive the Venom.

As a result of the decision in mid-1956 to station a British battalion in Aden the RAF presence at Khormaksar expanded, so that at the end of the year there was, in addition to No 8 Sqn's Venoms, 78 Sqn with six Twin Pioneers, and 1426 Flight with four Lincolns. The Aden Comms Squadron had added Pembrokes and Sycamore helicopters to its Valettas, and No 20 Wing RAF Regiment was also on strength. Over the next two years this expansion increased, No 8 Sqn establishing a Flight of Meteor FR9s for visual and photo-reconnaissance, and the Lincoln Flight being replaced by a permanent Shackleton Squadron, No 37, which was posted in from Malta in July 1957. The versatile Shackletons were

capable of a wide variety of roles, from bombing to search and rescue, and even the airlift of personnel. At the same time the transport force was reorganized, with the Aden Comms Squadron releasing its Valettas to form No 84 Sqn, and the Sycamores being incorporated into the Station Flight. Finally, a detachment of two Beverleys from 47 Sqn, Abingdon, was added in 1958.

The Beverleys increased tremendously the capability to deploy forces throughout the Arabian Peninsula, and No 84 Sqn re-equipped with the freighter in mid-1958. No 8 Sqn, on the other hand, was destined for the Hunter FGA9 and had completed conversion to the type by January 1960. The sonic boom of this, Aden's first aircraft able to fly faster than sound, was occasionally used as a ruse to simulate 1,000 lb bomb explosions during operations against tribesman. No 8's Hunters, together with two Shackletons from 37 Sqn, deployed to Bahrain and thence to Kuwait in mid-1961, in response to the Kuwait crisis of that year. Beverleys of 84 Sqn flew in No 8's groundcrew, and shortly afterwards airlifted in 45 Commando stationed in Aden. The Beverleys, supported by Valettas from 233 Sqn, which had been formed at Khormaksar back in September 1960 by expanding to squadron status the Valetta Flight of 84 Sqn, then took in heavy stores and other equipment for the forces already established. A force of Britannias also took part in the airlift of troops and equipment from Aden to Kuwait. The crisis highlighted the need to maintain an offensive capability in the Persian Gulf, within reach of Kuwait, and resulted in the formation of the 'Khormaksar Wing', comprising 8 and 208 Sqns whose Hunter FGA9s rotated between Khormaksar and Bahrain (Muharraq) at approximately monthly intervals.

No sooner had the Kuwait crisis died down than tribal unrest broke out again in the Western Aden Protectorate at the start of 1962, which necessitated bombing attacks by Hunters and Shackletons. One of the latter collected a bullet in its wheel bay, and a Beaver of 653 Light Aircraft Sqn, AAC, was hit in the cockpit while on the ground up-country. The size and strength of Khormaksar at this period, with a civil airport located at one end of its single runway, was considerable, but the completion of an extensive building programme meant that the Station could accept a squadron of Argosy medium-

Beverley of 84 Sqn unloading supplies at Beihan, north of Aden, in 1963. (MoD Crown Copyright)

range transports. The first five Argosys of 105 Sqn arrived in June and were able to provide some relief for the hard-pressed Beverleys. By now the Command had its own comms unit, the Middle East Communications Squadron which had been established the previous year. MECS's equipment comprised the Hastings, Valetta and Dakota, but by the spring of 1966 it had added the more modern Andover CC2.

Unrest inside Aden, fomented from across the frontier in Yemen, broke out in September 1962, and after a number of unidentified aircraft had crossed over into Aden air space from the Yemen and fired rockets at at village, Hunters of 8 and 208 Sqns maintained standing patrols of the frontier area. At the same time detachments of Canberras from 13 Sqn (Cyprus) and 58 Sqn (UK) carried out maritime photo-reconnaissance sorties for arms, which it was thought were being smuggled in from other Middle East countries. This activity continued into 1963, when the Station was further reinforced by Westland Belvederes which began to trickle in for No 26 Sqn.

Not only did terrorism in Aden make the headlines in December 1963, with a grenade attack on the High Commissioner on the

Hunter FGA9 XG296 'A' of 43 Sqn at Khormaksar c. 1964. (P Russell-Smith Colln)

apron of the civil airport at Khormaksar, but the beginning of 1964 saw the start of the Radfan operations. The forces ranged at Khormaksar, however, had reached a peak and in addition to the units already mentioned now included a third Hunter FGA9 squadron, No 43, together with the Hunter FR10s of 1417 Flight in the recce role, not to mention the three Sycamores of the SAR Flight. The RAF units played a major part in the operation, providing close air support to the ground forces moving against the dissident tribesmen, and airlifting men and materials to where they were needed. Within the operational area the Belvederes took the lion's share of the air transport work, the Hunters and Shackletons providing air cover and attacking fortified positions.

Due to the deteriorating political situation and the need for increased security, two and sometimes three RAF Regiment squadrons were required to guard the airfield, and so a number of changes were ordered. No 78 Sqn re-equipped with Wessexes in June 1965, relinquishing its Twin Pioneers to No 21 Sqn which, having disbanded in Kenya, now immediately reformed at Khormaksar and which was also equipped with the Dakota (e.g. KJ955) and the Andover CC2. The completion of this move permitted the disbandment of No 26 Sqn in November, that unit's Belvederes being flown aboard HMS *Albion* for

despatch to 66 Sqn in Singapore.

The beginning of the end for Khormaksar came in the Defence White Paper of 1966, which said that South Arabia should be independent by 1968 and that it would therefore be inappropriate for British forces to remain in the area after that. A withdrawal was inevitable. Terrorist activity began to mount, and with limited facilities for the dispersal of aircraft on the airfield, revetments were constructed from 40-gallon oil drums filled with water. The repatriation of families by air duly began in May 1967. Fuelling the fires of an already tense internal situation came the Arab-Israeli War, the success of the Israelis leading to an outbreak of anti-British feeling in Aden. Aden port was closed, but once again the amazingly capacious Beverley saved the day, airlifting in the food which had been diverted by ship to other Red Sea ports. With a pull-out imminent, a plan was formulated which called for the deployment of the majority of Khormaksar's squadrons to either Muharraq or Sharjah, in order to provide a comprehensive force of modern aircraft in the Persian Gulf.

Accordingly, in July 1967, 21 Sqn disbanded, its Twin Pioneers being passed on to 152 Sqn at Muharraq. No 105 Sqn's Argosys started to move to Muharraq at the same time, and 84 transferred to Sharjah in August. Lacking the necessary legs, No 78's

Wessex HC2 XS674 'H' of 78 Sqn at Khormaksar in July 1966. (P Russell-Smith)

Wessexes made the trip to Sharjah by sea. After flying their last ground attack sortie against dissidents on 9 November the Hunters, on the other hand, would maintain an air defence capability until the withdrawal airlift was complete. The date for final withdrawal, or 'W' day, was set at 29 November 1967, and the main airlift out of Aden took place over the week preceding this. Personnel and equipment were flown to Muharraq by Britannia, Belfast and Hercules, and thence to the United Kingdom by VC10 and Britannia. With the departure of 8 Sqn and the disbandment of No 43 in October, the last Hunters to leave were those of 1417 Flight, which flew up to Muharraq on 28 November to become part of 8 Sqn. By the end of the following day Britain had left Aden for good.

Kohat, India

For the Serviceman posted to Kohat in the 1920s and 30s, the very act of getting to this North West Frontier base was an epic of travel. The steamer voyage from the United Kingdom was followed by a lengthy train journey across the Sind Desert to Peshawar, the capital of the North West Frontier Province. Kohat itself, some 30 miles south-west of Peshawar, was finally reached by road. Amongst the first aircraft to appear at the base were the BE2cs of No 31 Sqn on mail runs as early as 1918, but between December 1921 and April 1923 Kohat was the HQ base for No 28 Sqn flying Bristol F2Bs in operations against raiding tribesmen. In 1925, however, it became a true bomber base with the arrival of No 60 Sqn and its de Havilland DH9As.

Conditions at this somewhat isolated location were surprisingly civilized, with bungalows for married personnel, an indoor swimming pool, tennis courts and a golf course, and 60 Sqn soon established a good rapport with the resident Army HQ. In 1926 the DH9s began live individual and formation bombing training on the newly-built Kohat range, in preparation for the Ellington Trophy which No 60 went on to win. Later in the year the Squadron began mounting detachments at other locations, notably Miranshar with its picturesque fort about 100 miles to the south-west of Kohat. In February 1927 No 60 took part in a spectacular air display at Delhi, which also featured the other RAF units in India. The Squadron also provided a pilot to demonstrate one of two Fairey IIIFs which had recently arrived in the country for evaluation trials. The following month

these two aircraft were both flown up to Kohat from the Aircraft Park at Lahore for trials by 60 Sqn, though sadly one of them was soon lost in a fatal crash.

The climate in India led, in early 1927, to the repatriation of No 60's CO, Squadron Leader T. Hazell, who had suffered severe head wounds in the First World War, and indeed the Squadron prudently had a 'hot weather routine' involving the detachment of one Flight to the cooler Hill Depot. The normal routine at Kohat was for flying to begin at dawn; there was a break for breakfast, and then flying continued until 1300 hours. Everyone rested during the afternoon heat, and sports fixtures kicked off at 1600 hours. Hazell's replacement, fresh from a modern, front-line fighter squadron in the United Kingdom, was somewhat startled by the backward conditions and ponderous DH9s at Kohat, and resorted to reading Kipling to put himself in a suitably Victorian frame of mind! However, he was soon in action with his Squadron, making demonstration flights over areas to the north of the base, where there was unrest between rival Muslim sects. Pamphlets were dropped and the Kohat Army GOC was taken up for a reconnaissance of the situation.

Under a general reorganization of the RAF in India in late 1928 No 27 Sqn, also with DH9As, joined 60 Sqn to form No 1 (Indian) Wing at Kohat, while in December the first issue of parachutes to aircrew caused a contemporary stir, even amounting to resistance in some cases. Competition between the two DH9 squadrons had always been fierce but they were soon facing a common challenge, the air evacuation of the British Legation in Kabul following the sacking of the Afghan capital. Orders were given for the DH9s to be stripped of military equipment and on 18 December a 27 Sqn aircraft flew the 150 miles to Kabul to drop a Popham Panel to the Legation, for use in passing messages to aircraft. Hit by rifle fire, the DH9 was forced to land at nearby Sherpur airfield. The DH9s flew several recce sorties to the beleaguered city, before taking part in the first airlift mission on 23 December, and in subsequent missions until the completion in February 1929 of the first-ever large scale aircraft.

The delivery of Westland Wapiti IIAs to replace DH9As at Kohat in the spring of 1930 was timely, for the new aircraft were immediately involved in operations in response to tribal unrest, mainly on a detachment basis from Miranshar. No 5

60 Sqn Westland Wapiti bombing over the North West Frontier from its base at Kohat. (MoD Crown Copyright)

Sqn with Bristol F2Bs was unexpectedly moved up from Quetta for a short reinforcement of Kohat's resident squadrons, though No 5 was no stranger to the place, having put in time during 1925 as a general purpose squadron on army cooperation duties. It was during these operations that Leading Aircraftman R. Douglas of 60 Sqn was awarded the Empire Gallantry Medal for his attempt to rescue the crew of a Wapiti that had crashed on take-off with its load of bombs. The first to arrive on the scene, Douglas found the gunner close to the wreckage with his clothes on fire. Dragging the man clear he next attempted to extricate the pilot. But after a first bomb had gone off Douglas realized that there was no hope for the remaining crewman, and only then made his way clear of the wreckage. He was only thirty yards away when a second bomb detonated, and he had been well aware of the risk he took in approaching so close to the burning Wapiti.

By 1933 an all-weather landing strip had been laid on the airfield, for use when monsoon and winter rain made the grass airfield unserviceable, and this was supplemented by another similar though shorter strip on the west side of the airfield, which sometimes made landing in the Wapiti, with its lack of brakes and tendency to swing, interesting.

In 1934 it was decided that No 60 Sqn would carry out a formation flight from India to Singapore, an activity initiated by No 28 Sqn the previous year. After HQ No 1 Wing at Kohat (numbering amongst its staff officers one Flight Lieutenant Basil Embry) had selected 'C' Flight for the job, the four Wapitis, left Kohat on 29 November, returning home on 21 December, minus one aircraft which had been abandoned in the air over Malaya after a fuel leak. A similar long-distance flight, though a more ambitious one since it involved twelve Wapitis, was mounted in 1936, while in 1937 it was the turn of No 27 Sqn (together with No 11 Sqn from Risalpur) to travel east. Throughout 1936 and 1937 the Kohat squadrons were heavily engaged in offensive action against rebel tribesman. In April 1937, for example, this consisted mainly of operations in

Hawker Audax K4844 of 20 Sqn at Kohat. (via R C B Ashworth)

Waziristan, the Wapitis rearming and refuelling at Miranshar, supported by Bomber Transport Flight Valentias operating out of Kohat. The Flight's four Valentias also carried out supply-dropping sorties, during the course of which one parachute was carried 3,000 feet above its delivery aircraft before coming to earth, due to air currents caused by the rugged terrain. Operations against such infamous dissidents as the Faqir of Ipi continued right up to 1939 when new aircraft (Blenheims), new locations and a new war began to occupy the minds of 27 and 60 Sqns.

Between 1939 and 1942 Nos 20 and 28 Sqns, both of which had served in India for many years, were based at Kohat with Audaxes and Lysanders, but continued to mount detachments at many other locations for North West Frontier work. By 1942, however, Indian Air Force squadrons began to appear on the Station and in September Nos 3 and 4 were there with Audaxes. When No 4 Sqn moved to Risalpur to convert to Hurricanes in June 1943 its place was taken by No 1 Sqn. The first Indian wing commander took over as Station Commander in August, and this remained the pattern for the rest of the war years. In December 1945 the Station strength comprised the following IAF Squadrons: No 1 with Spitfire VIIIs, Hurricane IICs, and a Harvard; No 6 with Spitfire VIIIs and XIVs; No 12 with Spitfire VIIIs; and a Station HQ Communications Flight with three

Harvards. The last reference to RAF flying is in October 1946, when arrangements were made to refuel Spitfire PR19 PS917 of 34 Sqn during a photographic survey of the Frontier.

Kuala Lumpur, Malaya

In its original form as a civil aerodrome, Kuala Lumpur had a grass landing area 800 yards long and 400 yards wide, running NE/SW. Home for 153 Maintenance Unit from June 1941, it was first used operationally during the Japanese advance on Singapore. In December of that year the five airworthy Brewster Buffaloes of 453 Sqn, RAAF, withdrew to Kuala Lumpur from Ipoh after a severe mauling by the Japanese. Replacement aircraft were flown up from Singapore, but the Buffaloes were patently no match for the enemy fighters. By 22 December, after fierce combats with Japanese Ki 61 'Tonys', only three serviceable Buffaloes remained, and these retired to Sembawang (Singapore) on Christmas Day.

At the end of the Second World War in the Far East, a number of operational and administrative units which had been earmarked for Operation Zipper, the now redundant Allied invasion of Malaya, landed in the country. Amongst these were 11 and 17 Sqns, both flying Spitfire XIVs which had been shipped to Malaya aboard HMS *Trumpeter*. Taking off from the carrier the 'Spits' flew to Kuala Lumpur via nearby Kelanang in September 1945, and they were probably the first RAF squadrons back into KL. Their stay was but a brief one, and they soon flew on down to Singapore. *Trumpeter* also brought in 656 AOP Sqn and its Austers, which again made initially for Kelanang, at the same time deploying one of its several Flights to KL. No 656 would, in November, move its HQ to KL for the remaining weeks of 1945. November also witnessed the arrival of Air Headquarters Malaya, complete with its own communications squadron, and during this period the airfield became the location for 154 Staging Post.

The Operation Zipper plans had included the employment of RAF Thunderbolt squadrons, and two of these, Nos 60 and 81, were deployed to Java, via Kuala Lumpur in October 1945, in response to nationalist unrest in that country. Two other Thunderbolt squadrons, Nos 131 and 258, remained at Kuala Lumpur over the final months of the year. No 131 flew low-level dummy attacks over North Malaya to discourage rioting in November. The following month leaflet raids were mounted over the Anambas Islands, after which 131 Sqn's aircraft were transferred to the two Java-based squadrons. A similar support role was performed by No 258 which fed 60 and 81 Sqns with aircraft and crews before disbanding at Kuala Lumpur on 31 December.

The tide of post-war reorganization brought several fighter squadrons to Kuala Lumpur for brief periods. No 28, flying Spitfire XIVs, had come and gone before 1945 was out. Arriving in November 1945, No 136 left for India with its Spitfire XIVs in May 1946, while the Spitfire PR19s of 681 Sqn were based here between December 1945 and January 1946, before moving on to India. Nos 11 and 17 Sqns with Spitfire XIVs arrived in January 1946, but had both left by May. A detachment of Mosquito FBVIs from 47 Sqn was also on strength in December 1945, together with Nos 7005, 7011, 7132, and 7136 Servicing Echelons.

With the arrival, if only for a short spell, of 28 Sqn (Spitfire FR18s) and 84 Sqn (Mosquito FBVIs) in April and May 1946 respectively, accommodation became a problem. Aircrew found themselves living in tents, and the ovens in the Messes were

Spitfire XIVs of Nos 11 and 17 Sqns make a ceremonial flypast at Kuala Lumpur prior to their departure for Japan in April 1946. Standing behind the reviewing officer, an Army General, is Air Commodore C A Bouchier. (D Healey)

constructed by the cooks themselves. However, the domestic situation eased once the repatriation of wartime personnel was complete. Kuala Lumpur was at this stage also serving as a civil airport, and in March 1947 the first Malayan Airways aircraft, an Airspeed Consul, landed (due to a defective tyre). In May a Beaufighter of 84 Sqn arrived to work in conjunction with the local CID in locating opium smugglers and pirates operating along Malaya's west coast. The CID had two launches standing off Port Swettenham, which the Beaufighter was to contact and direct on to anything suspicious. In February 1947 the RAF Regiment opened a Combat Training School, and in May a permanent depot for the RAF Regiment (Malaya) was established. In November, however, the Station closed and reverted to its previous civil role.

The Malayan Emergency was declared the following year and it was during the air operation of this protracted campaign (Operation Firedog) that Kuala Lumpur carved itself a niche in RAF history. An RAF Task Force was formed here in July 1948, this particular airfield being selected due to its central position and its proximity to the seat of government. The Task Force was commanded by Wing Commander H. N. G. Wheeles, the OC Flying from Changi, and consisted initially of detachments from 60 Sqn (Spitfire FR18s) and 110 Sqn (Dakotas). The initial Task Force personnel found conditions at Kuala Lumpur somewhat basic, since the Station had run down since November 1947. In

spite of this, the Spitfires immediately began daily strikes against suspected communist terrorist (CT) positions using cannon and rockets, while the Dakotas carried out patrols, supply and leaflet dropping. By August detachments of 84 and 45 Sqns (Beaufighters) and 28 Sqn (Spitfire FR18s) had been added to the Task Force. The scale of activity resulted in the airfield being reinstated as an RAF station proper in September.

KL now became the main centre of air operations against CTs, though as the ground force effort moved north so part of the offensive support force was moved to Butterworth. Monthly activity followed a similar pattern, with the Singapore-based squadrons detaching aircraft and personnel to Kuala Lumpur where they were controlled by an Advanced Air Headquarters. By the end of 1949 Tempest F2s of 33 Sqn were operating alongside the Spitfires against bandit camps.

Early in June 1950 operations in Johore State intensified, when the Briggs Plan was launched to clear the State of terrorist gangs. Dakotas from KL played an important part in supplying the security forces engaged in the drive, and the following month dropped the millionth ration produced on the Station to a patrol in Negri Sembilan. The Dakotas frequently had to search for crashed aircraft and, for example, were looking, in August 1950, for a strike marker Dakota which had gone down in South West Kelantan. The search Dakota eventually located the wreckage with no sign of life and dropped parachute

Beaufighter TF10s of 45 Sqn starting up at Kuala Lumpur c. 1949. (R A Cook)

canopies to guide ground search parties to the spot. Later another Dakota dropped wreaths and crosses over the crash site, and two padres on board conducted a burial service from the air. On other occasions dummy supply drops were performed to mislead the enemy over the position of the British troops. In addition to Nos 48, 52 and 110 Sqns, other transport units providing six-monthly detachments throughout the Emergency, included 41 Sqn, RNZAF, 38 Sqn, RAAF, and the Far East Communications Squadron. Supplementing the Dakotas, Vickers Valettas and Bristol Freighters were used in some 37,000 Firedog supply dropping, trooping and transport sorties, mainly from Kuala Lumpur.

The 45 Sqn detachment was changed to a full squadron presence when the unit was posted here from Ceylon in May 1949. A move followed in December down to Tengah, where Bristol Brigands replaced the Beaufighters. In February 1952 the Squadron returned to KL, at the same time re-equipping with de Havilland Hornets, with which it moved back to Tengah later in the year.

The Royal Malayan Air Force, which would form later on in 1958, had its origins in the Malayan Auxiliary Air Force consisting of a small number of 'fighter' squadrons which were constituted at the beginning of the decade. The third of these auxiliary squadrons was formed at KL in December 1951, and its Tiger Moths, Harvards and later Chipmunks carried out a limited number of Firedog reconnaissance sorties and leaflet drops over Northern Malaya.

Casualty air evacuation played an important part in the jungle operations of the Emergency, and helicopters for this purpose were introduced into the Far East at a time when rotary wing aircraft generally were still at an experimental stage. Malaya proved a tough testing ground, particularly for the early Westland Dragonfly which 194 Sqn took to Kuala Lumpur in May 1953. A similar move from Sembawang was made by 848 Naval Air Sqn, with its rather more capable Sikorsky Whirlwind HAR21s. No 848 was awarded the 1953 Boyd Trophy for its activities during the year. The following year No 194 replaced its Dragonflies with Bristol Sycamores, which could lift two stretchers, had a better performance, and, of great importance, had better visibility for the pilot when entering jungle clearings. From September 1954 (when it was formed at Seletar) another helicopter unit, No 155

Sqn, was tasked with providing detachments of its Whirlwind HAR4s. This unit merged with 194 in June 1959 to become 110 Sqn.

Complementing the limited capability helicopters, 267 Sqn was formed here as a communications and army support unit on 15 February 1954. In addition to Scottish Aviation Pioneers and Hunting Percival Pembrokes it flew several Dakotas fitted with loud speaker ('sky shouting') equipment, with which to broadcast messages to terrorists in the jungle below. For three years the Squadron flew in and out of jungle strips on casevac and freight missions in support of ground forces, before being renumbered 209 Sqn in November 1958.

Kuala Lumpur continued life as the last RAF station in Malaya but, with Firedog drawing to a close, the process of running it down began in April 1959 when HQ 224 Group (originally known as AHQ Malaya) moved back to Singapore. Operational forces were redeployed, detachments returning to their parent bases and complete squadrons transferring to other stations – for example, 110 to Butterworth in September 1959 and 209 to Seletar a month later. On 25 October 1960 the base, which had played such a central part in the longest campaign since the Napoleonic Wars, was handed over to the Federation of Malaya for use by the Royal Malayan Air Force.

Laarbruch, Germany

Set in the Lower Rhine some two miles from the Dutch border, Laarbruch was the last of the airfields to be built by Germany as part payment for reparations after the Second World War. Construction, which first involved the clearance of large numbers of trees, began in 1953 and the airfield opened for flying in October 1954.

Planned as a reconnaissance base, three squadrons specializing in this role were transferred here from Gütersloh in November/December 1954. These were No 79, whose Meteor FR9s performed low-level and tactical reconnaissance, No 541 with the PR10 version of the Meteor, and No 69 on Canberra PR3s for both tactical and strategic work. From August 1955 onwards the Canberras mounted detachments to Luqa, Malta for reconnaissance over the Central Mediterranean. Early in 1955 two Light Anti-Aircraft Wings of the RAF Regiment were established, followed, between March and August, by no less than three Canberra PR7 squadrons, Nos 31,

Above *Canberra B(I)8 XM244 of 16 Sqn at Laarbruch in 1971.* (P Russell-Smith)

Right *XV Sqn's Hunter T7 WV318 at Laarbruch in June 1971.* (P Russell-Smith)

Below *Buccaneer S2b XW530 of XV Sqn in June 1971.* (P Russell-Smith)

214 and 80 which all reformed here. This made conditions somewhat crowded, and to alleviate the situation the two Meteor squadrons were relocated to Wunstorf in November 1955. Of the remaining Canberra squadrons, No 214 Sqn was, in August 1955, renumbered 80 Sqn and transferred to Brüggen two years later, while No 69 left for Malta in April 1958.

This reshuffle of squadrons left Laarbruch with just one Canberra recce unit, 31 Sqn (which would serve on here until disbandment in March 1971). By 1957 the need for LAA Wings had disappeared and the accommodation built for the RAF Regiment units was handed over to the Army's 21 Signals Regiment. The year also witnessed a change of role for the Station, 68 Sqn moving in from Wahn with its Meteor NF11s in July. No 68 took over 5 Sqn's numberplate in January 1959, re-equipping with Javelin FAW5s in January 1960. The Squadron's normal complement of fourteen aircraft was increased to eighteen in September 1961 as a result of the Berlin crisis. No 5 eventually relocated to Geilenkirchen in December 1962.

Meanwhile, in March 1958, the first of two Canberra B(I)8 squadrons to be taken on establishment was reformed here. This was No 16 and its role was light bomber and night interdiction. It was joined, in January 1968, by a sister squadron, No 3, which

transferred from Geilenkirchen when that Station closed. Of the two squadrons No 16 would become a more or less permanent feature at Laarbruch while 3 Sqn disbanded here in December 1971.

Nineteen seventy one was an eventful year, January ushering in the first Buccaneer squadron, No 15, which had first reformed at Honington before moving to Laarbruch. 'C' Flight of 25 Sqn (HQ at Brüggen) with Bloodhound Mk 2 missiles was now located here to provide an air defence capability. The Canberra B(I)8 lingered on for another 18 months until 16 Sqn disbanded in June 1972, but in October 16 Sqn (Designate) began working up on the Buccaneer, reforming as an operational squadron in January 1973. Assigned to SACEUR, the role of the Buccaneers was low-level overland strike attack. Complementing the RAFG Jaguars, the Buccaneers' standard weaponry was 1,000 lb HE bombs, but they could also carry Paveway laser-guided bombs and cluster bombs. In addition to their nuclear capability an ECM pod could be fitted externally. In 1978 Buccaneers of 16 Sqn defeated 14 Sqn's Jaguars from Brüggen to win the Salmond Trophy in the annual RAFG bombing and navigational competition. Further afield the Laarbruch Buccaneers were regular visitors to Nellis AFB, USA for the Red Flag series of exercises which began in 1977, and to CFB Cold Lake, for the Canadian Maple Flag exercises.

After sixteen years of continuous service with Canberra PR7s at Laabruch, 31 Sqn disbanded in March 1971, but was replaced two months later by 2 Sqn which flew its Phantom FGR2s over from Brüggen in May. Equipped to carry a centreline pod containing EMI infra-red linescan and sideways looking radar, the principal role of the Phantoms was reconnaissance, which had been No 2's specialization for many years. This was but a temporary measure pending the availability of the Jaguar, which was used to work up a 2 Sqn (Designate) alongside the Phantoms, which were relinquished in September 1976. No 2 (Jaguar) Sqn then reformed on 1 October, continuing in the tactical recce/attack role.

It was next the turn of the Buccaneers to bow out, with 15 Sqn first being absorbed by 16 Sqn. Then, again using the system of overlapping Designate squadrons, No 15 reformed as a Tornado GR1 unit in September 1983, followed by 16 Sqn in March 1984. A third Tornado (Designate) squadron, No 20, worked up during 1984, becoming operational in June when 20 (Jaguar) Sqn disbanded at Brüggen. On 13 May 1987, 2 Sqn celebrated the 75th anniversary of its formation and the fact that, alongside 3 Sqn, it was the oldest aeroplane squadron, and to mark the occasion six Jaguars were flown from Brüggen (Laarbruch's runways were being resurfaced at the time) to Farnborough. The last operational sortie by a Jaguar in Germany on 16 December 1988 brought to an end thirteen years of continuous RAF Jaguar operations in the Command, and in January 1989 2 Sqn finally became a Tornado unit.

Laarbruch is, in mid-1990, one of RAFG's two main strike/attack bases – the other being Brüggen. The RAF Regiment provides the other units based here, and these are the light armoured 1 Sqn (a lodger unit assigned to the Gütersloh Harriers in time of war), and 26 Sqn with Rapier SAMs.

Labuan, Borneo

One of the first references to Labuan is in the description of the RAF Far East Flight's 1928-9 cruise of the China Sea. The Flight's Supermarine Southamptons left Seletar, Singapore in November 1928 and made for Borneo, calling first at Kuching and then at Labuan, an island

twenty miles off the coast of North Borneo. This 'isolated outpost of the British Empire' formed a natural staging post on the Singapore-Philippines-Hong Kong route. In September 1948 it was used as a base for a detachment of 81 Sqn Mosquito PR34s from Tengah, tasked with a photographic survey of Sarawak and British North Borneo. By July 1950 a monthly courier service from Changi was in operation, and in October of that year a Hastings from Singapore made the first of many visits.

It was the Indonesian Confrontation which brought Labuan to prominence, although when the campaign began in December 1962 the airfield was no more than a small staging post run by a detachment of approximately 80 personnel from Changi. However, its fine runway, capable of taking the largest aircraft, coupled with its secure off-shore location, led to its use as the RAF's main base in Borneo in the 1960s.

Accordingly, a rapid development pro- gramme was begun. By May 1964 the unit strength had risen to around 500, and a year later to over 1,000. The increase in manpower outstripped permanent accom- modation, and tentage had to be used. Such was its size and operational importance that on 1 August 1963 it became an RAF station in its own right, with permanent personnel posted in on one-year unaccompanied tours.

One of the first aircraft to arrive after the outbreak of the Brunei Rebellion in 1962 was a Bristol Britannia carrying troops to quell the unrest. It was during the initial ensuing operations that a low-flying Canberra of 45 Sqn, detached to Labuan, made dummy attacks on rebels, bluffing them into releasing a number of hostages that they were holding.

Following the declaration of an Air Defence Identification Zone (ADIZ) along Borneo's Malaysian/Indonesian border in 1963, four 20 Sqn Hunters and two 60 Sqn Javelins from Tengah were based here. They were joined by Canberra PR7s, also from Tengah, which began photo- reconnaissance sorties along the the border to pinpoint incursions. Two Shackletons of Changi-based 205 Sqn were usually on strength for maritime reconnaissance of the waters around Borneo. A steady stream of Hastings, Argosys, Beverleys, and Bristol Freighters flew in from Singapore with the men and equipment needed to support the ground operations in Borneo. In addition, there were normally at least two Beverleys

Above *On the pan at Labuan in 1965. Left–right: Borneo Airways Dakota VR-OAH, 48 Sqn Hastings C1a TG526, and 205 Sqn Shackleton MR2 'H'.* (E B Goldsmith)

Below *Canberra B15s of 45 Sqn fly over Labuan in 1965. The Squadron mounted many detachments to the Borneo base.* (via C Jefford)

and one or two Argosys actually attached to the Station from the Singapore squadrons. Numerous forward airstrips were constructed 'up-country' and these themselves were supplied by Scottish Aviation Pioneers and Twin Pioneers of 209 Sqn (home base Seletar) operating from Labuan (and Kuching – the other main RAF airfield in North Borneo). The RAF Pioneers were supplemented by others from the Malaysian Air Force, Westland Whirlwinds of 103 and 110 Sqns, Westland Belvederes of 66 Sqn, and, on occasions, Royal Navy Whirlwinds. With such a diversity of types the Station could truly claim to be one of the most versatile in the RAF. Whilst this force had so far been comprised exclusively of detachments, Labuan gained its first established squadron in March 1965 when 230 Sqn with Whirlwind HAR10s arrived from the UK, aboard HMS *Bulwark*.

By early 1966 Indonesian forays had become fewer in number but larger in scale, and the Commonwealth could still not afford to lower its guard. As a result, Beverleys operating from Labuan were dropping more than one million pounds of supplies each month to forward areas at this point. Hostilities ended in the summer but even as peace was announced the Station's transport aircraft were working at full tilt supporting a ground operation against Indonesian raiders. Peace held, but in order to provide some relief for the hard-pressed Hunters and Javelins in policing the ADIZ, a detachment of Sabres from the RAAF's 78 Wing was sent in from Butterworth.

In October 1966 230 Sqn returned to Odiham, its UK base, the Whirlwinds being flown home in Belfast transport aircraft. The gap left by 230 was filled by 110 Sqn whose own Whirlwinds helped with the resupply of troops and the running down work generally. October proved a busy month with large numbers of aircraft engaged in the withdrawal from Borneo staging through.

Less than two years now remained under the RAF ensign, a period which saw the gradual handover of the Station to the RMAF, in line with the policy for the Malaysian Government to meet military commitments in Borneo. RMAF personnel first took over the refuelling and general handling of all visiting aircraft and RAF strength was gradually reduced. The last RAF personnel left on 16 June 1968.

Lahore, India

So successful were the operations carried out by No 31 Sqn, the first Royal Flying Corps unit to be sent out to India's North West Frontier at the end of 1915, that a second squadron, No 114, was formed at Lahore, capital of the Punjab, in September 1917 from a nucleus of 31 Sqn. Equipped with Farmans and BE2cs No 114's task consisted primarily of frontier patrols, although it joined with No 31 in raids on the Marri tribal areas, before disbanding in 1920.

When the pioneer No 31 Sqn had embarked for India back in 1915, it had been accompanied by the nucleus of an Aircraft Park which, by 1916, was located

Left to right: Bristol Fighter, DH9A, Handley Page Hinaidi, and Westland Wapiti at the Aircraft Park, Lahore. (MoD Crown Copyright)

Handley Page Clive at Lahore in 1932. (MoD Crown Copyright)

at Risalpur. However, in March of that year the Aircraft Park moved to Lahore, forming the main element of the Station. Staffed by twelve officers and 420 other ranks, the Park comprised an Engine Repair Shop, Aeroplane Repair Section, Test and Despatch Section, and MT Repair Section, together with a small stores. The aircraft in use were two BE2cs, two Sopwith Camels and 'two Handley Pages'. When 97 Sqn arrived in India in August 1919 it based an aircraft erection party initially at Lahore. Between November 1919 and March 1920 the Squadron was headquartered on the Station, but mounted detachments at a number of locations for operations in support of the Army on the frontier, and for India's first airmail service (between Bombay and Karachi).

Resources from the Park were used to form an Aircraft Depot, which moved to Karachi in February 1921. The Aircraft Park itself remained at Lahore primarily in the role of of a stores distribution unit. Aircraft were flown in from Karachi to be held in reserve, with very little work being carried out on them apart from routine maintenance. The Park provided assistance for the quelling of riots in Amritsar in 1923.

In 1927 the Secretary of State for Air, Sir Samuel Hoare, inspected the unit and was flown round India on the remainder of his inspection in DH9As specially equipped for the task by the Aircraft Park. Early in the year the unit provided refuelling facilities for a number of aircraft making their way

to and from Delhi for an air display. Additionally, a number of aircraft were actually housed at Lahore for the display, including one Iraq-based Vickers Victoria, two Armstrong Whitworth Siskins and three Fairey IIIFs.

In the course of its duties the Park was required to erect and test a variety of interesting aircraft, notably a DH9 for a flight to England which ended in a fatal crash; the first Hawker Hart to arrive in India; and Handley Page Hinaidi J7745, which was used as the personal transport for the Under Secretary of State for Air, Sir Philip Sassoon, during his 1928 inspection of RAF stations in India. The Hinaidi, together with two Handley Page Clives, was used to equip the Heavy Transport Flight which formed at Lahore in March 1929. A Photo Section was formed to cope with the extra work anticipated from the use of the Clives on survey work, while in February 1931 the Hinaidi was fitted with coloured lights at night for the inauguration of New Delhi.

Throughout 1929–31 an 'HQ Communications Flight' flickers in and out of Lahore's history. Initially equipped with three DH9s and two Bristol Fighters, it later received two Westland Wapitis and one de Havilland Moth before disbanding in April 1931. Out of this was born a so-called HQ Flight which became part of the Aircraft Park, being detached to Delhi for the winter months. The Park provided the pilot and maintenance facilities for the

Avro Ten VT–ACT delivered to India in December 1931 for the use of the Viceroy.

The vicissitudes of the Heavy Transport Flight included a change of title to Bomber Transport Flight in July 1932, and a hangar fire the following March which gutted one Clive and damaged the Hinaïdi. However, in June 1933 a Victoria was loaned by Iraq for trials, which resulted in the purchase of the aircraft for the Flight as K2340. The Viceroy was also the recipient of a replacement machine, an Avro 642, VT–AFM, named 'Star of India' which was flown in for trials before delivery to Delhi. The Victoria, Avro 642, and three Wapitis were also used on relief work after the Quetta earthquake of June 1935. Not long afterwards the Victoria was replaced by Vickers Valentia K4634 which was ferried out from England and which later took part in long-distance flights to Singapore, having been named 'City of Lahore'. K2340 reappeared on the books after conversion to a Valentia at Karachi, while 'Star of India' (serialled L9166) was damaged in Singapore in February 1938. Two Airspeed Envoys, N9107 and '9108 were brought on strength in September 1938 and one of these, in company with Hawker Audax K4862, was used to evacuate a member of the Frontier Constabulary severely injured in an encounter with dacoits.

With effect from 1 October 1938 the unit relinquished the title of 'Aircraft Park' in favour of 'RAF Station Lahore', other changes including the arrival of No 31 Sqn with Wapitis. The Squadron completed its conversion to Valentias, absorbing the Bomber Transport Flight in the process; the Valentias flew many frontier reconnaissance sorties. No 31's stay lasted until April 1940, when it moved on to Peshawar to make room for two Blenheim squadrons, Nos 11 and 39, which both left for the Middle East in May. Their place was, in turn, taken by No 5 Sqn which, leaving its Wapitis behind at Port Sandeman for No 1 Sqn, Indian Air Force, reformed at Lahore in June as a Light Bomber Sqn with Hawker Harts (India), before transferring to Risalpur in February 1941. Another squadron, No 60 with Blenheims, departed at the same time, thought its stay was so brief that there is no record of its arrival! Later in the year a Blenheim of 20 Sqn, which had remained behind at Lahore after an air defence exercise, was used for the photo reconnaissance of certain parts of Persia. Westland Lysanders now began to appear in increasing numbers, five arriving

from Karachi in January 1942. The original intention was for these to be stored pending issue to other units, though in the event they left the following month for the Far East. The Lysanders of No 28 Sqn staged through on 26 January 1942 and would suffer heavy casualties in the coming months in operations against the Japanese. In March the RAF Station HQ disbanded and was absorbed by No 307 MU.

'An ideal place for the formation of a new squadron' enthuses the history of 194 Sqn, 'The Friendly Firm', which formed at Lahore in October 1942 with resources, including its CO, Wing Commander Alec Pearson, from 31 Sqn. The task of 194's Hudsons was to provide a regular communications service for mail, passengers and stores within India and Ceylon, and the first schedule to Colombo was performed in November. Flights to Cairo and Chittagong were initiated a month later. By the end of January 1943 No 194 had twelve Hudsons at Lahore, plus detachments of five aircraft at Dum Dum (Calcutta) and three at Tezpur over near the Burmese border supplying Orde Wingate's Long Range Penetration Group. The last British squadron to be based at Lahore, No 194 moved on in February 1943 (to distinguish itself in the Burma War flying Dakotas), and the only unit of any significance here after that date was 307 Maintenance Unit.

Luqa, Malta

Although destined to become the principal RAF station on Malta, Luqa was younger than the other main bases on the island, construction beginning in October 1939 and reaching completion by May 1940. The airfield saw limited commercial use by the Italians before they entered the war in June, and there is reference to Imperial Airways staff here towards the middle of the year. Probably the first permanent unit to be taken on strength was Fighter Flight, Malta which, with its handful of Sea Gladiators and Hurricanes, transferred from Hal Far in June 1940, and which was in action against Italian bombers attacking the island practically daily in June and July. Fighter Flight's aircraft, together with twelve Hurricane Is of 418 Flight flown off the carrier HMS *Argus* on 2 August, were then used to form 261 Sqn that same day, ground crews arriving by submarine.

With its proximity to Italy, Malta was ideally situated as a reconnaissance base and in September three Marylands were sent out from the UK to form 431 Flight for

The three Gladiators, 'Faith', 'Hope' and 'Charity' at Luqa in September 1940. (via J Pickering)

long range recce over the Mediterranean. It was one of the Marylands that brought back photographic proof of the success of the attack on the Italian Fleet in Taranto harbour in November. The need for intelligence information increased with the reformation at Luqa in December 1940 of 148 Sqn, whose Wellingtons began the bombing offensive against Italian supply lines to Libya, embracing targets in Italy, Sicily and Tripoli.

On 10 January 1941 No 69 Sqn was reformed from 431 Flight, the Marylands continuing to seek out naval targets, harbours and airfields; by April No 69 had also acquired Hurricanes for photo-reconnaissance, to which were later added Beauforts and Blenheims. A historic raid took place on 10 February when Armstrong Whitworth Whitleys of Bomber Command, temporarily based in Malta, dropped British paratroops over Southern

RAF personnel construct a blast wall for a Wellington at Luqa during the Second World War. (Nat War Museum — Malta)

Italy in a bid to destroy the Tragino aqueduct. Codenamed Colossus, this was the first such operation by British Airborne Forces.

Throughout the year Blenheim squadrons from No 2 Group were detached to Luqa from the UK on a rotational basis to attack Axis shipping sailing between Europe and North Africa. First to arrive was No 82 in April, followed during the succeeding months by Nos 21, 139, 110, 105, 107 and 18. In May half of 252 Sqn flew in from Aldergrove, and the unit's Beaufighters were immediately in action carrying out dusk strafing attacks on the airfields at Catania and Comiso. No 38 Sqn provided a detachment of Wellingtons in August for the war against enemy shipping, followed in mid-October by the entire complement of 104 Sqn with its fifteen Wellingtons (which remained until January 1942). Throughout September Blenheim fighters of 113 Sqn mounted anti-submarine patrols, while 272 Sqn's Beaufighters attacked E-boats and the Marsala seaplane base. Yet other Wellington squadrons operated from the base during October, including No 221 for shipping searches, and No 40 which raided Tripoli. One of the more interesting detachments during October/November comprised two Whitleys of 138 Sqn, based here for SOE drops into Yugoslavia.

1942 opened with detached Wellingtons of 156 Sqn bombing Catania and Comiso, but in March Luqa itself became the target for repeated attacks by Ju 88s escorted by Me 109s. To counter these raids 601 Sqn flew in its Spitfire Vs off the USS *Wasp* on 20 April, and by the end of the day had seen combat with the enemy, with losses on both sides. Other units operating from the Station on detachment throughout the first half of the year included 605 Sqn from Hal Far with Hurricane IICs, 37 Sqn's Wellingtons, and 252 Sqn again, whose Beaufighters provided continuous cover for the Malta convoys. Following 261 Sqn's move to Ta Kali in May 1941 a detachment of the unit's Hurricanes had remained at Luqa, and in May 1942 this was reinforced by 126 Sqn which, with Spitfire Vs, stayed on until the summer of 1943. There is reference at this point to 'Special Duties Flight' Wellington VIIIs, which were probably the aircraft of 38 Sqn detached here from Egypt in the maritime role. Yet another fighter squadron, No 1435, was added in August when 1435 Flight (which had moved over from Ta Kali earlier in the year) was elevated to squadron status. This

unit's Spitfire Vcs were very active against the mounting Italian raids on Malta.

For some time a detachment of 235 Sqn's Beaufighters had been on strength, and in August this was formed into 227 Sqn in the shipping strike role. Like so many of the Luqa squadrons this unit was in action on the first day of its existence, escorting a 39 Sqn attack on a convoy, in which two of the 'Beaus' were lost. No 227 moved on to Ta Kali in November. During September a detachment of Wellingtons from 162 Sqn carried out a radar survey of Taranto, Sardinia and Tripoli, while in December the Mosquitoes of 23 Sqn arrived to begin long range intruder operations over Sicily prior to the forthcoming Allied landings there. Throughout the winter 458 Sqn, based in Egypt with Wellingtons, mounted detachments at a number of airfields, including Luqa, for mining and torpedo operations.

Activity during 1943 centred around the Allied invasion of Sicily in July. In preparation for this, No 683 Sqn was formed (from 'B' Flight of 69 Sqn) for photo-reconnaissance work on 8 February, the unit's Spitfires and Mosquitoes covering Italian-held airfields and harbours. P-38 Lightnings of the USAAF's 3rd Photo Reconnaissance Gp flew similar missions, while 126 Sqn's Spitfires escorted US Liberators attacking Augusta harbour. A detachment of 221 Sqn's Wellingtons was on hand for daylight operations against ships and subs, with night coverage in April being provided by a detachment of Leigh Light-equipped Wellington XIIs from 172 Sqn. June and July brought in a flood of squadrons taking part in the invasion: fighter cover was provided by Spitfires of 73, 92, 417 and 601 Sqns, together with Beaufighters of 600, 219, 272 and 108 Sqns, while Kittyhawk fighter bombers of 250, 260 and 450 Sqns attacked targets on Sicily itself. Two tactical recce Mustangs of 1437 Flight were based here in late July, leaving for Sicily at the end of the month, and the landings also drew detachments of Baltimores (Nos 55 and 223 Sqns) and Bostons (No 114 Sqn) from Tunisia.

In the wake of the Sicilian landings many of the squadrons had moved on, or were shortly to do so, and the pressure on Luqa eased. Before leaving in September No 23 Sqn received the AOC's congratulations for its contribution to Malta's 1943 offensive – 1,000 sorties in which 24 enemy aircraft were destroyed, 25 ships attacked and 172 locos destroyed or damaged. September also saw the inevitable stream of post-assault transit aircraft. No 683 Sqn was still here (but only until November), its Spitfires carrying out recce flights, while 69 and 221 Sqns were mounting A/S patrols. No 256 Sqn with Mosquito XIIs arrived for night defence and convoy escort work in October, remaining until April 1944, while 108 Sqn moved over to Hal Far in July, receiving the Mk XII Mosquito in the interim. The long-serving No 69 had finally left in February, and a detachment of 458 Sqn's A/S patrol Wellingtons had also gone by June.

There were now (mid-1944) no front-line units based at Luqa and the accommodation made available was utilized by No 64 Staging Post whose task was to handle transit aircraft. There were visits from RN and USN carrier-based aircraft, but it was not until the arrival of 38 Sqn with its air-sea rescue Warwicks and Wellington XIVs in July 1945 that the Station regained a resident squadron. No 1357 Meteorological Flight, formed on 1 February 1946 with Mosquitoes, was practically stillborn, since it disbanded on 10 April. The Malta Communications Flight, on the other hand, had begun a more assured existence and was at this point operating Anson XIIs and Wellington Xs. No 38 flew to Egypt to convert to Lancasters in July and then moved to Palestine in December, leaving behind a detachment of two aircraft for ASR duties.

Post-war the number of visiting aircraft had risen, exceeding the 1,000 mark by May 1947. The statistics had included BOAC traffic, but in June the company began re-routeing their four-engined types via Castel Benito, resulting in a decrease in civilian movements. In addition, RAF Bomber Command had begun a series of 'Sunbronze' detachments from the UK, and by the turn of the decade the Lincolns of 100, 57, 214, 83, 97, 9 and 7 Sqns had become a familiar sight.

In October 1947 the first Anson XIXs arrived for the Malta Communications Flight, and by December the Flight also had a Proctor III on charge. For VIP work the Mediterranean/Middle East VIP Pool was operating Dakota KN279. The build-up of permanent units proceeded apace, with the return from Palestine of 38 Sqn HQ in April 1948, together with a sister squadron, No 37. Now flying Lancaster GR/ASR 3s, the activities of the two units continued to centre around the Jewish immigration problem, both squadrons providing aircraft for Operation Thug, the airlift of Jewish detainees from Nairobi to El Adem in July. The Lancasters also exercised with RN and US naval units, and it was during one such exercise in September that TX269 'N' of 38 Sqn was lost with all its crew, when it flew into the side of Monte Cristo island.

The USAF in Germany was now eyeing Malta for armament practice activities, and

Lancaster ASR3 RE123 'R' of 38 Sqn takes off from Luqa. (Nat War Museum — Malta)

in February sent down sixteen F-47 Thunderbolts, two B-26 Invaders and a B-17 Flying Fortress, supported by two C-47s, for air firing practice. Two months later four F-80 Shooting Stars arrived to assess the Station's suitability for gunnery training exercises, which led to a larger USAF contingent in May. Meanwhile, in April, Devon VP953 had arrived for the Malta Comms Flight, and 240 OCU had carried out a proving flight from the UK with one of its new Valettas. By mid-1950 the Comms Flight had received its own Valettas, and the year also saw the start of periodic detachments of 109 Sqn's Mosquito B35s from Hemswell.

A prime location for detachments of maritime aircraft, Luqa began hosting visiting Shackleton squadrons in October 1952 when four aircraft of 240 Sqn arrived for exercises with the Mediterranean Fleet. The majority of the RAF's Shackleton squadrons put in an appearance at one time or another throughout the 1950s, and Luqa's own two maritime squadrons began re-equipping with the type at the end of July 1953. The protracted sorties over the sea mounted by Nos 37 and 38 included, for example, searches for the BOAC Comets which broke up in mid-air in January and April 1954. A detachment of Neptunes from the RAF's 217 Sqn arrived in August 1954 for one of the aptly named 'Fair Isle' maritime detachments.

Luqa took on its first squadron of jet aircraft in January 1955 when 39 Sqn was posted in with Meteor NF13s, and at about the same time the Station assumed responsibility for No 1151 Marine Craft Unit based

at Marsaxlokk with its High Speed Launches. With its role widened, the Comms Flight had by now expanded into the Malta Comms and Target Towing Sqn, receiving a Vampire FB9 (soon handed over to 39 Sqn) plus two Pembrokes, and controlling a Flight of Beaufighter TT10s. From August 1955 No 69 Sqn, based at Laarbruch in Germany with Canberra PR3s, maintained a detachment at Luqa for reconnaissance of the Central Mediterranean, the demands of which eventually resulted in the move of the entire Squadron to Malta.

Although more distant from Egypt than the Cyprus airfields, Luqa nevertheless played a prominent part in the Suez crisis of 1956, and elements of a number of Bomber Command Squadrons were based here for the brief operation which ensued. These were Canberra B2/6s of 9, 12, 15, 101, 109 and 139 Sqns, together with Valiants from 138, 148, 207 and 214, the majority of which arrived in October. At the same time 39 Sqn moved to Nicosia to be nearer the action. In the course of raiding Almaza airfield, Cairo, on 31 October Valiant XD814 of 148 Sqn became the first V-bomber to drop bombs 'in anger'. The main body of the reinforcements had returned to the UK by the end of the year, though a 12 Sqn detachment remained behind until March 1957.

No 37 Sqn transferred to Aden in July 1957, leaving No 38 to soldier on in the maritime recce role. The following year (on 1 July) No 69 Sqn was disbanded and reformed as 39 Sqn – a familiar unit at Luqa, but this time in the photo-recce role.

Shackleton MR2s of 37 Sqn airborne over the Mediterranean in the mid-1950s from Luqa. Nearest is WR954 'C', behind is WL800 'Z'. In the distance are nine Lockheed Neptunes. (Fairbairn Colln)

Canberra PR9 XH174 of 39 Sqn at Luqa in January 1965. (R C B Ashworth)

The departure of the last Shackletons of 38 Sqn to Hal Far in September 1965 ushered in 13 Sqn from Cyprus, the Near East Air Force's main photo-reconnaissance unit, flying the Canberra PR9 which now began a comparatively long association with Malta. In addition, the Shackleton reappeared, this time in the shape of the MR3s of 203 Sqn which flew in from Ballykelly in January 1969. No 203's area of operation was the whole of the Mediterranean, and the Squadron was increasingly turning its attention to the movement of Soviet naval vessels in and out of the Black Sea. No 39 Sqn, on the other hand, flew home to Wyton in October 1970. The maritime capability of 203 Sqn was greatly improved by the arrival, in July 1971, of Nimrods which went on to take part in numerous NATO and CENTO exercises.

Political differences between Britain and the Maltese government led to a withdrawal of British forces in the winter of 1971/72. No 203 Sqn was detached to Sigonella, Sicily on 12 January 1972 while the problems were sorted out, but returned on 23 April, some three weeks after the signing of a new Anglo-Maltese Agreement. No 13 Sqn, for its part, was sent further east to Akrotiri, Cyprus (where some of its PR9s were exchanged for the more plentiful PR7), remaining there until 10 October before returning to Luqa. Back in Malta, 13 Sqn maintained its programme of exotic detachments, one of the most unusual of which was to Sana'a, capital of the Yemen Arab Republic, for an aerial survey of that country, codenamed Operation Hayrack.

Throughout its final years Luqa remained a principal maritime airfield, as well as forming a stepping stone down the Mediterranean not only for transport aircraft but also for a host of additional types flying Lone Rangers, training and other sorties. In addition, it was being used increasingly for civil traffic. No 203 Sqn disbanded *in situ* on 31 December 1977, 13 Sqn went home to Wyton the following October and the Station finally closed on 31 March 1979.

Masirah, Muscat and Oman

'Two dhows arrived from Aden at the beginning of the month bringing goats, sheep, firewood and dates. Most of the goats died *en route* and the rest are in poor shape.' This entry in the Station records for February 1947 sums up the remoteness and rudimentary lifestyle at this desert island airfield, located fifteen miles off the Arabian mainland near the entrance to the Persian Gulf. Conditions were no doubt infinitely more primitive back in April 1930 when the island was visited by an RAF party who examined its potential as a staging post and flying boat anchorage. In October 1932 No 203 Sqn, then operating Short Rangoon flying boats from Basra, Iraq, was given authority to pay petrol store guards here, and it was subsequently utilized as a landing site for the RAF and for Imperial Airways aircraft flying to India.

A temporary flying boat base was eventually established on the south-west corner of the island and, utilizing abandoned concrete huts previously erected by Civil Aviation India, this was used from 1942 onwards by detachments of Catalina squadrons, including Nos 209, 265 and 321. Meanwhile, in 1943, an airfield with accommodation for one GR squadron was constructed on the north-east end of the island. The first permanent use of the airfield was by a detachment of Bristol Blenheim Vs of 244 Sqn based at Sharjah. As late as 1974 the wreck of one of these Blenheims could be seen about 100 yards off the shore of Masirah, not far from the flying boat anchorage.

By 1943 No 33 Staging Post had been established at Masirah, with the task of handling the flow of aircraft being ferried along the southern reinforcement route to India. All supplies for the Station arrived by sea, and because of the distance of the jetty from the airfield, together with the limited supply of road building material, a narrow gauge railway using three diesel locomotives was constructed in November 1943. This was the celebrated 'Masirah State Railway' and many years later one of the locomotives would end up as an exhibit in the RAF Museum.

No 244 Sqn moved in on a permanent basis in February 1944, at the same time re-equipping with Wellington XIIIs which joined the Catalinas on convoy escort work and anti-submarine patrols. The flying squadrons also assisted No 214 Air Sea Rescue Unit, which had been established by 1944, to locate torpedoed ships and ditched aircraft.

The end of hostilities in 1945 resulted in a number of changes: the Catalinas moved on, and No 244 Sqn disbanded to be replaced by a detachment of Warwicks from 294 Sqn, an ASR unit. A Marine Craft Unit detachment (replacing 214 ASR Unit) was established, and using the Umm Rasas anchorage, was equipped with High Speed Launches.

BOAC began to take an increased interest in the place in August 1946, when a number of the company's staff were drafted in, their duties including the operation of the D/F station on the island. The role of the Station was now to provide staging post and navigational facilities for both civil and military aircraft operating not only in the Persian Gulf area but also on the Far East routes. In addition to the weekly Aden Communications Flight Wellington, visitors in the late 1940s included Skyways Yorks, Dakotas of Indian Overseas Airlines and Ethiopian Airlines, Airspeed Consuls of Chartair,

and Handley Page Haltons of the Lancashire Aircraft Corporation. For the protection of the Station there was a Squadron of Aden Protectorate Levies whose CO (a Flight Lieutenant) also doubled as station commander.

Throughout the last three months of 1951 single US Navy Liberators made short stays, carrying out a photographic survey, one of the aircraft being flown by the squadron commander of VP-61. Political unrest in Oman between 1957 and 1959 involved British forces operating against rebel tribesmen, and Masirah's role in the air action was to host detachments of Shackletons from Nos 37, 42 and 224 Sqns, which dropped 1,000 lb bombs on the water tanks, dams and aqueducts upon which the villages depended for the irrigation of their cultivated areas. Later the Shackletons bombed caves, sangars and machine-gun posts in support of a squadron of the SAS preparing for an assault on the Jebel Akhdar (Green Mountain). A second SAS squadron was flown into Masirah early in 1959 to be discreetly infiltrated into Oman for the final successful push against the three rebel villages.

With the focal point of British military power in the Middle East switching from Aden to the Persian Gulf, Masirah grew in importance. Accordingly a £3 million development programme was drawn up, beginning, in 1962, with the construction of a 9,000 ft asphalt runway. Before the year was out the first large jet, a Comet, had been handled, and seven Hunters of 8 Sqn had made the first night landing. When the time came for withdrawal from Aden in 1967 No 8 Sqn was one of several units to be relocated, and *en route* to its new base at Muharraq it spent several weeks at Masirah for training and to be on call during the final stages of withdrawal. During June of that year the Lightning F6s of 74 Sqn staged through on their way out to Tengah, Singapore. The first Lightning detachment from the United Kingdom, to exercise the reinforcement of air defence in the Gulf, took place in 1969, swiftly followed by the first Vulcan detachment from the recently formed NEAF Bomber Wing (9 and 35 Sqns) at Akrotiri, Cyprus. The Vulcan detachments, three or four aircraft for ten day periods, became a regular feature at Masirah in the early 1970s.

With the imminent withdrawal from the Persian Gulf, two Andovers (from the disbanded 84 Sqn) were flown to Masirah in September 1971 to form a detached Flight of 46 Sqn, which at that point had its

Andover C1 XS601 of Masirah's resident 46 Sqn detachment prepares to take off on a routine sortie to Muscat in 1972. (T Fairbairn)

headquarters at Thorney Island. Known locally as 'Yimkin Airways', the Andovers flew regular schedules to Muscat, Salalah and Dubai, in addition to a stand-by commitment for aeromedical and search and rescue duties. The RAF's last remaining base in the Gulf, Masirah finally closed in March 1977.

Mingaladon, Burma

When No 60 Sqn, the first operational unit to use the Station, moved to Mingaladon in great secrecy in February 1941, they found the airfield to be still under construction. Located some 40 miles north of Rangoon the base boasted only one hangar at this point, in which No 60 made themselves at home. Initially the Squadron pilots shared accommodation with the Gloucester Regiment. Bristol Blenheims formed No 60's equipment, although due to a shortage of fighters for the defence of Rangoon the Squadron now formed 'C' Flight with Brewster Buffaloes. The tubby little fighters were embarassingly outclassed by the larger Blenheims, and it was probably something of a relief when, in October 1941, No 67 Sqn arrived from Kallang, Singapore to take over the Buffaloes.

Following the outbreak of war with Japan in December, No 67's Buffaloes were in action strafing enemy-held airfields, and when Mingaladon was attacked a few days later the Buffaloes claimed six Japanese aircraft destroyed. No 60 left for Malaya during the month, but No 67 fought valiantly on in the face of the Japanese advance from the south, supply support for the Station as a whole being provided by the Douglas DC-2s of No 31 Sqn. On Christmas Day another Japanese air raid damaged many of the Buffaloes, while in January 1942 one of the DC-2s (DG474) was written off in an attack on the airfield. Reinforcements in the shape of Hurricanes of Nos 17 and 135 Sqns arrived during January, and the units had some success against Army 97s. The Japanese, however, were hammering at the door and during February and March all units retired to India. The airfield itself, littered with wrecked aircraft, was abandoned to the enemy.

As the Japanese floodtide ebbed, so the airfield passed back into Allied hands, and amongst the first RAF aircraft to appear, in May 1945, were two Lysanders of No 357 Sqn, a special duties outfit, carrying infiltrators. The Hurricane IICs of No 28 Sqn flying tactical reconnaissance sorties were not far behind (though bad weather and unserviceability caused the Squadron to grind to a halt by the summer). Two other fighter squadrons, both with Spitfire VIIIs, moved in during May, No 273, which in addition to standing patrols over Rangoon later flew bombing and strafing

Special Duties Lysander V9289 of 357 Sqn at Mingaladon for work with Force 136 behind enemy lines. (Bruce Robertson Colln)

attacks, and No 607, whose duties included leaflet raids calling on the Japanese to surrender. The war, which was now drawing to a close, was photographed by detachments of No 681 Sqn's Spitfire XIs.

In the post-war clear up there was a need to relocate men and materials on a vast scale, and no less than three Dakota transport squadrons took up post in August 1945 to perform this role. All three were housed in tented accommodation set in clearings cut out of the scrub and trees around the edge of the airfield. Of these, Nos 62 and 194 carried out supply dropping and troop carrying, while No 267 started scheduled services throughout South East Asia to such destinations as Hong Kong, Saigon and Bangkok. Food, clothing and medical supplies were flown to POW camps and POWs brought back to be repatriated. Such was the scale of movements in and out of the Station (there were, for example, 1,946 in April 1946) that a Land Rescue Team was formed and in a typical month (June 1946) was called out to search for missing Spitfire XIV RM974 and Expediter KJ479. No 1300 Meteorological Flight was on the strength of the Station at this time, putting up daily PAMPA weather sorties with its Mosquito VIs.

In September (by which time 194 and 267 Sqns had disbanded at Mingaladon, and 62 had moved on) the Burmese Government asked the RAF to supply rice by air to some ten thousand Karens who were near to

starving in the hills. Four Dakotas were therefore detached from No 48 Sqn in Singapore and began operations on the 25th of the month. Each aircraft carried 6,000 lbs of rice, which was dropped on a small disused landing strip. A general strike in Rangoon during late September resulted in a possible requirement to move troops to disaffected areas, and in response to this an entire Dakota squadron, No 52, moved in from India.

In order to provide better support for the RAF Avro York schedule from the United Kingdom to the Far East, No 1300 Met Flight moved to Butterworth in November, but the following month a detachment of four Mosquito PR 34s from No 81 Sqn (Java) flew in to carry out a survey of Siam (Thailand). The Siamese Government had asked for four Siamese officers to be attached to the Squadron to learn photo-recce techniques. Unfortunately the Mosquitoes were grounded on arrival due to technical reasons, and two Spitfires were flown in from Seletar, Singapore, during January 1947 to carry out the task. An early Monsoon prevented the completion of the survey (which was eventually finished after a return visit by 81 Sqn in October 1947). The rice dropping operations were completed in March (Operation Hunger IV) after an epic 366 sorties, and during the month No 48 Sqn's Dakotas began a two-month stay. The need to provide weather data was met by the deployment of No 18

Sqn with its Mosquito FB 6s in April 1947, and by now No 52 was carrying out scheduled services. The following month the Station began training recruits for the Burmese Air Force.

This latter role was a sign of the times, and indeed there was actually political unrest in Burma at this juncture. Consequently, No 52 Sqn's planned transfer to Singapore was postponed while No 18's Mosquitoes were fully armed during July. At the same time a special HQ to form 25 Brigade was flown in from Singapore aboard four Dakotas of 48 Sqn. One other event in July was the arrival for 18 Sqn of two Bristol Buckmaster trainers, which were immediately grounded due to suspected corrosion. The year saw Burmese independence, and the Station closed down as an RAF unit in December 1947.

Minneriya, Ceylon

One of the lesser known Ceylon airfields, Minneriya nevertheless had a most interesting and varied career, particularly in the final year of the Second World War when it became an important base for RAF Liberator operations. Its development began in July 1942 when orders were given for it to be opened up with a small advance party made up chiefly from ground personnel of 217 Sqn (then a Beaufort unit making its way out east from the UK). The balance of the Squadron would follow as soon as the Station was ready.

In the meantime various units began to use the airfield, mainly on a detachment basis. August saw the arrival of four Blenheims of XI Sqn under the command of Wing Commander R. N. Bateson, which were refuelled, bombed up and declared operational. Jungle at the edge of the airfield was cleared for bomb dumps, while on the fighter front Hurricanes of 258 and 261 Sqns visited from other bases in Ceylon. Throughout September 1942 the build-up of the Station continued apace, with the arrival of two Hurricanes on detachment from 30 Sqn which undertook the first night flying from the airfield. Four Swordfish of 814 Sqn FAA and six Beauforts from 22 Sqn began anti-submarine patrols. Hudsons from India started to reach 217 Sqn in October, joining 22 Sqn for A/S patrols the following month; these, however, were short-lived, both units moving on in February 1943.

Apart from a refusal by the Air Ministry Works Department labour gangs to go to work on the construction of facilities due to

a grievance over pay, 1943 saw few changes, but early in 1944 a fresh crop of units began to appear on the Station. First there was 733 Sqn which formed as a Fleet Requirements Unit on 1 January. A number of Albacores, Defiants and Beaufighters for No 733 had arrived safely the previous month, but some of its subsequent machines were not so fortunate. When Beaufort JM515 was delivered by a New Zealand pilot in February it crashed on landing and was badly damaged. The same month Defiant AA500 crashed in the jungle, the crew being taken to hospital in Kandy. Two Hurricane units took their place alongside 733 Sqn in January and these were 17 Sqn which flew convoy protection patrols, and 135 Sqn which took part in harbour defence exercises at Trincomalee. The exercises involved the interception of Corsairs which, if nothing else, proved that the Corsair could outclimb the Hurricane IIC!

The Corsairs were from the Royal Navy, and plans were already being made to receive two squadrons of the aircraft (Nos 1837 and 1838), together with the RAF's 89 (Beaufighter) Sqn. To make way for these units 733 Sqn was relocated elsewhere in Ceylon. The start of 89 Sqn's operations in April, which included many night patrols, was marred by the loss of Beaufighter X8001, which crashed fatally in a moonlight take-off. The Corsairs, which had flown in from the escort carrier HMS *Atheling*, were for their part forbidden from carrying out carrier-style landings which took them out of sight behind trees on the downwind leg at Minneriya - this edict resulting from an attempt by one of the 'bent-wing birds' to land with its wheels still up. Conversion on to new types now became the order of the day for the Hurricane squadrons, No 17 to the Spitfire VIII and No 135 on to Thunderbolts. August brought two more fighter squadrons, No 81 with Spitfire VIIIs and No 176 flying Beaufighters, both in a non-operational role. No 136 Sqn, also with Spitfire VIIIs, would follow at the end of the year.

When Liberators 'J' and 'C' of 354 Sqn took off from Minneriya on an anti-submarine patrol in November 1944 they marked a change in role for the Station to a General Reconnaissance base. Once a submarine had been sighted the Liberators carried out what was known as the 'Hunt to Exhaustion', which involved an aircraft being airborne continuously over the sub's reported location. To this activity No 354 added convoy escort work until departing in January 1945. By this time, BOAC Liberators were also making refuelling stops here *en route* to Australia.

Throughout the early months of 1945 Liberator activity was stepped up, 160 Sqn replacing No 354 in February. Mining operations, which were now the primary task, took eleven of 160 Sqn's aircraft to the port of Chumphon in Thailand for a record drop (by Ceylon-based aircraft), of 59 mines. In March the Squadron not only flew an eighteen-hour mining raid to Penang, but also carried out a photo-reconnaissance mission to Nias Island, south-west of Sumatra, where leaflets were dropped for good measure. The following month Liberator 'X' of the India-based 159 Sqn was attached for special reconnaissance operations over the north coast of Sumatra, and thence up to Malaya.

A halt to 160 Sqn's mining operations was ordered in May and the Squadron began training vigorously for a new role, that of Special Duties. The Squadron's Liberators were supplemented in this important task by additional aircraft from 200 Sqn (which renumbered to 8 on arrival), and a detachment of four machines from 357 Sqn. Beginning in June the SD sorties, mounted in support of partisans in enemy-held Burma and Malaya, resulted in some very long-distance flights. In July, for example, Flight Lieutenant J. A. Muir of 160 Sqn flying aircraft 'J' was airborne for 24 hrs 10 mins. The Japanese surrender offered no immediate respite for the Liberators, for in August leaflets were scattered over villages and Red Cross parcels were dropped to POWs in Operation Mastiff. SD ops were officially concluded in September, to be replaced at the beginning of November by a ferry service to the Cocos Islands.

The end of hostilities in the Far East resulted in the inevitable squadron disbandments, and No 8's was set for November. The unit had, however, expected Lancasters by the end of the year and their disappointment was such that it drew a personal placatory letter from the Allied Air Commander, Sir Keith Park. The demise of 8 Sqn was not unique though, and by February 1946 no aircraft remained at Minneriya.

Mount Pleasant, Falkland Islands

'Smile - happiness is Mount Pleasant-shaped. If you weren't here you'd have to be somewhere else!' Thus proclaimed the banner jauntily draped over a waiting fire tender, which greeted a fresh load of Servicemen and civilians disembarking from their TriStar at Mount Pleasant in early 1986 at the start of their tours in the Falkland Islands.

The need for Mount Pleasant had arisen from the limited capability of RAF Stanley (the only other airfield in the Islands) to cope with the influx of men and aircraft which a reinforcement of the Falklands might demand. Accordingly, in June 1983 Mr Michael Heseltine, the then Defence Minister, announced that a new airfield capable of accepting wide-bodied jets would be constructed at March Ridge/Mount Pleasant on East Falkland. It would have an 8,500 ft runway which would enable larger aircraft such as TriStars and Boeing 747s to fly direct from Ascension Island without in-flight refuelling.

The project was an extensive and costly one, embracing plans not only to centralize a number of RAF units operating from widely scattered, improvised bases around the Falklands, but also to bring together units of the Army, and ultimately even to provide accommodation for Commander British Forces Falklands Islands and his HQ staff. As well as a front-line RAF station, Mount Pleasant would in effect be a custom-built joint-Service military complex, and its often-used title 'MPA' (Mount Pleasant Airport) underlined the civil role it would play and which would hopefully blossom in the future. The airfield would have its own military port constructed on the coast nearby for the movement by sea of bulky goods.

Work on the basic facilities required for the operation of large transport aircraft (the main runway, air traffic control equipment, and a large hangar known as the 'TriStar hangar') proceeded apace and on 1 May 1985 an RAF TriStar of 216 Sqn arrived on a route-proving flight. The choice of HRH Prince Andrew to carry out the airfield opening ceremony on 12 May was an apt one, for he had flown helicopters in the Falklands war. British Airways Boeing 747s now began twice-weekly trooping flights from the UK under a contract lasting until November 1985. RAF TriStars then took over the route, although due to their smaller capacity the schedule increased to three flights per week - resulting in more frequent mail deliveries, which was guaranteed to boost morale. RAF TriStars were still in short supply,

Hercules of 1312 Flight and a TriStar of 216 Sqn, Brize Norton, on the apron at RAF Mount Pleasant. (MoD)

though, and for short periods in 1986 British Airways 747s and later Virgin stood in while the RAF's 'big white bird' underwent routine servicing.

Up to this point the airfield had been run by a small group of RAF personnel working alongside the enormous contractor's workforce still beavering away to meet the target date for completion. Then, in April 1986, the RAF began moving in from Stanley and other outlying locations. Amongst the units and organizations which repositioned were 23 Sqn (Phantom FGR2s), 1312 Flight (Hercules), 63 Sqn, RAF Regiment (Rapier Missiles), and Bristow Helicopters (Sikorsky S–61Ns), together with the Chinooks of 1310 Flight from Kelly's Garden and 1564 Flight's Sea Kings from Navy Point. The transfer was accomplished smoothly if hectically, enabling RAF Mount Pleasant to be officially opened as an RAF station on 1 May 1986.

The dispersed and protected airfield accommodation for the flying units was vastly superior to the ramshackle improvisation of RAF Stanley, though life in general inevitably became a little more formal. A number of organizational changes were made, one of the first of which was the grouping together of the RAF helicopter Flights into a single squadron. Initially this was known as the Mount Pleasant Helicopter Sqn, but soon received the 78 Sqn numberplate. Tragically one of the Chinooks was lost in May 1986 when it crashed on Mount Young in a heavy snowstorm while on a flight from Byron Heights to Mount Alice, West Falkland. Two of the crew and a Gurkha soldier were killed.

The role of the Phantoms remained the same, to patrol and if necessary defend the Falkland Islands Protection Zone (FIPZ) and, should the need arise, provide the air power necessary to keep Mount Pleasant open as a reinforcement airhead. Quick Reaction Alert (QRA) aircraft were routinely scrambled to investigate radar contacts: on 12 August 1986, for example, one of the fighters came across an Argentinian Lockheed Electra and flew alongside it – without any beligerance on either side. Armament for the Phantoms comprised Skyflash and Sidewinder missiles plus a Vulcan 20mm cannon. On 1 November 1988 the Phantom unit here became 1435 Flight, to enable 23 Sqn to re-role as a Tornado unit in the UK.

Tanker support for the Phantoms was provided by the Hercules of 1312 Flight, which could be airborne within fifteen minutes of a QRA scramble. 1312's other main role, maritime radar reconnaissance

A wintry start to the day at RAF Mount Pleasant. This view from the TriStar hangar shows a Hercules of 1312 Flight and a Chinook of 78 Sqn in the background. (MoD)

(MRR), involved the Hercules maintaining close contact with RN ships patrolling the FIPZ, while secondary tasks included the provision of a search and rescue facililty, and regular mail drops to the garrison on South Georgia some 900 miles away to the east.

The high alert state that was a constant feature of RAF Stanley was perpetuated at Mount Pleasant. Frequent training exercises were held and in 1990 the RAF's youngest station was well prepared for any eventuality.

Muharraq/Bahrein, Persian Gulf

RAF Station Bahrein was formed on 2 April 1943 under the control of Air Headquarters Iraq and Persia. It retained this title until 1 December 1963 when, to avoid administrative confusion, it was renamed Muharraq. The airfield was located on the island of Muharraq, which itself is joined to the island of Bahrein by a causeway. The establishment of No 43 Staging Post during April reflected the primary role which the airfield would play throughout its existence, that of a major

staging post on the strategic air route to the Far East. At the same time work began on the construction of an RAF pier at the Muharraq causeway.

Throughout May and June visiting aircraft began to arrive on both land and sea. Anchorage facilities were used by Catalinas of 191, 240 and 413 Sqns, while on the landward side a special Lockheed Lodestar arrived to convey a Saudi Royal Family party to Bombay. A Catalina detachment, comprising one machine from 191 Sqn and two from 212 Sqn, was mounted in July and Power Boat No 567 arrived from Basrah, Iraq to operate with the aircraft.

In addition to RAF traffic, Bahrein was also handling aircraft from other organizations, notably BOAC which, through its Imperial Airways lineage, had first established a presence here in November 1932. In April 1944, for example, the company's throughput was 26 Armstrong Whitworth Ensigns, 20 C Class Flying Boats and 30 Sunderlands. One of the 'boats' was called on to rescue the Senior Naval Officer Persian Gulf after his Westland Walrus had made a forced landing. The other major user of the airfield was the USAAF, and in January a detachment of No 5051 Airfield Construction Sqn arrived to begin building facilities for the Americans. No fewer than 166 US transport types staged through in July 1944, and two of these picked up the crew of a 19th Photo Sqn B-17 which crash-landed on nearby Yas Island.

The regular flow of RAF, USAAF and BOAC aircraft continued until the end of the war, when a detachment of Vickers Warwicks of 294 Sqn was mounted from Basrah. This lasted until 1946 when the Squadron as a whole disbanded. By 1947 the Station had its own Anson PH538, and the following year was handling traffic from another war, that in French Indo-China (Vietnam), when a French civil Skymaster landed with wounded troops from Saigon, *en route* for Paris. The first Vampires seen on the Station, for the Indian Air Force as it happened, staged through in September 1950, followed in November by RAF Vampires being ferried out to FEAF.

The essentially transitory nature of Bahrein's work was perpetuated with trials on the Boulton Paul Balliol trainer involving WG153 and '154 during 1953, but in September of that year the Station gained its own flying unit when No 1417 Flight was formed with six Ansons for reconnaissance duties, following the start of political unrest in Oman. In 1955 Pembrokes superseded the Ansons, and the recce commitment was further met by the attachment, in October, of two Bomber Command Lincolns, which were later formed into 1426 Flight. From July 1957 onwards Valettas of 84 Sqn (Khormaksar) were detached in to provide logistical air support in the Oman campaign.

The Kuwait crisis of 1961 saw the Station adopting a more offensive role with the deployment of Nos 8 and 208 Sqns from Aden and Nairobi respectively, with their Hunter FGA9s. Arriving on the afternoon of 30 June they were refuelled and rearmed by nightfall, ready to react to any attack on Kuwait by Iraq. The next day the Hunters flew into Kuwait itself. Throughout the airlift of forces into Kuwait, Bahrein was used as the main terminal for long range aircraft, with AFME Beverleys and Valettas shuttling between Bahrein and Kuwait. By now 1417 Flight had become 152 Sqn, whose Pembrokes and Twin Pioneers also took part in the operation. When tension began to ease towards the middle of July, twelve Beverleys of 30 and

84 Sqns, together with detachments from 13 Sqn (PR Canberras) and 37 Sqn (Shackletons) remained at Bahrein on standby. Detachments of Hunters and transport aircraft continued after the Kuwait crisis had blown over.

The presence of Hunters became permanent in June 1964 with the arrival on the Station (now renamed Muharraq) of 208 Sqn. The fighters were joined four months later by 30 Sqn's six Beverleys for transport duties throughout the Gulf stations. Under the general redeployment of forces as part of the withdrawal from Aden, in 1967 Muharraq gained 105 Sqn with its Argosy medium range transports, and a second Hunter squadron, No 8, which joined 208 to form a fighter ground attack wing. As well as its Mk 9 aircraft, No 8 Sqn took over the FR10s of Khormaksar's disbanding 1417 Flight to form a reconnaissance element. The Station played a pivotal role in the airlift out of Aden in November 1967, handling the many VC10s, Britannias, Belfasts and Hercules, together with AFME's own transport force, used to ferry people and equipment from Khormaksar to Muharraq, and from Muharraq to the United Kingdom.

No 105 Sqn disbanded at the end of January 1968, but Argosys remained on strength in the shape of regular detachments from Nos 114 and 267 Sqns in the United Kingdom. Known as 'Ardet' and sporting a triple 'A' on the fins ('Associated Argosy Airways') it was one of these aircraft that collected the wounded Sultan of Oman from Salalah, following a *coup d'état*. The other unit on the Station

Bahrein Marine Airport in 1947. (J Beel)

Wessex HC2 XR522 detached to Muharraq (from home base of Sharjah) for search and rescue duties, in June 1968. (P Russell-Smith)

was the Gulf Communications Sqn with its Pembrokes, an Andover on loan from 84 Sqn, and a Flight of Wessex HC2s for search and rescue duties.

Not only was Muharraq the outbound refuelling stop for the daily VC10 schedule to the Far East, it also provided facilities for other RAF aircraft using the CENTO route through Turkey and Iran to Cyprus. An unusual event during 1968 was the trial by the RAF Regiment of the Tiger Cat surface-to-air missile, while the following year saw the first visit by four Lightnings non-stop from Binbrook, refuelled by Victor tankers.

Air Support Command aircraft flying on reinforcement exercises from the United Kingdom to the Far East stretched resources in 1970, and by now withdrawal from Muharraq and Sharjah was being mooted. No 84 Sqn transferred from Sharjah in December, absorbing the Gulf Communications Flight in the process, only to disband here in September 1971. The two Hunter Squadrons (8 and 208) disbanded during the course of 1971, and by now the airfield had become an international civil airport. Muharraq handed over its mantle

One of Muharraq's Pembrokes WV744 airborne over Bahrein in 1969. (via P Porter)

of the RAF's major staging post in the Middle East to Masirah, and the ensign was lowered for the last time on 15 December 1971.

Negombo/Katunayake, Ceylon

Thousands of palm trees in one of the best coconut plantations in Ceylon were felled to make way for Negombo, on a site some 28 miles north of Colombo, selected for a Very Heavy Bomber station in 1944. Originally known as Katunayake, it was renamed Negombo in March 1944. However, it was never to parent its own heavy bomber squadrons, and instead became primarily an important staging post for transport aircraft flying to and from the Far East. Halifax VIIIs, attached from 298 Sqn, carried out transport support operations from here between December 1945 and May 1946, at which time 1303 Meteorological Flight was also on strength. During March 1946 RAF Liberators from Kankesanturai (another Ceylon base) used the airfield to mount sorties in search of Lancastrian G-AGLX, which had vanished after taking off from Negombo to Australia.

When Negombo's first resident squadron, No 45, took up post in April it changed role from light bomber to maritime strike. Initially the Squadron was equipped with Mosquito VIs which were also used for twice-weekly meteorological flights, from which TE640 was lost in November. During the same month Avro Yorks on the UK – Singapore route began scheduled services through Negombo, and this four-engined transport would become a very familiar sight, later building up to a peak of around seven per day.

Mosquitoes were not a success in the Far East, and in December 1946 No 45 Sqn began training on the Bristol Buckmaster, prior to converting to Beaufighters. The flow of heavy transport aircraft gradually increased, reaching a figure of over 200 per month in September 1947, this total including Skymasters, and the Constellations of KLM which had also begun using the airfield. Another civilian user was BOAC, which by March 1948 was operating a weekly Lancastrian service between the UK and Singapore. The Station also became home for Air Headquarters Ceylon, which was relocated here early in 1948. The AHQ Communications Flight had already been based at Negombo for some time.

The Station assumed something of its originally intended heavy bomber role when five Lincolns from 97 Sqn (Hemswell – UK) were attached in May 1948 for Operation Red Lion II. Joined by 45 Sqn, the Lincolns mounted two practise bombing operations before leaving for Singapore.

The requirements of the Berlin Airlift resulted in a temporary break in York traffic in July, but there were always other visitors to keep the Station busy: for example, two USAF B-29 Superfortresses ('Gas Gobbler' and 'Lucky Lady' of the 43rd Bomb Group) which later left to continue their round-the-world flight.

The Malayan Emergency prompted a 45 Sqn detachment to Kuala Lumpur in September 1948, the remainder of the Squadron following permanently in May 1949. During the month No 45 had received Bristol Brigand Met3s, but these remained behind at Negombo to form 1301 Meteorological Flight, which specialized in weather reconnaissance flights in the South West and North East Monsoon areas. The RAF Transport Command schedules which were resumed in July 1949 were now being flown by Hastings alongside the older Yorks. BOAC was still a regular operator, and October saw the proving flight of the Canadair C-4 in the airline's livery. Other civilian operators to be seen at the beginning of 1950 included Air India and Air Ceylon. For Ceylon's Independence Day celebrations on 4 February 1950 the Station put up formations of Dakotas, Brigands and Sunderlands, extra aircraft being 'borrowed' from Singapore. By May it was the practice of a Dakota to be attached from one of the Singapore transport squadrons for air/sea rescue duties, and under this long-standing arrangement the 'Daks' could also be employed on communications flying, Army cooperation, and jungle rescue cooperation work as necessary. *Ad hoc* tasks taken on by 1301 Met Flight (which also had its own Harvard), on the other hand, included ship interceptions, though the unit ceased to function towards the end of the year.

The air/sea rescue detachment also began to feature Vickers Valettas by early 1952, and in April, for example, VX555 (from 52 Sqn) took part in the search for a Ceylon Air Academy Auster which had ditched at sea. Negombos's Staging Aircraft Servicing Flight were presented with plenty of traffic on which to exercise their talents, including four Lancasters of 38 Sqn (Malta) attached for exercises with

Above *Saturday 3 February 1951 and RAF Negombo holds its first ever air display. Taking part is this Lancaster GR3 from St Eval in the UK. Aircraft serial is SW368.* (Fairbairn Colln)

Below *February 1952 brought five Shackleton MR1s of 220 Sqn from St Eval to Negombo for exercises. WB825 'T — M' was one of them.* (Fairbairn Colln)

the Fleet, Transport Command Hastings, the AOC's York (LV633) and even the Station Flight Harvard (FT186). Due to its location the Station naturally attracted maritime-related visitors, including Dakotas of 38 Sqn, RAAF, for ASR work, and in August 1952, six Shackletons from 224 Sqn (Gibraltar) for various exercises which also drew Beaufighters from Singapore. A sign of the times was the increasing number of training flights by the Royal Ceylon Air Force.

Undoubtedly the most interesting event of 1953 was the England to New Zealand Air Race which produced a crop of unusual visitors, not only in the form of competitors but also preparatory 'hangers on'. In the months leading up to the race RAF Canberra WE139 and '142 both carried out proving flights, while Boeing Washingtons brought in teams of RAF engineers surveying the route. On the day of the race itself (9 October) the RNZAF competitor, Hastings NZ5804, landed after three attempts, on three engines during a heavy thunderstorm. The Hastings' flaps were badly damaged by runway water, and a spare engine was later flown in aboard Bristol Freighter NZ5901. Other competitors noted that day included Canberras and Viscount G-AMAV.

The location filming of H. E. Bates' novel *The Purple Plain* brought Negombo immortality in January 1954. For this, two 81 Sqn Mosquitoes (RG238 and RE177 – the former replaced later by PT669) were flown in from Singapore, and the Station also provided much other material for this production. The spring months saw many Lincolns, Canberras and Shackletons transitting to the Far East, and by now a Rescue Coordination Centre had been established here.

For some time HQ FEAF had planned to send six Vampires from Singapore to Ceylon to prove the ability to reinforce the island with interceptor fighters. The visit was finally scheduled to coincide with an air display at neighbouring Ratmalana in January 1955, and the Vampires (from 60 Sqn at Tengah) plus shepherding Valetta duly arrived, remaining for ten days.

'Jet 55' was the name given to an exercise with local naval units held in August 1955, for which four Shackletons from 224 Sqn were attached. The pattern was repeated the following year, with 220 Sqn providing the Shackletons, which again flew sorties in the Trincomalee area.

With the takeover of the Station by the Royal Ceylon Air Force in 1957 came a reversion to the name of Katunayake. Up

This visiting Hastings crash landed at Negombo on the night of 5 April 1952. (Fairbairn Colln)

until November Air Headquarters Ceylon functioned alongside a disparate collection of units including Ceylon Air Traffic Control Centre; Signals Centre, Ceylon; No 41 Movement Unit; No 7 Mobile Oxygen Unit; and an RAF Hospital, but even this activity ceased in September 1960.

Nicosia, Cyprus

Before Akrotiri opened in the mid-1950s Nicosia was, for many years, the main British airfield on the island of Cyprus. A landing ground for civil use already existed here when the decision was made, in 1940, to establish an operational RAF station on the site. A stone quarry was opened up nearby and the necessary plant was shipped in from Egypt. Then, using local labour, tarmac runways and dispersals were constructed, together with technical and domestic accommodation for two squadrons. The airfield was completed in about nine months.

Nicosia's wartime activity can be divided into two distinct periods, the first starting around April 1941 and lasting until early 1944, during which numerous units were based here, mainly on a detachment basis reflecting the ebb and flow of hostilities. Amongst the earliest of these (in April/May 1941) was a detachment of Tomahawks of 250 Sqn from Palestine. After a brief detachment from its Lydda base, 213 Sqn moved across permanently in July to provide a fighter defence force for Cyprus with its Hurricanes, remaining until December. No 80 Sqn, also on Hurricanes, was here in a similar role during the summer. Yet another Hurricane unit, No 261 Sqn, mounted a detachment from Egypt during the latter half of the year, its task to provide day and night readiness over Haifa. Between mid-1941 and mid-1942 convoy escorts, fighter patrols and recces over the Mediterranean were carried out by detachments of 272 Sqn's Beaufighters, while the following twelve-month period saw a detachment from 162 Sqn. Equipped with Wellingtons and Blenheims, this latter unit was closely concerned with radio and radar activity, jamming the enemy's equipment and calibrating our own. Spitfires in the air defence role were first seen in December 1942, consisting of a one-month detachment of four aircraft from 417 Sqn, but further detachments from 127, 74 and 243 Sqns would follow in the succeeding months. The airfield was even used as a photographic reconnaissance base, 'B'

Flight of 680 Sqn (probably with Spitfire IVs) arriving in April 1943 to cover the Dodecanese Islands, and 'C' Flight taking its place the following month. Finally, 227 Sqn was based here from September to December in order to cover the Aegean Sea more effectively in its anti-shipping strikes.

The start of the second stage of Nicosia's war service could conveniently be put at 1 February 1944 when the Station was formed under RAF Middle East to control No 79 OTU. The task of the OTU was to train Allied crews on Beaufighters and Blenheim Vs. In addition to these main types, the OTU was established with an Anson Flight, and used Boulton Paul Defiants for target-towing. Hurricanes replaced the Defiants in late 1944, and a small number of Fairchild Arguses were on strength for communications duties. Such was the intensity of the flying training that Nicosia's aircraft also flew from the nearby airfields of Tymbou (to the east of the town) and Lakatamia (to the south-west), while regular use was made of the Larnaca firing range.

With the cessation of hostilities in 1945 the OTU's flying hours dwindled and the majority of the Blenheims and Beaufighters were ferried over to 168 MU in Egypt for disposal. Final disbandment took place at the end of July. The Unit's Ansons, however, were formed into a Communications Flight whose main task was leave flights for station personnel, until it was disbanded in September. Whilst the emphasis had been on OTU flying over the last two years of the war, the Station had also hosted other operational units for short periods. These had included the Marauders of 24 Sqn SAAF in April 1944, Venturas of 459 Sqn in June for patrol and escort work over the sea, and the following month No 46 Sqn's Beaufighters for 'special operations'.

The latter part of 1945 saw some organizational changes, for in November both 1565 Meteorological Flight and BOAC moved in from Lakatamia, the civilian airline having examined Nicosia the previous year in connection with a proposed Cairo-Nicosia-Ankara service. Nicosia's other role as a civil airport now began to gain momentum with a survey flight by Middle East Airlines, for a proposed thrice-weekly service to Beirut, being made on 28 December. This led in turn to the opening of a new civil airport, constructed on the old RAF site, on 24 May 1949.

Meanwhile, the RAF for its part began taking in the odd stray unit thrown up in the post-war contractions. First of these was 256 Sqn (July-September 1946) which had been reduced to a single Flight of Mosquito NF19s. Then came No 6 Sqn whose Hurricane IVs and Spitfire LF9s had given way to Tempest F6s by the time it left in July 1947. The last operational Hurricane in the RAF left the Squadron on 15 January 1947. Close on No 6's heels came 213 Sqn with Mustangs in October 1946, which similarly re-equipped with Tempests in early 1947 before moving on to Egypt in the autumn.

Although no less busy, 1948 marked the start of more regulated peacetime activity, with two Spitfire FR18e squadrons being taken on strength, No 208 in March and No 32 in May. A detachment which 208 had mounted was withdrawn to Nicosia after its base at Ramat David had been attacked by Egyptian Spitfires. No 208 had moved on by the end of the year but 32 Sqn remained here to convert to the Vampire F3. The following year, 1949, saw the first of many visits by front-line fighter squadrons based in the Middle East and the Mediterranean to attend No 26 Armament Practice School, which included air-to-air ground firing on the Morphou range. Another notable event during the year was a visit by a Turkish Spitfire squadron which proceeded to beat the resident No 32 Sqn in the-air-to-ground shoot. The APS activity drew visits not only from the Bomber Command Lincoln squadrons but also the Malta-based maritime squadrons for fighter affiliation work. It was also

customary to send across two or three Beaufighters from Shallufa for target-towing duties.

The regular pattern of APCs and exercises was maintained, with the occasional search for a missing aircraft. In February 1952 it was a US Navy Martin Mercator which had gone down off the north coast of Cyprus, and the following June a Meteor flown by AVM D. F. W. Atcherley, overdue from Fayid. During the year there were visits by Vampires from both the RAAF's 78 Wing and the RNZAF's 14 Sqn, (the latter remaining until April 1955), and the RAF's No 185 Sqn, also with Vampire, served here briefly in the autumn. While an exercise in 1953 brought in the Varsities of 201 Advanced Flying School perhaps the most unusual visitors of the year were three Savoia-Marchetti SM. 79s of the Lebanese AF, on loan to Mayflower Films for filming on the airfield. By May a Target Towing Flight had been established with Meteor F8s, alongside an Instrument Training Flight which had Meteor T7 WF879. In August five Austers of No 651 AOP Sqn flew in from Beirut for artillery cooperation work with the Army, while a bad earthquarke in the Paphos area resulted in an influx of Hastings, Valettas and Lincolns in September with supplies for the homeless. Boeing Washingtons of Bomber Command were no stranger to the station, a number staging through in September 1953, but in September 1954 two of these aircraft from the UK were

Miles Magister of Levant Communications Flight, Nicosia in 1948. Behind is one of 32 Sqn's Spitfire FR18s. (P Russell-Smith Colln)

Here are three Savoia-Marchetti SM 79s, L-112, '113 and '114, of the Lebanese Air Force on loan to Mayflower Films at Nicosia in April 1953 for film work. (D Davies via T Fairbairn)

attached for thirteen days to trial some classified equipment.

Ten years of comparative calm came to an end in 1955 with the erruption of the EOKA troubles in Cyprus. For the Station this meant not only handling the troop reinforcements which were flown to the island (a large force of Hastings brought in Battalions of the Gordon Highlanders and the Norfolk Regiment in October), but also a build-up of its own flying units to work with the security forces. Thus, by November a Helicopter Flight operating the Bristol Sycamore, and 1910 AOP Flight

with Auster 6s, had been taken on strength. Besides cooperating with Commandos on search duties, the Sycamore was soon also performing in the casevac role. Three Fairey Gannets of 847 Sqn, formed for duty in Cyprus, flew out from the UK in April 1956, their task being to search for ships attempting to infiltrate arms into the island by sea.

As if internal strife was not enough, the international crisis of Suez loomed to stretch resources even further in 1956. For its part in Operation Musketeer (the landing of a joint British/French force in

Pembroke WV700 with Meteor F8s WK954 and '952 of the Levant Communications Flight, Nicosia. (D Davies via T Fairbairn)

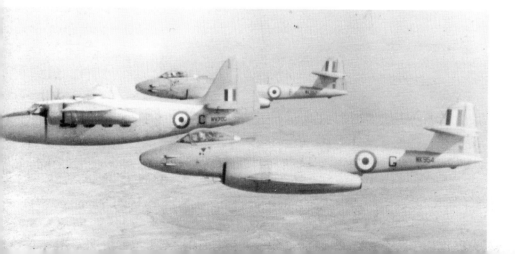

Egypt) Nicosia was reinfored in August with the Hunter F5s of the 'Tangmere Wing' (Nos 1 and 34 Sqns), followed in October by a Canberra Wing comprising over 60 aircraft from Nos 10, 15, 18, 27, 44, 61 and 139 Sqns in the UK. The Meteor NF13s of 39 Sqn also flew in from Malta during October. Canberra bombing raids from Nicosia began on the evening of 31 October, and one of 114 Sqn's Valettas led the airborne assult. During operations against Egypt the following numbers of sorties were flown by Nicosia-based aircraft: Canberra – 266; Hunter – 39; Hastings – 22; Valetta – 37; Beverley – 4.

In retrospect 1956 had been a vintage year for Nicosia with 70 Sqn (Hastings) arriving in February and 114 Sqn on the smaller Valetta following a month later. By mid-year the Middle East Communications Sqn (Pembrokes) and the Levant Communications Sqn (Pembrokes and Meteor F8s) had both signed on, and 1910 Flight had been joined by a sister Flight, now 1915. Both AOP Flights were squeezed out to a new airstrip at Dernia in September. The next month the Helicopter Flight was redesignated 284 Sqn, and flew 78 operational sorties in support of ground force engaged against terrorists.

No 114 Sqn disbanded in December 1957, followed by the Levant Communications Flight (as it had become) in March 1958, but from 1957 onwards the System of providing a day standby and a night standby air defence squadron meant that there was at least one day fighter and one night fighter squadron present on a detachment basis from either the UK or Malta. When Operation Fortitude required reinforcements to be sent to Jordan in 1958, Nicosia had Nos, 43, 54 and 66

Hunter Squadrons on standby duties and sent 208 (which had been posted in with Hunters in March) on to Amman. In response to this new crisis a Transport Task Force was also established, consisting of Hastings of 24, 99 and 511 Sqn, and Beverleys of 30, 47 and 53 Sqns, which airlifted the 16th Parachute Brigade Group into Amman.

Meanwhile the Cyprus Emergency rumbled on, prompting the deployment in of 230 Sqn during November 1958. The unit's Pioneers went on to mount anti-arson patrols, recce and comms flights. The following month the Joint Experimental Helicopter Unit was attached for a period of training and liaison work with the security forces, at the same time as 114 Sqn arrived with its Chipmunks for anti-EOKA patrols, having been formed in the UK specifically for this purpose. However, the political settlement reached in early 1959 enabled 230 and 114 to be withdrawn after only four months. The end of strife also led to 284 Sqn with its Sycamores being renumbered 103 Sqn (on 1 August) and tasked simply with search and rescue, rather than internal security. Similarly, 847 Sqn's Gannets were released in November.

Activity at Nicosia during 1958-9 was characterized by a constant stream of visiting Hunter and Javelin fighter squadrons for training under Operation Quickfire, which included practice interceptions and cine exercises. No 70 Sqn's Hastings were now flying to such destinations as Libya, Greece, Iran, Aden and Malta.

From June 1961 the resident fighter squadron was No 43, whose Hunter FGA9s were replaced in March 1963 by the Javelin FAW9s of 29 Sqn. The latter unit departed

Dakota G-AGND of Cyprus Airways at Nicosia in 1955. Note the armed guard — for 1955 saw the start of strife in Cyprus. (E B Goldsmith)

Above *Hastings of Nicosia's resident 70 Sqn, together with visiting Beverleys, during the airlift of British forces to Jordan in July 1958.* (MoD Crown Copyright)

Below *Chipmunks of 114 Sqn over northern Cyprus in 1959.* (MoD Crown Copyright)

Westland Whirlwind HAR10s of 230 Sqn (supported by an Argosy) arrive at Nicosia to take up the UN support commitment. (MoD Crown Copyright)

after exactly a year, but when deployed to Zambia (in May 1966) was resupplied with Firestreak missiles by 70 Sqn's Hastings.

The helicopter commitment had now diminished and hence 103 Sqn was reduced to Flight status, becoming 1563 Flight on 31 July 1963, and finally moving across to Akrotiri in April 1964. However, following fighting between Greek and Turkish Cypriots in 1964 a UN peacekeeping force was established on the island and a permanent helicopter detachment to support the force, initiated by 230 Sqn with Whirlwind HAR10s from Germany, was maintained at Nicosia. Throughout the late 1960s No 230 shared this task, which involved routine supply schedules to Observation Posts, troop rotations and VIP flights, with 72 Sqn (whose Wessexes were airlifted in by Belfast – still on trial – in November 1966) and 18 Sqn.

The 1966 Defence Review announced that Nicosia would run down and that 70 Sqn would move to Akrotiri in July of that year. With the departure of the Hastings the Station became an exclusively helicopter unit, and early in 1967 large areas were being handed back to the Cyprus Government. The closure of Akrotiri's

runway for repair for many months in 1968, and the deployment of that unit's front-line squadrons, plus visiting transport aircraft, to Nicosia was an echo of grander days. A more satisfactory solution to the helicopter UNFICYP support commitment was reached in January 1972 when 84 Sqn reformed at Akrotiri (from 1563 Flight) and deployed 'B' Flight to Nicosia to take over the detachment task from the UK/Germany squadrons. Apart from five RAF Hercules detached from Lyneham in February 1973 for stream assault training in an overseas environment, 84's Whirlwinds in their distinctive UN livery were Nicosia's only tennants until the detachment ceased to operate on 28 February 1982. In the meantime the Station had closed formally back on 2 Feburary 1975, though a small detachment remained alongside the Whirlwinds, forming the RAF Element of the Nicosia Air Traffic Control Centre.

Peshawar, India

Strictly speaking, Peshawar did not become an RAF station proper until 1940, but it is one of those bases that is prominent in the

Bristol Fighter of 20 Sqn flying over Khyber from its Peshawar base in 1925. (MoD Crown Copyright)

annals of the RAF in North West India between the wars. Located 30 miles or so from the Khyber Pass it was first used by No 31 Sqn which arrived from Cawnpore with Bristol F2Bs in October 1921 for a five-month spell of duty. No 31 had been in India since 1915, taking part in sporadic action against dissident tribesmen. The CO at this point was one Squadron Leader A. T. Harris (later C-in-C Bomber Command), who described Peshawar as an improvement on Cawnpore, though just as hot! Here, as at Cawnpore, No 31 continued to suffer from a severe lack of spares for its aircraft.

It was next the turn of No 28 Sqn to move in for ops against raiding tribesmen in April 1923. The rugged mountainous country over which the Squadron's Bristol F2Bs were required to fly, together with small arms fire from the ground, resulted in the occasional casualty. When No 28 left for Quetta in January 1925 its place was taken by another Bristol F2B unit, No 20 Sqn, destined to remain for a comparatively long fourteen years.

Due to its proximity to Afghanistan, Peshawar was called upon to play an important part in the relief of Kabul, the Afghan capital, in what has become recognized as the first significant airlift in

history. The British Legation in Kabul had requested an evacuation of British and other nationals after tribesmen had attacked the city in protest against proposed domestic reforms in November 1928. The limited range of No 20's F2Bs rendered them unsuitable for the airlift; as the Squadron was operating two Westland Wapitis on wireless trials at this time, it was decided that these could be employed. Led by one of the Wapitis, which landed first at Kabul to check conditions, the first wave of aircraft, consisting of three DH9As (from 27 and 60 Sqns at Kohat) and one Vickers Victoria of 70 Sqn, flew in to the capital on 23 December. After a brisk turn-round in which the Victoria picked up 23 passengers and the DH9As one each, all the aircraft made their way back to Peshawar. During the course of this first mission the Wapitis had been able to keep Group HQ at Peshawar informed of progress by wireless telegraphy. Other aircraft operating from Peshawar included Handley Page Hinaidi J7745, normally based at Lahore. The airlift, carried out in particularly bad weather, lasted until February 1929.

Aside from the evacuation activity, North West Frontier operations continued apace and in 1930 No 20 Sqn was involved in sorties on behalf of the Army Brigade

HQ against the 'Red Shirt' movement. The 'Red Shirts' were fomenting trouble amongst the tribes in Waziristan, as a result of which civil disturbances broke out in Peshawar in April. No 20's role was to fly aerial recces reporting on the movement of people in and around villages in the area.

Although No 20 had already made limited use of the Wapiti, it was not until January 1932 that four aircraft arrived at Peshawar to re-equip the Squadron as a whole. The final flight of F2Bs took place on 13 March, when the last five aircraft were flown to Lahore to make No 20 the RAF's longest operator of the type (nearly fifteen years). Whilst frontier policing duties remained the stock in trade for the Wapiti, No 20 also flew relief missions following the 1935 Quetta earthquake. Wapitis made way for the Hawker Audax (India) in December 1935, and these were soon employed on trials of the Vickers-Bomb-Lewis type of attack. This involved the aircraft diving at its target using a forward-firing Vickers gun to suppress enemy fire, the dropping of bombs, followed by fire at the target with a Lewis gun as the aircraft climbed away. In May 1939, 20 Sqn collected four Hawker Hinds from Drigh Road (Karachi). Destined for the Afghan Air Force, the Hinds gave a demonstration of message-snatching and supply-dropping for Afghan officials, before being flown on to Kabul. Another new type to appear on No 20's books in May was the Westland Lysander, the second prototype (K6128) of which the Squadron trialled for Army Cooperation duties. Over the years No 20 had mounted a number of detachments to Miranshah and the Squadron as a whole moved there in August 1939.

RAF Station Peshawar was officially sanctioned as a separate unit by the Air Branch of the Defence Dept of the Government of India on 16 November 1940. By this time 31 Sqn had returned for a ten-month period of minor operations with ten Wapitis. The other unit on the Station was No 1 (Indian) Group Flight, with one Wapiti and one Hart. Wapitis, together with Audaxes, also formed the equipment of No 1 Sqn Indian Air Force which arrived from Ambala in February 1941. Throughout 1942 other fresh units began to appear: No 155 Sqn formed (although it was to be several months and another location before it received its planned Curtiss Mohawks), a 223 Group Communications Flight was formed with 'one twin-engined and four single-engined aircraft',

and No 319 MU formed as an Aircraft Storage Unit able to handle up to 50 Hurricanes or light bombers. In July five Blenheims of 34 Sqn arrived to begin bombing dissident tribal villages, while the following month Hudsons, Mohawks and Hurricanes began to filter in for storage by 319 MU. At about this time a Miles Hawk and a Piper Cub were bought from their civilian owners for communication flying.

On 25 November 1942 RAF Peshawar disbanded, and the unit was retitled No 152 OTU. This in turn was replaced by No 151 OTU in 1944. Peshawar remained primarily a training base throughout the latter war years, and by 1945 the main task was the training of Indian Air Force officer pilots by RAF instructors. Students came from basic training at Ambala for advanced training (Fighter Reconnaissance/Ground Attack etc) on Harvards, Spitfires (mainly Mk VIIIs but also the odd Vc), and Hurricanes, with Vengeances used for target-towing. When spares for these types became critical in March 1945 the Station Airspeed Oxford was despatched to Lucknow and Cawnpore to scrounge the necessary parts. This remained the general pattern of activity until the base was made the HQ of No 1 (Indian) Group in early 1946. Probably the last RAF unit to use Peshawar before Independence was No 5 Sqn which, with Tempest IIs, had its HQ at the Station from February to April 1947.

Ramat David, Palestine

It is difficult to be precise as to when construction of this airfield, located some ten miles south east of Haifa, was begun, but it was certainly after the start of the Second World War. The first RAF squadron to appear on the books was No 74 which arrived for a two-month spell in July 1942. A famous fighter unit, 74 was, at this point, without any aircraft (having relinquished its Spitfire IIas in December 1941) and the task of its ground personnel throughout the latter half of 1942 was to assist with servicing of the B–24 Liberators of the US 376th Bombardment Group ('The Liberandos') which was activated in Palestine in October of that year.

The first permanent squadron to be based in full strength here was 127 Sqn, which took up station in January 1943 with Hurricane IIBs and Spitfire Vcs and mounted standing patrols. Another important unit here in the first half of 1943, and indeed one which dictated the role and designation of the airfield, was No 4

Middle East Training School equipped with Hudsons. On 1 August 1943 it was announced that 4 METS was to form RAF Station Ramat David. The main task of the Hudsons was to provide supply drop training, and trials in this activity were also conducted with the Long Range Desert Group using equipment containers. In addition, the Parachute Regiment used the Hudsons to carry out refresher jumps. Early in August a detachment of three Dakotas of 216 Sqn arrived for para drop training.

Following this training 216 Sqn, together with 267 Sqn – a sister Dakota unit, began using Ramat David as a forward base from which to drop supplies on the Greek islands of Kos and Leros as part of the Allied efforts to gain a foothold in the Aegean Sea. These operations, which took the Dakotas at low-level through valleys in Turkey, were extremely hazardous, and 216 Sqn in particular played a gallant part in keeping the invading forces supplied from the air, at a time when shipping was at a premium.

No 26 Anti-Aircraft Cooperation Unit arrived in December 1943 and, using Hurricanes and Spitfires, provided the usual training facilities for local air defence units. Hudsons were still being used here for para drop training, but this activity

formally ended in April 1944. At the tail end of April, No 14 Staging Post was established and this unit was responsible for handling many visiting aircraft moving to and from points further east. The period December 1943–March 1944 had also seen detachments of Spitfires from 154, 232, 242 and 243 Sqn from bases in Syria, prior to their moving west up the Mediterranean to take part in the spring 1944 offensive on the Italian mainland. After operating purely in the bomber role the Australian 459 Sqn moved here for six weeks in April 1944, its Venturas concentrating on convoy escort work.

Apart from visiting aircraft, which included Ansons, Fairchild Arguses and Beechcraft of the Lydda Comms Flight, Beaufighters from 79 OTU in Cyprus, and Wellingtons from nearby 78 OTU, Ramat David remained operationally quiet until early 1945 when, in February, 32 Sqn brought in its Spitfire Vcs for internal security duties, which included oil pipeline patrols and exercises with the Army. June 1945 saw some flying from here by an Anti-Malarial Unit Baltimore. Arriving in early July the Spitfire IXs of 208 Sqn remained only briefly, moving elsewhere in Palestine in mid-August. September saw the departure of 32 Sqn but the addition of two fighter squadrons, 213 with Mustang IVs

208 Sqn operated its Spitfire IXs from several airfields in Palestine in the summer of 1945 including Ramat David. This aircraft is PV117 'RG-E'. (T Scott via P Green)

and 6 Sqn on Hurricane IVs, which were also engaged in Army cooperation and internal security work.

Now that the European war was several months into history the Station found itself involved in much goodwill activity. The Emir Adbullah of Transjordan inspected Lancaster PB698 in September, while the following month saw visiting training flights by Egyptian AF Ansons. In November, for the benefit of the Overseas Staff College located just up the road at Haifa, a demonstration was laid on and the display included a Proctor, Auster, Lancaster PB873 ('Thor' of the Empire Air Armament School), Liberator, Fairchild Argus, Mosquito, Baltimore, 6 Sqn's Hurricanes, 32 Sqn's Spitfires, and 213's Mustangs. Following an acute shortage of spares for the Mustangs during the month, a Ju 52 was sent to Italy for replenishment stocks.

1946 began with threats of sabotage stemming for the internal unrest, and the Station was reinforced with RAF Regiment units. In February more than twenty Halifaxes of 620 and 644 Sqns landed with elements of 6th Airborne Division in 34 minutes, and were airborne again in eighteen minutes. During the month 6 Sqn exchanged its ageing Hurricanes for Spitfire LF9s. June saw the departure of 6 Sqn to Ein Shemer, but at the end of the month a detachment of three Austers of 651 Sqn flew in to cooperate with Army units searching local settlements.

Between September 1946 (when 213 Sqn transferred its Mustangs to Nicosia) and March 1948 there was little activity, but in April 1948 nine Lancasters of 37 and 38 Sqn flew in from Ein Shemer, while at about the same time a detachment of Spitfire FR18s was provided by 208 Sqn at Nicosia. Political events at this period were marked by Arab attacks on Jewish settlements, and the Lancasters flew recce sorties near the Syrian border, 'flag-waving' patrols, and illegal immigrant shipping patrols. On 28 April four Spitfires were sent out to attack the Gold Star brewery near Jaffa, which was being used as an HQ by the Jewish forces, the cannon and machine-gun strikes forcing the evacuation of the building.

With the British Mandate in Palestine due to end at midnight on 14 May, a detachment of four Tempests from 249 Sqn in Iraq was sent in to cover the British withdrawal. Arriving on 13 April the Tempests carried out tactical reconaissance in the Jordan Valley, but in the event the withdrawal was peaceful and the fighters returned to Habbaniya on 17 May. Although the official records for RAF Station Ramat David end in April 1948, both 32 and 208 Sqn continued to provide detachments of Spitfire FR18s here to cover the evacuation of British forces from what was, with effect from 15 May, the State of Israel. Ironically these RAF Spitfires were scrambled to intercept what proved to be Spitfire LF9s of the Egyptian AF, which attacked what was now an Israeli airfield on 22 May. The Egyptians apologized to Britain for the raid, in which two of 32's aircraft were destroyed and seven of 208's damaged. Following this twist of fate, Ramat David passed into RAF history.

Ratmalana, Ceylon

The Japanese, in their relentless drive towards India in 1942, did not neglect the southern tip of the country and Ratmalana was one of two bases in Ceylon (the other being China Bay) prepared for the defence of the island now renamed Sri Lanka. Located some ten miles south of Colombo the airfield had served as Colombo Civil Airport and when RAF records started in March 1942 it was still being used by the Ceylon Flying Club and Tata Airways. Indeed the Flying Club still occupied one of three small hangars, though by now little or no civilian flying was actually taking place. The initial RAF presence consisted of a small refuelling party which provided a handling facility for transit aircraft. The Royal Navy, though, had used the airfield as far back as June 1941 when 814 Sqn brought in its Fairey Swordfish for trade protection duties. Several other Fleet Air Arm squadrons visited for short periods in the first half of 1942, including 800 and 806 (Fairey Fulmars), 803 (Sea Hurricanes), 818 and 831 (Fairey Albacores), 880 (Sea Hurricanes) and 888 (Martlets). Certain of these RN aircraft were placed under the command of the RAF Station Commander in March 1942 alongside the RAF squadrons which now began to arrive or form at the base.

The first of the new units was 258 Sqn (reformed here on 1 March from 'K' Sqn, whose Hurricanes had already been carrying out dawn and dusk patrols), followed by another Hurricane unit, 30 Sqn, which had arrived off Ceylon aboard HMS *Indomitable*. No 261 Sqn's Hurricanes refuelled here on 6 March on their way from *Indomitable* to China Bay, and the Squadron would later send back detachments of its fighters. Five days later yet more resources, in the form of a detachment of three Vickers Vildebeests of 273 Sqn, arrived from China Bay for patrol duties. A reminder of the plight facing the Allies further to the east was provided by the appearance of a Netherlands East Indies Lockheed 12 flown by a Dutch and Australian crew, who had made a daring escape from Java by fitting long-range fuel tanks inside the fuselage of the aircraft.

Early in April, all of 30 Sqn's Hurricanes were hastily made serviceable and manned, following confirmation that enemy naval forces, possibly including aircraft carriers, were in the vicinity of Ceylon. The Hurricanes were soon airborne when the Station was dive-bombed on 5 April. Nos 803 and 806 Sqns also took part in the ensuing dog-fights, many of which were fought in and out of low cloud. After the attack, which caused no damage or injury, the airfield Bofors battery could claim two enemy aircraft shot down.

The departure of 806 Sqn made room for the arrival in May of 22 Sqn's Beauforts, which began torpedo exercises with the Fleet. The venerable Vildebeests, which included K4601, K4160 and K4162, also played their part by providing drogue-towing facilities and in searchlight cooperation duties. In addition to two Tiger Moths and a Gypsy Moth taken over from the Ceylon Flying Club, the Station Flight operated a Fairey Seal K4779, which was used on spotting duties for shore-based artillery batteries. By August these numbers had been swollen to include Fulmar X8743 and Lysander N1209. The Station Flight aircraft went on to fly numerous so-called OCHAYE anti-submarine patrols, in addition to army cooperation reconnaissance sorties, photography for mass formations, and air sea rescue work.

By September 1942 the Station had gained something of a reputation as a haven for battle-damaged aircraft, due to its proximity to the nearby No 62 Repair and Salvage Unit! This, together with the steadily increasing flow of reinforcement aircraft, led to protestations of vulnerability from the Station, due to the sheer bottleneck of traffic on the airfield.

When 1943 opened Harvard FE420 had joined the Station Flight, and in March Hudsons began a weekly service to and from India. In February 160 Sqn with Liberator IIIs began maritime reconnaissance patrols over the Indian Ocean, to which were added photo-recce sorties of the

Nicobar Islands and Sumatra towards the middle of the year.

For the period April-August 1943, Ratmalana was home for the Vengeance dive-bombers of 84 Sqn, the presence of which no doubt assisted the energetic Station Flight in obtaining its own Vengeance, AN934. The Flight had also acquired an Anson and a de Havilland Dragonfly. At about this time construction work on a Torpedo School began on the airfield boundary.

August 1943 saw a number of changes, with 160 Sqn making way for the Hurricanes of 273 Sqn, a General Reconnaissance and Air Navigation training unit being established with eleven Ansons, and the arrival of a detachment of three Catalinas of 321 Sqn. The Dutch 'Cats' had positioned here to escort convoys and to search for torpedoed vessels. This detachment was joined by another from 89 Sqn, whose Beaufighters were soon making their presence felt, shooting down a Japanese flying boat a few miles out to sea from Colombo. The incident drew as much interest as the arrival of Ratmalana's first visiting Lancaster in December, apparently from Salbani in India.

The New Year brought new arrivals in the form of three air/sea rescue Walruses from 292 Sqn, together with 1579 Calibration Flight and 1303 Meteorological Flight, both with Blenheims. In addition to these permanent units, Wellingtons of 203 Sqn dropped in to refuel during the course of anti-submarine patrols in the Colombo-Bombay area. In March the Station Flight was retitled 222 Group Communications Flight, while the following month 22 Sqn returned for a second time to begin escort duties for naval forces. In the event 22 Sqn's Beauforts were to see little action and left in July, by which time the Squadron had re-equipped with Beaufighters. A sister coastal unit, 217 Sqn, followed a similarly fruitless pattern, arriving a month before No 22 and departing with Beaufighters in September.

During the summer, 292 Sqn's Walruses were replaced by Vickers Warwicks from 'C' Flight of the same squadron, 136 Sqn arrived in a non-operational role with Spitfire VIIIs, and 89 Sqn was exchanged for a detachment of 176 Sqn Beaufighters. At around this time the Communications Flight was operating a Dakota, FL510, named 'Sister Ann', which flew as far afield as the United Kingdom carrying VIPs, in addition to a Beechcraft Expediter HB175. The Flight was joined in September

1944 by the South East Asia Command Communications Sqn whose eqiuipment comprised not only Avro Yorks but also apparently a Spitfire PRXI, which in December caught fire while being flown by a SAAF major. Pilot and aircraft parted company over the sea, the former being retrieved half an hour later with extensive burns.

There was no operational activity in the first half of 1945 but the number of aircraft using the base grew over the months, until by August there were 92 dispersed around the airfield. Station records end on a sad note with the mention of the the loss of a Royal Navy Expediter on 15 October. The aircraft, HB759, had arrived overhead from China Bay, but due to heavy rain and low cloud had been instructed to divert to another airfield. However, the pilot decided instead to land at Ratmalana. At low altitude and in a steep turn the Expediter stalled and crashed, killing all eight on board.

Salalah, Muscat and Oman

In August 1949 a Dakota of the Aden Communications Flight with a crew of three and nine passengers hit a 3,000 foot escarpment on its approach to Salalah, killing all on board except one, who died on the way to hospital. The weather at the time was severe and the incident underlined the treacherous conditions at this particular Middle East airfield, where good visibility could swiftly deteriorate into monsoon and thick dust.

Located in the province of Dhofar of the Sultanate of Muscat and Oman, the first recorded use of the airfield is in 1942 as the location for No 32 Staging Post, although the landing ground already in existence here was inspected by a party from RAF Khormaksar on 22 May 1941 with a view to its use on an alternative mail route from India. As one of the 'route stations' on the South Arabian route it handled reinforcement aircraft being ferried to the Far East.

The presence of enemy submarines in the Gulf of Aden during August 1942 produced a need for shipping lanes to be patrolled continuously and to achieve this No 8 Sqn, then based in Aden, mounted a number of detachments at various landing grounds, including Salalah. Wellington XIIIs formed the equipment for the detachment, which ended in May 1945, though official records mention the use of Liberator GR VIs in the final two months. A detachment of USAAF servicing personnel was based

here until 1945, and in July 1943 the CO of this detachment was killed in an air crash at Masirah. Signals facilities were constructed during 1944 and 1945 and these provided the navigational and communications links around the edge of the 'Empty Quarter' stretching for 1,000 miles between the coast of South Arabia and the upper part of the Persian Gulf. Such facilities were vital to the small but steady flow of transport aircraft using the South Arabian route which, from October 1945, was supervised by No 115 Wing of Transport Command headquartered at Sheikh Othman, Aden.

The endless procession of visitors included Liberators, Venturas, Bostons and Albacores. Wellingtons of the Aden Communications Flight and Dakotas of 216 Sqn brought in fresh vegetables, while in July 1946 Mosquitoes TE770 and '821 arrived from Aden (probably No 114 Sqn) to search for a missing tug believed to be on the rocks on the South Arabian coast. When '770 went unserviceable it was replaced by TE756 and spares were brought in by Wellington. Alongside the military traffic BOAC had been using the airfield for some time, but its operations were now drawing to a close. After the airline's last eastbound Lockheed Lodestar took off in January 1947 the company's superintendent began handing over signals facilities, vehicles and buildings to the RAF. The final BOAC aircraft departed for Karachi in February.

Prior to this, in fact in April 1946, the Station had been reduced to a Care and Maintenance basis due to manpower shortages in the Command, and designated 'RAF Unit Salalah' it was commanded by a Flying Officer. By 1948 the Aden Communications Flight had established the so-called 'South Arabian Service' routeing Khormaksar - Riyan - Salalah - Masirah and return using Dakotas. When Vampire VG703 (supported by Dakota KN231) passed through on its way home from Singapore in March 1949 it became very clear that jet efflux would erode the compacted sand runway. Throughout the early 1950s movements built up steadily, with the accent on twin engine aircraft. Daily RAF Valettas began to replace the Dakotas, and civilian visitors included Captain Paul Mantz in a B-25 Mitchell in January 1955.

During the same month two Bomber Command Lincolns were brought to readiness at Salalah to search for a Saudi Arabian Government official who, with an armed band, was reportedly making unauthorized incursions into central Oman. The Lincolns were to be used if a target within 150 miles of Salalah presented itself. Monthly aircraft movements reached a peak of 709 in May 1957, by which time several civilian operators were using the airfield. A Viscount of Pakistan International Airways was the first of its type to use Salalah in May 1962.

Political instability in Oman, particularly in Dhofar (the Omani province around Salalah), now began to flavour life on the Station. In August 1963 Omani rebels laid land mines on roads and tracks around Salalah, one of which destroyed an RAF stores vehicle, killing the driver. Beverleys of No 30 Sqn immediately flew in six Ferret cars from Sharjah, and the Sultan provided reinforcements of his own forces. The Station was again threatened by hostile rebels in 1965, and on two occasions during the year troops from the Parachute Regiment had to be flown in from Bahrein to protect the airfield which, from 1968 onwards, came under rebel mortar attack. Although the RAF was not called upon to provide air support, the SOAF operated a detachment at Salalah and SOAF Provosts carried out attacks on Omani rebels.

Under the arrangements for withdrawal from the Persian Gulf, Britain agreed to staff the airfield at Salalah and to maintain its support for SOAF, in return for which the Sultan of Muscat would agree to Britain's continued use of Masirah as an important staging post. However, before these plans reached fruition the Station was at the centre of another political upheaval when, in 1970, the Sultan was deposed by his son. The letter of abdication was signed at the airfield on 23 July and the next morning an RAF Argosy arrived to take the slightly injured outgoing Sultan to Bahrein. The *coup d'état* had not placed Station personnel in any danger, and the new Sultan visited the station at the end of the month to inspect a guard of honour.

The SOAF presence gradually built up during the 1970s (Strikemaster had arrived back in 1969) and the base also became the HQ of the Dhofar Army Brigade. Control of the airfield services was handed over to Panam acting as agents for the Omani Civil Aviation Authority, and the RAF Detachment was finally withdrawn in March 1977.

Sek Kong, Hong Kong/New Territories

Somewhat overshadowed by Kai Tak, its elder and more famous Hong Kong sister

airfield, Sek Kong's history nevertheless dates back to the 1930s, when it was decided to build a second military airfield in the Colony. Accordingly, work began in 1938 at a site near Pat Heung (later known as Sek Kong) in the New Territories. Designed to accommodate three squadrons, the ground was levelled and grassed over, but work stopped in 1940 when it was realized that the site would be within range of artillery fire from the Japanese, whose invasion forces had overrun areas just over the border in China. The airfield was then used as a refugee camp, up until the Japanese invasion of the Colony in December 1941.

After the defeat of Japan in 1945 civil war again broke out in China, which led to increased tension in Hong Kong. Sek Kong, some four miles from the Chinese border, was therefore reopened to provide a forward base for the air defence of the Colony, the teeth being provided by the Spitfire FR18s of 28 Sqn which moved in from Kai Tak in May 1950, the month before the outbreak of the Korean War. Between 1949 and 1957 the airfield was visited by the AOP Austers of the RAF's 1903 and 1900 Flights from their base at Sha Tin, marking the start of a long association between Sek Kong and what would later become the Army Air Corps. In October 1950 28 Sqn moved back to Kai Tak to enable a proper runway to be laid. This was completed by March 1951, enabling No 28 to return once again with its newly-delivered Vampire FB5s.

Early the following year the Vampire FB5s were replaced by FB9s, a popular move in Hong Kong's steamy climate, due to the latter's cockpit cooling. The Station's limited facilities made the task of maintaining the jets a difficult one, and deep servicing had to be carried out either at Kai Tak, or at Sek Kong using personnel flown in specially from Kai Tak. The Squadron found the airfield, surrounded on three sides by mountains and with the end of the runway only two miles from the Colony's highest peak (the 3,187 ft high Tai Mo Shan), a difficult one to operate from, and this was made no easier by the stiff, frequent crosswinds. It was therefore something of a relief when it was announced that 28 Sqn would replace 80 Sqn at Kai Tak following the latter's disbandment in April 1955. The move took place in August of that year.

In 1955, however, it was Kai Tak's turn for major runway work, and to allow this to go ahead 28 Sqn moved back to Sek

Kong in December of that year. Here it re-equipped with Venom FB1s and joined another newly-arrived Venom unit, 45 Sqn. When Kai Tak's runway reopened for use in June 1957, 28 Sqn moved back to the airport, while 45 Sqn remained *in situ* patrolling the 'bamboo curtain', until disbandment in November. The airfield was then declared too dangerous for modern jet fighters, relegated to emergency use and later handed over to the Army.

Army aircraft started using the airfield on a regular basis in Ocober 1969 when an amalgamation of Far East Army Air Corps units resulted in the deployment from Kai Tak of the newly created 656 Sqn, at this point operating Bell Sioux helicopters. In the spring of 1970 the Sioux were supplemented by Westland Scouts. When, in 1974, the time came to replace the Sioux, Gazelles were tried but proved unsuitable. Thus, in 1975, 656 was left with a fleet of ten Scouts, the last Sioux going on display on the roof of the Squadron offices until 1982. On 30 June 1977 the Squadron was downgraded and renamed 11 Flight AAC,

but a year later on 1 August 1978 the AAC again renumbered its units and the Flight became, a little confusingly, 660 Sqn.

Since then 660 Sqn's Scouts have performed observation, recce, liaison and troop lifting roles, supporting the Army on exercises and on the Sino-Hong Kong border. From June to October 1979 and again during 1981 and 1982 it was heavily involved in stemming the flood of illegal immigrants from China. During this period it was reinforced by a detachment of 656 Sqn.

Meanwhile, in May 1978, 660 Sqn was joined at Sek Kong by the RAF's 28 Sqn (from Kai Tak), which had itself become a helicopter unit, using Wessex HC2s. The move was prompted by a general RAF exodus out of Kai Tak, following which Sek Kong became the main RAF base in the colony. In addition to support for the Army, the roles of the Wessexes included search and rescue, aeromed evacuation, fire fighting and VIP flying. 28 Sqn's rescue missions, which included the in-flight birth of a baby in June 1981 and the

Westland Scout of Sek Kong-based 660 Sqn Army Air Corps over Hong Kong in 1989. (660 Sqn AAC)

uplift of two badly injured fishermen from a boat 70 miles from Hong Kong in 1986, passed the 1,000 mark in 1982.

In addition to the resident units, the airfield has, for a number of years, been used by the Royal Hong Kong Auxiliary Air Force for annual two-week training camps, as well as for *ad hoc* individual flights. This activity has involved Bulldog and Musketeer trainers. A somewhat older trainer was hangared here in 1979 – Tiger Moth T6645, privately owned by a Cathay Pacific TriStar captain. The home base for 28 Sqn RAF and 660 Sqn AAC, Sek Kong is, in 1990, the only British military airfield in Hong Kong.

Seletar, Singapore

Of all the Singapore airfields, Seletar takes pride of place in terms of both longevity and variety of activity. Its origins date back to 1921 when the British government decided to build a naval base in Singapore. At the same time, the need for an airfield and seaplane base was recognized. In 1923 the locations of the two bases were finalized: the naval base was to be built at a point on Singapore's north coast, with the air base a few miles to the east at a place called Seletar.

The proposed site was photographed by an RAF Survey Flight of Fairey IIIDs in January 1925. With a Flight Lieutenant G. E. Livock as one of its pilots the Flight had

arrived in Singapore by sea the previous year, and was the first RAF unit to visit the Far East. The task of constructing the RAF's first base in Malaya and Singapore began in earnest in 1926, the mixture of mangrove swamp, trees and vegetable gardens which covered the area making the project a daunting one. By March 1927 sufficient land had been cleared for a landing strip.

The construction work was no doubt given added impetus by the planned visit of the Far East Flight, consisting of four Supermarine Southampton flying boats, detailed to fly by stages from Felixstowe to Singapore under the command of Group Captain Henry Cave-Brown-Cave. Leaving England in October 1927 the Southamptons, with Gerry Livock as Senior Pilot, arrived at Seletar in February 1928. By this time a concrete slipway had been constructed. In January 1929 Cave-Brown-Cave left for England, and the Far East Flight was renamed 205 Flying Boat Sqn with Livock as its CO.

Up until 1929 Singapore had lacked a civil airport, but on completion of the grass landing ground at Seletar, permission was given for the airfield to be used by civil visitors, the base thus becoming the island's first international airport. Seletar had actually received its first visitor the previous year, on 7 November 1928. This was a Ryan Brougham, G-AUIX, flown by Australian Captain Frank Hurley and crew in an

Supermarine Southamptons of the Far East Flight at Seletar on 29 February 1928. (MoD Crown Copyright)

Vickers Vildebeeste of 100 Sqn at Seletar in 1936. (MoD Crown Copyright)

attempt on the Australia to England record.

For the next nine years or so Seletar was to host many such pioneering flights and aviation personalities. One of the earliest was Charles Kingsford-Smith who route-stopped in his Avro Sports Avian G–ABCF 'Southern Cross Junior' in October 1930 during the course of a record-breaking England-Australia flight. Other notables included Charles Scott, Jim Mollison, Jean Batten, Bert Hinkler, Francis Chichester and Amy Johnson. Many of the competitors in the 1934 MacRobertson England to Australia Air Race made refuelling stops here, the winning de Havilland Comet establishing a new record. In 1935 Kingsford-Smith, by now a familiar figure at Seletar, decided he would make one last record-breaking flight and try and better the Comet's time. Leaving England in November in his Lockheed Altair 'Lady Southern Cross' he made his way safely to India, from where he took off for Seletar on 7 November, but he disappeared *en route*. Seletar-based aircraft set out to search for the missing airman, but their efforts proved fruitless and the search was called off after two weeks.

Some five years earlier Seletar's RAF pilots had provided instructors for the newly-formed Singapore Flying Club. Due to a lack of suitable landing grounds within range of Seletar, the Club's activities tended to be confined to seaplane flying, making it the first seaplane club in the British Empire. Three of the Club's Moth seaplanes escorted Amy Johnson into Seletar when she flew there in June 1930.

Singapore received its first commerical

aircraft on 11 February 1930 when a Fokker FVIIB of the Royal Dutch Indies Airline Company landed at Seletar, bringing fruit, airmail and passengers from Java. Commercial traffic expanded with the arrival on 16 April 1931 of Singapore's first British airmail on board Imperial Airways de Havilland Hercules G–EBMW. The Station relinquished its auxiliary role as an Asian airport in 1937 when Kallang was opened as Singapore's airport.

Seletar's role was, of course, a military one and it was officially opened on 1 January 1930 as RAF Base Singapore. The Station's first permanent land-based unit arrived in December of that year in the shape of 36 Sqn's Hawker Horsley torpedo bombers. Initially No 36 flew survey flights over Malaya in search of landing ground sites, but in March it sent a detachment to Burma to bomb rebels. In December 1933 the HQ of the Far East Command was established separately on the Station, and the following month 100 Sqn arrived with its Vickers Vildebeests, bringing Seletar up to three squadrons. The Straits Settlement Volunteer Air Force formed in December 1935 with Avro Tutors, Hawker Harts and Audaxes for training. A fourth squadron, 230 flying Short Singapore IIIs, arrived in October 1936 to join 205 (which had re-equipped with Singapores in April 1935), and in November 1936 the Station was retitled RAF Seletar.

The Short Sunderland's long association with Seletar began in 1938 when 230 Sqn took delivery of its first machine, which had been flown out from the UK. Three of 230's original Sunderlands were paid for by the Sultans of individual Malayan States,

Marine aircraft at Seletar in February 1937. Left–right: Osprey K3625 of 714 Catapult Flight, Tiger Moth K2590 of 36 (TB) Sqn, and Singapore III of 203 Sqn visiting from Basra (Iraq). (R Mager via P Porter)

and in recognition of this the aircraft concerned were officially named 'Perak', 'Selangor' and 'Pahang' in October. The later 1930s saw Seletar's flying boat unit taking part in Far East cruises and in exercises with the Fleet.

Apart from the fact that Seletar's aircraft were camouflaged and armed, the declaration of war in Europe had little immediate impact on the Station as a whole. For the next year 36 Sqn was primarily involved in photographing the surrounding operational area. No 230's first wartime tasks were meteorological flights, but the Sunderlands were soon performing coastal, anti-submarine and anti-sabotage patrols. These were short-lived, for in October the Squadron left for Ceylon.

Although 230's departure had reduced the number of operational squadrons to three, other support units had appeared on the scene. No 4 Anti-Aircraft Cooperation Unit had been formed in 1939 using radio-controlled de Havilland Queen Bees and Blackburn Sharks, while in October of that year a Spotter Unit was formed to help in the defence of Singapore. In 1941 Engineering and Equipment Wings were amalgamated to form 151 Maintenance Unit, whose primary task was the servicing of Far East aircraft.

Catalinas had replaced Singapores in 205 Sqn in 1941, and one of the 'Cats' entered

the history books as the first British aircraft to be shot down in the Pacific war. The aircraft in question was sent out to shadow an approaching Japanese invasion convoy on 6 December, and was downed by the convoy's air escort. Following the Japanese landings at Kota Bharu on 8 December, 36 Sqn's Vildebeests were detached up to airfields in Northern Malaya for torpedo attacks on Japanese ships, while 205 Sqn flew reconnaissance and bombing sorties. Much-needed fighter reinforcements in the shape of 232 Sqn's Hurricanes became operational in mid-January 1942.

By the end of January enemy air attacks had made Seletar untenable, and so the Vildebeests were withdrawn to Java, followed in February by 232 Sqn. It was a scorched earth airfield that was left for the Japanese to overrun on 14 February. For the next three years it was in the hands of the Imperial Japanese Navy whose aircraft, including those from vessels visiting the nearby naval base, made extensive use of the airfield facilities. A concrete runway was laid by the Japanese, who remained here until September 1945.

The first RAF units to return after the Second World War were 205 and 209 Sqns (both flying Sunderlands), the crews of which found the airfield and nearby beach littered with abandoned Japanese aircraft. Due to the unserviceability of runways all over the island the Sunderlands now played an important role ferrying food and medical supplies, and repatriating Allied personnel. During September and October 1945 many new units arrived, including 84, 89 and 110 Sqns, all on Mosquitio FBVIs, together with 11 and 17 Sqns operating Spitfire XIVs. In November Nos 314, 389 and 390 MUs were established, while the following year 81 Sqn reformed with Mosquito PR34s.

In mid-1948, by which time the majority of the front-line squadrons had moved to Changi or Tengah, Seletar and its MUs were reorganized into a composite Maintenance Base which provided engineering support for Singapore-based aircraft during Operation Firedog, the Malayan Emergency.

In March 1950 81 Sqn, using Spitfire PR19s in addition to its Mosquitoes, returned from a spell at Tengah, followed in June 1951 by 88 (Sunderland) Sqn which joined 205 and 209 in the Far East Flying Boat Wing. After flying sorties in both Firedog and the Korean War, 88 disbanded in October 1954. Nos 205 and 209 then merged (as 205) in January 1955. Later in the year, on 15 December, 81 Sqn flew the RAF's last operational Mosquito sortie. After a Shackleton Flight of 205 Sqn was formed at Changi in May 1958, the Squadron flew the RAF's last Sunderland sortie in May 1959. Five months later a reborn 209 Sqn brought its Pioneers and Twin Pioneers down from Kuala Lumpur. The Beaufighter was still active here, and

on 10 May 1960 the Station and Towed Target Flight flew the RAF's last Beaufighter sortie. During the 1950s the Flight had used an interesting variety of types, including the Spitfire, Dakota, Anson, Harvard, Valetta, Hornet, Meteor and Pembroke.

Throughout the 1950s the emphasis on Seletar's role had been on Maintenance; 309 MU had provided engineering support for FEAF and its aircraft, while 389 MU was an Equipment Supply Depot. But now it began to take on a new role as a short and medium range transport base, which would later play an important part in the Borneo Campaign resulting from the Indonesian Confrontation that began in 1963. The build-up started in October 1960 when 34 Sqn reformed with Beverleys. Then, in April 1962, the first of several helicopter squadrons was taken on strength – No 66 with Belvederes. Two further helicopters squadrons, 103 and 110, were added in mid-1963 and early 1964 respectively. Next, on New Years Day 1964, No 65 (Bloodhound) Sqn was established to become the RAF's first overseas SAM squadron. A peak was finally reached in December 1966 when 52 Sqn was sent out from the UK with Hawker Siddeley Andover tactical transports.

Throughout the Borneo Campaign FEAF tactical aircraft had been controlled by HQ 224 Group (under HQFEAF), located at Seletar since 1959. Following the ending of the Campaign in 1966, Seletar's flying

Sunderland MR5 NJ193 'P' of 205/209 Sqn at Seletar in 1957. (R Cook)

Belvedere HC1 XG466 'L' of 66 Sqn at Seletar — 1965. (P Russell-Smith Colln)

squadrons took part in many 224 Group/Army exercises in Malaysia, but, with the imminent British withdrawal from the Far East, its days as an RAF station were numbered. Thus, on their return from Exercise Crowning Glory in March 1969, Seletar-based aircraft deployed to Changi, and flying officially ceased on the 28th of that month.

For the next two years its role was again to provide engineering and supply support for FEAF as the Command ran down, and during this period facilities were gradually handed over to the Singapore government.

Beverley C1 XB260 of 34 Sqn at Seletar in 1966. Behind are 52 Sqn's Andovers. (P Russell-Smith Colln)

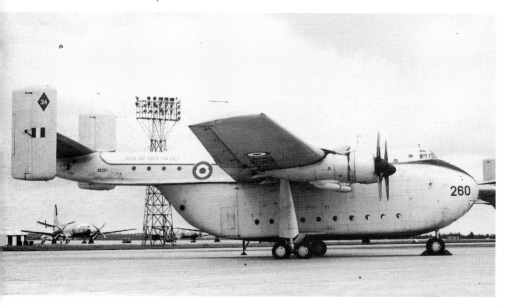

After a parade and flypast on 31 March 1971 it ceased to function as an RAF station. Since then it has been a Republic of Singapore Air Force base for Strikemasters, Jet Provosts and Bloodhound SAMs.

Sembawang, Singapore

The Air Ministry first considered developing 'this difficult site' early in 1935, and the construction of a landing ground was authorized the following year. The dimensions of the landing ground were split into three strips running N/S, NE/SW and NW/SE. Authority for the NE/SW and NW/SE strips to be lengthened by approximately 300 yards was given in March 1940. During the same month the Air Force List first mentions it – as an unoccupied RAF station, while *The London Gazette* refers to it as an airfield designed in peacetime for two bomber squadrons. The construction of two hard runways was deferred. There is no trace of the precise opening date, but this would seem to be either 1937 or 1938.

On 4 July 1940 No 1 (GR) Sqn, RAAF, arrived with Hudsons from Australia via Sourabaya, to be joined on 9 August by another Australian Hudson squadron, No 8. The latter unit departed for Kota Bharu

in November. When 453 Sqn brought its Brewster Buffaloes to Sembawang in August 1941 another Australian Buffalo unit, 21 Sqn, was already resident on the airfield. No 21 was, in November 1941, despatched to Sungei Patani in Thailand as part of NORGROUP to take part in Operation Matador, a plan (subsequently cancelled) to counter possible Japanese landings on the Kra Isthmus just over the Malayan border in Southern Thailand.

With the Japanese advancing rapidly towards Singapore, the airfield defences in December 1941 were listed as: 'no anti-aircraft guns, but within the zone of the Naval Base anti-aircraft cover'. In mid-December two Dutch squadrons with Martin Marylands arrived. They are shown in the Order of Battle to have had sixteen serviceable aircraft on 10 January 1942, but there is no mention of them after that date. By the end of January there were only six serviceable Buffaloes – the remnants of 21 and 453 Sqns, while the Hudsons had already been withdrawn to Sumatra. Like Tengah and Seletar, Sembawang was located on the northern edge of Singapore, within shelling range of the mainland-based Japanese artillery. This soon made the airfield untenable, and in the first week of February all airworthy fighters were flown out to Sumatra.

During the Japanese occupation of

Scottish Aviation Twin Pioneer CC1 XN320 of 209 Sqn Seletar 1966. (E B Goldsmith)

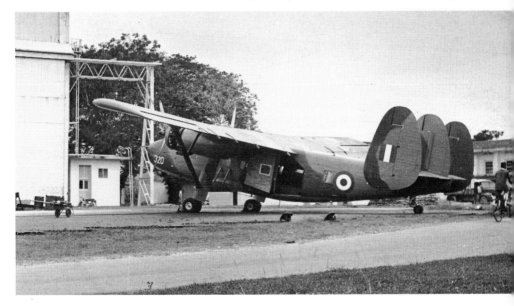

Singapore, Sembawang came under the control of the Japanese Army. However, it was also used for a time by the Japanese Navy, whose aircraft were initially unable to make full use of Seletar due to the energetic work of the British demolition teams immediately prior to Singapore's fall.

Following the Japanese surrender in September 1945, a Royal Navy advance party returned to take control. Approximately 90 Japanese aircraft were found on the airfield, and the area was honeycombed with tunnels and foxholes. Rehabilitation work began immediately utilizing Japanese personnel who helped lay a 1,200 yard PSP runway. The Station received a new nautical name, HMS *Nabrock*, on 1 October when No 9 Mobile Naval Air Base (MONAB) took over. This was changed to HMS *Simbang* when *Nabrock* paid off in December. Later in December 791 Sqn, a Fleet Requirements Unit operating Corsairs, Vengeance target tugs and a Harvard arrived. Adding Seafires, Austers and Expediters to its establishment in 1946 the Squadron also operated air/sea rescue and communications Flights, before

disbanding here in June 1947. Throughout 1946 and 1947 Sembawang hosted various FAA fighter squadrons, such as 802, 804 and 806, operating Seafires disembarked from visiting carriers. HMS *Simbang* itself paid off on 31 December 1947 and the Station was temporarily reduced to Care and Maintenance, until being transferred to the RAF on 16 January 1948.

On that date RAF Station Sembawang officially opened and an advanced party of 60 Sqn arrived. The Squadron's Spitfire F18s and a Harvard followed later in the month and began a daily meteorological flight, practice dive-bombing sorties, aerobatics and communications and ferry flights. The airfield formally opened for flying on 27 January.

Another new arrival was 1914 Flight which transferred across from Changi with Auster 6s. One of the Flight's first tasks was to photograph Singapore's Kranji cemetery in response to an urgent UK Parliamentary Question. A second Spitfire unit, 28 Sqn with FR18s, began to filter into Sembawang from Tengah and the two fighter squadrons now trained alongside each other in formation bombing, gunnery

Spitfire F18 TP217 'G' of 60 Sqn at Sembawang 1948-9. The incomplete stripes on the nose are due to the fitment of a new top cowling. (60 Sqn)

and cine camera work. Dive-bombing was carried out at Seletar, and air-to-sea firing at North China Rock. 'Cab Rank' exercises were mounted, and 'Rhubarb' sorties were flown up to Butterworth. Much work was carried out on the airfield during this period.

In addition to 1914 Flight's exercises with artillery units, the Austers also took on another important task, that of internal security. This embraced reporting shipping movements and monitoring street disturbances in Singapore itself. In April 1945 Sembawang's Technical Wing was tasked with the preparation of three Spitfires for sale to the Burmese Air Force. The airframes selected were SM943, TP198 and NH853 and 60 Sqn was given responsibility for converting the Burmese Air Force pilots to the Spitfire FR18. This was successfully achieved via a couple of circuits in the Harvard.

The ripples of the Malayan Emergency and Operation Firedog spread to Sembawang in July 1948 when both 28 and 60 Sqns detached Spitfires up to Kuala Lumpur as part of the Task Force formed there. Not since their time in the Netherlands East Indies had the two units fired at 'live' targets. The Communist Terrorist (CT) activity also led directly to 1914 Flight being expanded to full squadron status in July, and retitled 656 AOP Sqn. The unit at first comprised four widely detached Flights, all equipped with Austers, of which the Sqn HQ remained initially at Sembawang. Extra Flights were soon added, and in August 1949 the HQ moved to Changi. The Flights moved around periodically, with the result that 1911 was at Sembawang in early 1951, 1907 moved here in March 1952, and 1902 in December.

When supporting troops, and with the likelihood of a good target, the Austers carried a Bren gun operated by the observer. A spate of accidents by 656 Sqn, usually involving forced landings in padi fields with the aircraft turning over, led in October 1948 to the following ribald comments in the Station records: 'It appears that many pilots in the Sqn have a fixation about inverted flight'; and 'It is understood that the Air Ministry, in consequence of certain accidents being brought to their notice, are considering renumbering the RAF Accident Report Form, the new number to be 656'!

Meanwhile, the main task of the two fighter squadrons was to provide serviceable aircraft for the Kuala Lumpur detachment, which they achieved but somewhat to the detriment of operations at Sembawang. When the 60 Sqn detachment returned from Kuala Lumpur in December 1948 it was rumoured that this was an end to the commitment. The rumour, however, proved false and just after Christmas the squadron was again tasked with providing aircraft and crews up-country. At this point operational sorties against CTs were also being flown from Sembawang. The daily meteorological flight originally mounted by 60 Sqn had been taken over by 28 Sqn in April 1948, and a year later No 28 was allotted Spitfire TP329 solely for 'met' duties. No 28's Kuala Lumpur Firedog commitment was officially ended in April 1949, and the following month the Squadron moved to Hong Kong, one Spitfire crashing at Kuching on the way. Meanwhile, 60 Sqn began operating a shuttle strike system between Sembawang and Kuala Lumpur, the aircraft arming at either end. The 'Spits' also carried rockets, and 60 Sqn reached a peak in operational sorties in July 1949. During this month the Squadron took part in a new type of maximum effort against CTs, involving six Spitfires, a Sunderland armed with over 300 fragmentation bombs, and up to eleven Harvards. The target on each occasion was a jungle clearing in Malaya.

August 1949 saw the arrival in Singapore abroad HMS *Ocean* of replacement Spitfires for 60 Sqn, which moved to Tengah at the end of the month. Another visiting carrier HMS *Triumph*, disembarked the Seafire F47s of 800 Sqn (in October and December), which also mounted strikes against jungle targets from Sembawang. No 60's exit had been as a result of the decision of transfer Sembawang back to the RN, and after a gradual handover that Service gained control on 16 January 1950. Under its previous title of HMS *Simbang* the airfield was again used by visiting FAA squadrons. Apart from a brief period under RAF auspices which ended in July 1953, Simbang remained in Naval hands until reduced to Care and Maintenance in April 1957. Two helicopter squadrons were based here during this period: first to arrive (in January 1953) was 848 Sqn of the FAA with ten American-built Whirlwind HAS21s, followed in February by the RAF's 194 Sqn, reformed from the Far East Casualty Evacuation Flight and operating the Westland Dragonfly. The two squadrons formed the UK's first operational helicopter Wing, No 303, which moved up to Kuala Lumpur in May

Westland Wessex HAS1 of 820 Sqn visiting Sembawang from HMS Eagle in 1966. (C Simlett)

to be near the Firedog action. No 848 disbanded back at Sembawang in December 1956, and the period also saw numerous visits by disembarked FAA Firefly and Sea Fury squadrons.

Early in 1959 work was begun to prepare the airfield as a base for a Royal Marine Commando and a Naval helicopter squadron. The advance party of 42 Commando arrived in January 1960, and the following June 42 Commando together with 848 Naval Air Sqn disembarked from HMS *Bulwark*. HQ 3rd Commando Brigade was piped aboard in March 1961.

HMS *Simbang* again recommissioned on 4 September 1962, and throughout 1962 and early 1963 814 and 815 Naval Air Sqns spent periods disembarked here. The years between 1963 and 1966 saw HM Ships *Victorious*, *Centaur*, *Eagle*, *Ark Royal* and *Hermes* operating in Far Eastern waters, and on each occasion anti-submarine squadrons from the warships operated from the airfield. This spasmodic Naval air activity meant that Sembawang could be used for various other functions, such as supply drop training by the RAF, parachute dropping by students of the Far East Parachute Training School, and Commando exercises.

In 1966 a Fleet Amphibious Forces Base was established, leading to the arrival of 40 Commando in March. This prompted the constitution, on 12 August 1968, of No 3 Commando Brigade Air Sqn operating Sioux helicopters, the first full operational Army Air Corps squadron to be formed for many years. Additional air support for the Royal Marines was provided by 847 Sqn

which, with its Wessex HU5s, was officially commissioned the following April. On 1 September 1971 administrative control of the Base was handed over to ANZUK Support Group HQ, and HMS *Simbang* finally paid off on the 30th of that month.

Shaibah, Iraq

Immortalized in its own song 'Those Shaibah Blues', the enervatingly humid location of this particular base in southern Iraq, down near the Persian Gulf, was no doubt a source of inspiration for the composer. Shaibah's first operational unit was 84 Sqn, which began a twenty year occupancy in September 1920. The Squadron's DH9As were in action, alongside other Iraq-based units, in November 1923 when a number of dissident tribes began revolting in the Samawa area of the Euphrates valley. Reconnaissance patrols, followed by offensive sorties, soon prevented the trouble from spreading. The following year No 84 was involved in quelling another uprising in the Lake Hammar area. A more peaceful task for No 84 during its first two years at Shaibah was a photographic survey for the remapping of southern Iraq, while in January 1928 the unit contributed aircraft to 'Akforce', formed for operations against the Akhwan. Re-equipment with Westland Wapitis began in September.

Apart from policing duties, the 1930s were quiet for Shaibah and during this period No 84 Sqn also administered the Station. This arrangement changed in September 1940 with the departure of the

Squadron (whose Vickers Vincents had given way to Blenheims) for Habbaniya and the formation of a Station Headquarters. At the same time 'S' Sqn arrived with twelve Vincents, and its CO, Sqn Ldr H. V. Alloway, additionally assumed command of the Station as a whole. 'S' Sqn was redesignated No 244 Sqn on 1 November, and the following January put three Vincents, armed with 250 lb bombs, on standby after an enemy submarine had been reported in the Indian Ocean. In February 244 made preparations to operate from Muscat or Sharjah following a signal from Air Headquarters reporting the presence of a German pocket battleship in the vicinity of Zanzibar.

In addition to the war with Germany, Britain was also faced with hostility from within Iraq itself during April 1941, and all ranks were confined to camp. Iraqi attentions were concentrated on Habbaniya, which was besieged, and Britain responded by sending in reinforcements to the country. These included elements of the King's Own Royal Regiment which were flown to Shaibah in May aboard Douglas DC-2s and Vickers Valentias of 31 Sqn, together with civilian Armstrong Whitworth Atalantas impressed into service in military markings, for onward movement to Habbaniya. In addition, detachments from two Egypt-based Wellington squadrons (Nos 37 and 70) were sent to Shaibah in May, from where they raided the Iraqi forces surrounding Habbaniya. Meanwhile, fighting had also broken out nearer to Shaibah itself, and the Vincents of 244 Sqn, aided by a number of

Fairey Swordfish which were flown in specially off HMS *Hermes*, were called on to support British ground forces operating in the area. Shortly after its arrival, one of 37 Sqn's Wellingtons crashed on take-off, its bombs exploding in the ensuing fire. The crew were rescued but two were seriously burned, one of whom later died. No 31 Sqn's 'A' and 'B' Flights (Valentias and DC-2s respectively) were detached to Shaibah during this period.

In June 1941 the Station was allotted its own Airspeed Oxford (L4667), but was so dismayed at the aircraft's unserviceability that Air Headquarters was asked to re-allot it to 244 Sqn, which earlier in the year had begun receiving Blenheims.

Under the command of its celebrated CO, Squadron Leader E. M. 'Imshi' Mason, No 261 Sqn moved to Shaibah in August with thirteen Hurricanes and six Gladiators for Operation 'Y' – offensive action against Persia (Iran). During the course of this the Hurricanes attacked Persian airfields and barracks, shooting down one enemy Audax, while 244's Vincents and Blenheims, together with a detachment of No 84 Sqn's Blenheims, flew tactical reconnaissance sorties over Ahwaz airfield and the oil refinery at Abadan, and dropped leaflets over Isfahan and Shiraz. One Vincent was mistakenly shot down by a Hurricane and its pilot wounded. After the Shah of Persia had ordered an end to hostilities, No 261 and the 84 Sqn detachment went their separate ways in September.

By April 1942 reinforcement Bostons for the Russians were routeing through

DH9A of 84 Sqn flying from Shaibah. (MoD Crown Copyright)

Westland Wapiti of 84 Sqn at Shaibah. (MoD Crown Copyright)

Shaibah, while in July the first Baltimore to be tested on the Station crashed, fatally injuring its USAAF pilot. In a rather depressing period two Bostons, one Russian and the other British, collided in mid-air, Baltimore AG967 crashed killing the pilot, and several Station personnel simply died of heat exhaustion.

After the differences with Iraq and Persia had been resolved, Shaibah would not again be called upon to play an offensive role through the war years. Instead it became the location, in September 1942, for the Aircraft Depot (which moved in from Habbaniya), the main task for which was now the assembly and delivery of Spitfires to the Russians. First deliveries were made in February 1943 when 38 'Spits' were completed by No 119 MU and flown to Abadan for handover. The scope of this lease-lend scheme was widened in mid-1943 to include Hurricanes, 111 being transferred in August. The Russians, however, could be difficult customers, refusing to accept any aircraft that had flown in excess of 40 hours from brand new!

Preparations in 1944 for the use of the Station as a reinforcement transit airfield included the establishment of No 42 Staging Post. In April of that year Shaibah came as close as it ever would to operational activity when the Station

Commander, accompanied by the 119 MU test pilot, took off in a Tiger Moth to look for a submarine reported to have surfaced in the Shatt-al-Arab. Refuelling at Abadan they headed out over the sea, and spotted a dark object in the water. Descending, they soon realized that it was a school of sharks – and suddenly appreciated their reliance on the Moth's single engine!

The Station establishment in November comprised Nos 115, 119 and 127 MUs, together with 42 SP. By now the Aid-to-Russia programme was virtually complete and the emphasis was on the build-up of staging post activities. The immediate post-war months found the Station involved in large-scale trooping to and from the Far East, and handling Halifax, Stirling, Liberator and York transport aircraft. The provision of route support facilities remained the pattern through the late 1940s, during which period the Station gained its own Anson and Ventura. A new task taken on in the 1950s was the hosting of RAF Middle East Vampire squadrons making use of the Tuba weapons range. One of these aircraft (from 249 Sqn) crashed fatally in September 1951 while carrying out unauthorized low-level aerobatics.

In November 1952 the Station welcomed No 7 Sqn of the Iraqi Air Force for a short stay with its Hawker Furies and Austers, which carried out a successful exercise with the Iraqi army. With the arrival, in January 1955, of No 32 Sqn Shaibah at last gained a 'permanent' front-line unit, though morale on the Squadron was tempered by the news that the RAF was soon to leave Iraq. In the event, No 32, equipped with Venom FB1s plus a number of Vampire T11s, Meteor T7s and Vampire FB9s, was posted to Malta in October. At the end of the year Air Headquarters Levant announced that the Station had been sold to Iraq, and RAF control ceased with effect from 1 March 1956.

Shallufa, Egypt

The units that would make up RAF Shallufa (Station Headquarters together with Nos 37 and 38 Wellington Sqns) assembled at Fayid at the beginning of December 1940 and then transferred to Shallufa on the eighteenth of the month, personnel moving into tented accommodation at the new base, located some eight miles from Port Suez. The Wellingtons began night operations against such targets as Derna, Tobruk and Benghazi, often flying from Advanced Landing Grounds and detachments airfields.

During this period, Station records mention the presence of an OTU at Shallufa, though no details are given of its identity or aircraft types. In any event it disbanded in August 1941 and provided resources to reform No 108 (Wellington) Sqn at Kabrit. Air raid warnings had been increasing since the beginning of the year, and in June the airfield defences claimed a hit on an enemy machine, thought to be a Heinkel 111K, which dived and fired down a searchlight beam, smoke pouring from its port engine. The NAAFI was destroyed and one person killed when a twin-engined aircraft dropped a stick of bombs across the camp the following month.

Earlier in 1941 No 90 Sqn in the United Kingdom had started to receive Boeing Fortress Is, and in late October a detachment of three of these aircraft flew out to Shallufa from Polebrook for operations against enemy ports and shipping. The detachment suffered its fair share of attrition, beginning with the loss of AN529 which was destroyed by its crew after it force-landed behind enemy lines during a raid on Benghazi on 8 November. Then, in January 1942, AN521 crashed about six miles north-west of the airfield whilst engaged on fuel consumption tests, killing two SNCOs. The remainder of the crew escaped by parachute. Later in the month the Fortresses made several inconclusive attacks on enemy convoys making for Tripoli. During its time at Shallufa the 90 Sqn detachment was redesignated No 220 Sqn and left for the United Kingdom in February.

Radio countermeasures had been under development for some time, and in order to provide a capability in the Middle East No 162 Sqn was formed at Shallufa from a detachment of No 109 Sqn in January 1942. Its task was twofold: to monitor and jam

Boeing Fortress AN532 'WP-J' of 90 Sqn at Shallufa. (G White)

enemy signals, and to provide calibration facilities for Allied radio and radar installations. For these activities it was equipped with Wellingtons and Blenheims respectivity.

Following the disbandment of RAF Shallufa on 30 January 1942 and its reformation as HQ 238 Wing, the airfield hosted several bomber squadrons throughout the course of the year. These included No 76/454 with Halifaxes, and No 40 with Wellingtons. In addition, the Wellington VIIIs of No 221 Sqn were on strength between August and November. The task of 221's ASV-equipped Wellingtons (known as 'Goofingtons') was to search out enemy shipping at night as targets for the torpedo Wellingtons of No 38 Sqn. No 221 was joined in September by another maritime squadron, No 458, which re-equipped with Wellington Ics and VIIIs for operations over the Mediterranean. During the year No 39 Sqn alternated between Shallufa and Malta for torpedo attacks on enemy shipping using Bristol Beauforts, in the course of which the Squadron incurred heavy losses.

Torpedo dropping, particularly the training aspects, would now increasingly occupy Shallufa's time by way of No 5 Middle East Training School (METS). Eight Marauders of No 14 Sqn arrived for conversion training in February, and later in the month the US Army HQ in Cairo sent over a staff officer to study US

Mitchell torpedo trials. Marauders and Beauforts carried out tactical exercises against British ships. All Marauders were grounded for a spell after the tail of FK376 broke off and it crashed in May, killing all on board. By August 1943 No 5 METS was tasked with training twenty Wellington and ten Beaufighter crews in torpedo bombing, in addition to the occasional Turkish Beaufort crew. At the turn of the year arrangements were made to provide rocket projectile (RP) training for Beaufighter crews, and soon No 5 METS was running Torbeaux Training Courses, and Hurricane RP Courses. At the same time a Flying Instructors School was formed and allotted three Ansons. Instruction was also given on Harvards (e.g. EX119), Wellingtons and Beauforts.

Shallufa continued in the training role for the remainder of the war, although by February 1945 there had been considerable reorganization. No 5 METS had disbanded, leaving No 11 Flying Instructors School, No 7 Refresher Flying Unit, No 1342 (RP Training) Flight, No 1343 (Conversion) Flight, and the Middle East Armament School. But the Station had gained NO 75 OTU together with its 31 Martin Baltimores and three Hurricanes. The OTU's ten-week course trained Baltimore night armed reconnaissance crews.

Post-war Shallufa is best remembered for its Bomber Command Sunray

Beaufighter TT10 RD860 of Shallufa's Target Towing Flight. (via S Bond)

detachments from the United Kingdom, initially involving Lancasters but soon giving way to Lincolns. Practically every Lincoln squadron in the Command took its turn in these detachments, which were designed to provide training not only in long-range overseas flights, but also in visual bombing during clear weather when the English climate precluded this. Sunrays, which normally lasted about a month and involved entire squadrons, came to an end in 1953. During this period the Lincolns practised affiliation with several fighter squadrons based at Shallufa. Two Tempest VI squadrons, Nos 6 and 213, both spent periods here in 1947, while in 1951 jets came on the scene (January to October) in the shape of the Vampire FB5s of No 32 Sqn. This Squadron returned for a further two-and-a-half years spell in February 1952. Shallufa's last recorded resident aircraft were Beaufighters operating in the target-towing role in September 1954, and there was no activity after that date.

Sharjah, Trucial States

Although a primitive landing ground existed here earlier, Sharjah's history as a recognized airfield dates back to the early 1930s and to the old Imperial Airways route to India. After the 1929 three-year agreement with Persia had expired Imperial Airways was forced to adopt a more southerly route embracing Kuwait, Bahrain and Sharjah in the Trucial States on the north coast of the Arabian Peninsula. Thus, in July 1932, the British Government signed an agreement with the Sheik for the use of the airfield at Sharjah; in addition to a monthly rent of 800 Indian rupees and water charges, a fee of five rupees per aircraft was levied, and for many years payment was made to the Sheik in silver coinage, due to his distrust of paper money.

Imperial Airways was using Handley Page 42s on the India service at this point, the inaugural aircraft ('Hanno', under the command of Captain Alcock) having arrived at Sharjah from Bahrain on 6 June 1932, and the first mail being carried over the new route in October. Overnight accommodation was provided in a resthouse built in the form of a fort. By 1933 Sharjah, together with the landing grounds which the RAF had set out at Doha, Muscat and Masirah, was being used by the Vickers Victorias of No 70 Sqn and the Westland Wapitis of Nos 55 and 84 Sqns. The following year the first mail for

Australia staged through, and it was via the Empire Air Mail Scheme that Sharjah began its association with flying boats. The Scheme involved the use of Short C Class Empire Flying Boats carrying mail without surcharge throughout the Empire, and the first scheduled service from Alexandria to Karachi took place in October 1937. The boats operating this route alighted on the water off Dubai, some twelve miles south of Sharjah and an outpost of the Station, where transit facilities were established for both passengers and aircraft. Flying boat operations in the Persian Gulf, later under BOAC, continued until January 1947.

In the meantime, the Second World War had broken out, but it was not until June 1940 that operational aircraft were based at Sharjah. These consisted of a detachment of Blenheims of No 84 Sqn from Shaibah (Iraq). Another detachment from Shaibah, this time provided by No 244 Sqn, arrived in January 1942 and, with its eight Vickers Vincents and an Airspeed Oxford, began surveying landing grounds, during the course of which one Vincent (K4121) was lost. Armed with 250 lb anti-submarine bombs the Vincents started anti-sub patrols in February, but were replaced by Blenheim IVs two months later. The detachment became a full squadron presence in 1943, with 244's CO also assuming command of RAF Sharjah itself. During the year the Squadron re-equipped with Blenheim Vs, the engines of which gave endless problems following protracted storage in the Middle East. Before the establishment of No 4 Ferry Control Unit the task of handling the many aircraft transitting through to India fell to the lot of No 244's ground crew. In addition to RAF Hurricanes the visitors included USAAF P-38 Lightings and P-40 Warhawks.

By the beginning of 1944 the steady flow of transit aircraft included USAAF transport types, and the Americans embarked on an extensive building programme. With the departure of 244 Sqn to Masirah in March following re-equipment with Wellingtons, the principal unit on the station was No 44 Staging Post (ex-No 4 FCU), but during the final year of the war elements of two squadrons were attached to the station. These were No 294 Sqn, an air-sea rescue unit based in Iraq with Wellingtons, Warwicks and Walruses; and No 680 Sqn, whose Spitfire XIs carried out a photographic survey of Iraq and Persia. The last of No 294's Walruses staggered off in the direction of Iraq in April 1946, W3017 force-landing after take-off from Bahrein, and W3062 being burnt at Doha having suffered engine failure.

The immediate post-war years, during which the station came under the auspices of Air Headquarters Iraq, were quiet. In October 1948 Proctor G–AKIW arrived carrying two individuals engaged on 'Top Secret' work for the Government, while the following month three Vampires being ferried to the Indian Air Force introduced Sharjah to the jet area. Numerous VIP aircraft (e.g. Mauripur Communications Flight Dakota KJ880) rubbed shoulders with French transport types plodding to and from French Indo-China (Vietnam), and the Station gained is own Anson VL341 for local flying. Throughout the opening years of the 1950s convoys of jet aircraft passed through on their way to re-equip RAF squadrons in the Far East, while a wide variety of other visitors, British and foreign, civil and military, were also handled. The peaceful years came to an end in 1954 with the Buraimi affair.

Following the breakdown of discussions between Britain and Saudi Arabia on the subject of disputed borders, the latter country sent a small force to occupy a village near Buraimi Oasis in Oman. At this the tribal sheiks and the Sultan of Muscat asked Britain to protest to Saudi Arabia. The protest, however, was rejected and a show of force was considered necessary.

This included the deployment to Sharjah of three Vampires from No 6 Sqn at Habbaniya, supported by a Valetta, in September 1952. Later in the month the Vampires flew low-level sorties over the Buraimi villages while the Valetta dropped leaflets. A temporary agreement enabled the Vampires to return to Habbaniya in October, but the problem festered on, leading to the decision, early in 1953, to reinforce Sharjah with a large detachment of No 6 Sqn, together with two Flights of Armoured Cars from Habbaniya plus a number of Aden Protectorate Levies to boost the resident Trucial Oman Levies. The operation of jets from the airfield, however, presented two major problems: runway erosion from jet efflux, and the limited endurance of the aircraft themselves. The replacement of the Vampires by four Meteor FR9s from 208 Sqn in Egypt did little to ease these problems, which were only solved by the attachment of two Lancasters each from Nos 37 and 38 Sqns in Malta. This was a temporary measure pending the availability of photo-recce Lancasters of No 683 Sqn at Habbaniya. No 683, however, was due for disbandment and the air task in the overall blockade of Buraimi was finally met by the formation in November of No 1417 Flight with five Ansons, based at Bahrein but operating mainly from Sharjah.

It was often a motley selection of civil

208 Sqn's Hunter FGA9s during a detachment to Sharjah in 1968. (P Russell-Smith)

Wessex HC2 XR500 'A' of 78 Sqn — Sharjah June 1968. (P Russell-Smith)

aircraft that staged through, but one of the most celebrated was the KLM visitor of June 1954 carrying a large consignment of animals, including birds, four bears and three tigers. The machine promptly went unserviceable for two days, resulting in the harassed Station staff having to take on the secondary role of zoo keeping.

Internal political unrest within Oman itself from 1957 onwards led to the deployment of Venoms from Nos 8 and 249 Sqn, together with Shackletons of No 228 Sqn from St Mawgan. After the

Shackletons had dropped leaflets on the rebel positions, ten or even twelve Venoms would follow up with cannon and rocket attacks. In addition to leaflet dropping, Pembrokes, with which 1417 Flight had re-equipped, were used for 'sky shouting'.

An end to the Oman campaign in February 1959 enabled the Station to concentrate on its role as an Armament Practice Camp for the Middle East offensive squadrons, and a school would later be established for Forward Air Controllers and Air Contact Teams. But

84 Sqn's Andover C1 XS645 'E' at Sharjah in December 1969. (P Russell-Smith)

with the onset of the Kuwait crisis in 1961 the Station was again called to arms, albeit in a comparatively limited way. On 1 July the first four Canberra B(I)8s of No 88 Sqn from Germany flew in, joined a day later by eight B(I)6s No 213 Sqn. The presence of the Canberras again highlighted the need for permanent runways and other facilities, and at the end of the crisis (during which not a shot was fired) an extensive building programme was begun.

As a result of this redevelopment Sharjah was in a much better position to receive its share of the flying squadrons, which were being redeployed in 1967 in preparation for the withdrawal from Aden. These included Nos 8 and 208 Hunter FGA9 Sqns (temporarily, to ease congestion at Muharraq), followed by No 78 with Wessex HC2s whose tasks embraced that of search and rescue, and No 84, initially with Beverleys but soon re-equipping with Andover C1s. The latter's role was to provide Air Forces Gulf with air transport. Tactically it supported the Army units in the Trucial States, Muscat and Oman, as well as keeping one aircraft ready for medical evacuation duties. The presence of the Wessexes and Andovers meant that the Sharjah-based Flight of 152 Sqn (formed from 1417 Flight), equipped with Twin Pioneers, could be phased out. In addition, Shackleton MR2s of the Aden-based No 37 Sqn spent time at Sharjah during 1967. After No 37 disbanded at Khormaksar in September, Shackleton detachments at Sharjah were maintained from the United Kingdom. This arrangement was tidied up in November 1970 when five Shackleton MR2s were flown out to form No 210 Sqn.

Withdrawal from Aden was followed swiftly by withdrawal from the Persian Gulf, and the final two months of 1971 saw the disbandment of Sharjah's remaining squadrons, Nos 78 and 210. Back in September, however, they had been joined by No 8 Sqn, whose eight Hunters were now the last aircraft to leave before the Station was handed over to International Airadio. The station finally closed on 14 December.

Stanley, Falkland Islands

After a short period of comparative obscurity as a civil airport, Stanley airfield sprang to sudden and violent prominence in 1982 as a result of the Falkands War. Prior to this upheaval, aviation on a serious scale in the Stanley area can be traced back to 1948 when two Austers arrived in the Falklands for use on internal air services around the islands. The first of these began operating from Stanley racecourse in December 1948, with the second arriving in March 1949. The following year another Auster and a Noorduyn Norseman, both equipped with floats, began operating from Port Stanley, and shortly afterwards the tiny fleet was collectively titled the Falkland Islands Government Air Service (FIGAS).

The first of a small number of de Havilland Beaver floatplanes entered service in 1953. The opening of a proper airstrip at Hooker's Point, outside the town, enabled an external air service with Argentina using landplanes to begin in 1972. Built and operated by the Argentinians, the airstrip could accept types as large as the Fokker F-27 Friendship. Hooker's Point was in turn superseded by Stanley Airport, which began operating in December 1977 but was not officially opened until May 1979. Located some two miles from Stanley town on the Cape Pembroke Peninsula the new airport enabled the Argentinians to begin jet airliner services to the South American mainland, using Fokker F-28 Fellowships.

In 1977 a local review of the internal air services concluded that the sturdy and simple-to-operate Britten Norman Islander might be ideally suited to conditions around the islands. Additional airstrips would have to be prepared, but if the Islander proved successful then this would permit the phasing out of the seaplanes. Accordingly FIGAS acquired its first Islander VP-FAY in October 1979, and plans were made to increase the number of settlement airstrips. Due to careful pre-paratory work Islander operations got off to a sound start, but before they could flourish the Argentinians invaded on 2 April 1982.

Throughout the month a stream of Argentinian aircraft poured in, the first group consisting of four Pucaras, a Bell 212 and a Puma. A C-130 Hercules arrived with the vital AN/TPS-43F surveillance radar, and two Grumman S-2E Trackers began a ten day stay in the reconnaissance role. By mid-April an Argentinian evalu-ation of Stanley as an operating base for Argentine Navy (CANA) A-4Q Skyhawks and Super Etendards had concluded that this was only possible in fine weather. Such reservations did not apply, however, to the Macchi MB-339A light attack aircraft which the CANA flew in, and these were joined by Prefectura Naval Argentina (PNA) Skyvans is the coastguard role. Over the latter part of April the Argentinian airlift of men and equipment into Stanley increased in tempo, but on the morning of 1 May the airfield suffered its first raid by an RAF Vulcan, which dropped 21 1,000 lb bombs, cratering the runway. The raid was followed up the same day by Sea Harrier missions, and a second Vulcan attack took place on 4 May, with others later in the campaign.

After the Argentinian surrender on 15 June the first RAF personnel began moving in to what would swiftly become RAF Stanley. The assorted wreckage strewn around the airfield included Pucaras, MB–339As, Governor Six Rex Hunt's Cessna 172, and the hulk of the FIGAS Islander, which had been a casualty of the conflict. In order to support the rapid development of the new station, Hercules resupply flights were begun from Ascension, initially in the form of the airdrop of stores. These could be hazardous due to the presence of minefields, and it was something of a relief when, on 24 June in Operation Rosie, the first Hercules was able to land on the recently repaired runway. The main task was now to make the airfield suitable for accepting the various aircraft types that were considered necessary for the defence of the Falkland Islands, and one of the most significant measures towards achieving this was the laying of a 6,200 ft runway made up of aluminium matting by the Royal Engineers. The job was completed in October and was extended to include taxiways and parking areas.

Up to this point the air defence of the Falklands had been shared by RAF Harrier GR3s and RN Sea Harriers, but with the runway now suitably 'beefed up', Phantom FGR2s in the shape of a detachment of No 29 Sqn arrived on 17 October, via Ascension, to take over the role. An interesting feature of the Phantom operations was the use of the Rotary Hydraulic Arrester Gear (RHAG) for every landing, which resulted in a spectacular carrier-style arrival. Initially the Harriers and Sea Harriers (of 809 Sqn), which had moved into Stanley before the runway was restored, remained alongside the Phantoms, the GR3s providing an added offensive support capability. No 809 Sqn returned to the United Kingdom aboard HMS *Illustrious* in December 1982, but the RAF Harrier detachment (which had included resources from Nos 1 and 4 Sqns, together with 233 OCU) was redesignated No 1453 Flight in August 1983, remaining until June 1985, when the last aircraft returned to Wittering. On 30 March 1983 the No 29 Sqn detachment (known locally as 'Phandet') took over the numberplate of No 23 Sqn, which had disbanded at Wattisham. RAF Lyneham had, up to now, been providing a small detachment of Hercules and in August 1983 this became 1312 Flight, its C1P and C1K aircraft operating in the tanker, transport and maritime reconnaissance roles. (Throughout its short but busy life RAF Stanley was run on detachments, and every conceivable organization was bestowed with the suffix 'det'; hence 'Hercdet', and 'Jockdet' for the Scots fraternity. One unit, which shall remain nameless, was even known as 'Wimpdet'!)

In order to refuel a constant flow of visiting helicopters, Stanley was equipped with an elaborate system of aviation fuel field equipment, topped up from a dedicated ocean-going tanker, the mv

Phantom FGR2 of 23 Sqn at Stanley in April 1986. (T Fairbairn)

Hercules C1K XV203 of 1312 Flight at Stanley — November 1985. (P Russell-Smith Colln)

Lumiere, moored in a nearby cove. The visiting machines included Sea King HAR3s of 202 Sqn, later to become No 1564 Flight and based at Navy Point across the harbour from Stanley town; the Chinook detachment drawn from Nos 7 and 18 Sqns operating out of Kelly's Garden and forming No 1310 Flight on 20 August 1983; and finally Army Air Corps Westland Scouts and Gazelles. The Hercules airbridge from the United Kingdom had become a twice-weekly schedule, and detachments of RAF Regiment personnel provided a Resident Rapier Squadron, equipped with Rapier missiles and headquartered in the self-contained Black Eagle camp overlooking the airfield. The build-up of airlift capability was completed towards the end of 1983 when Bristow Helicopters began operating three Westland S-16Ns under an MOD contract to carry passengers and light freight over a network of routes throughout the islands.

Sea King HAR3 of 1564 Flight at Stanley in December 1985. (T Fairbairn)

Bristow Helicopters' S-61Ns — the celebrated 'Erics'. Stanley, December 1985. (T Fairbairn)

Whilst frequent exercises were held, No 23's Phantoms were occasionally scrambled for real. For example, on 13 June 1985 one of the fighters took off to look at an unidentifield radar contact which had appeared on the western edge of the Falkland Islands Protection Zone (FIPZ). The contact turned out to be an Argentinian Boeing 707, which turned away from the FIPZ in a northerly direction. Phantom and Boeing flew in company for some ten minutes in international airspace, with no aggression displayed on either side.

Stanley's severe operating limits for military aircraft in terms of runway length, crosswind, and sheer parking space had always meant that the RAF presence would be short-stay, and in mid-1985 the Station began planning its move to the new, purpose-built base being constructed at Mount Pleasant some 38 miles away. The main move was completed during 1986 in an operation which saw the transport of men and material by land sea and air. Chinooks plucked bulky equipment from inaccessible, remote locations, while Hercules airlifted critical or delicate spares which would not have survived the jolting road journey. Central to the move was the need to preserve No 23 Sqn's reaction capability.

The whole operation was completed in time, and on 30 April 1986 Stanley held a ceremony to mark its closure. Appropriately the Ensign was hauled down for the last time by Flight Sergeant 'Taff' Burton of No 63 Rapier Sqn, RAF Regiment, chosen for the task since he had been present when it was raised for the first time back in July 1982. Also very apt was the despatch, much later on, of the fourteen-seater Airfield Chapel to the RAF Museum. Constructed from a sea freight container, it epitomized Stanley's make-shift, temporary lifestyle. With the departure of the RAF the Royal Engineers moved in, tasked with erasing all trace of military activity and with returning a once-frantic RAF station to its former tranquility as a civil airport, operating nothing more warlike than the FIGAS Islanders.

Ta Kali, Malta

Prior to the outbreak of the Second World War, Ta Kali's role was that of a civil airport, its main customers being the Italians. By the time Italy entered hostilities in June 1940, however, obstructions had already been positioned around the airfield to prevent airborne landings. Ta Kali was soon to be put to use though, for on 30 October instructions were received at Hal Far from HQ Mediterranean Command for Wing Commander J. R. O'Sullivan to proceed to the airport with a small HQ staff, with the task of forming a one-squadron fighter station there. The following day the staff of fourteen duly took up post, together with seventeen men of the King's Own Malta Rifles to act as guards, and at the same time a servicing party from 261 Sqn at Luqa arrived to begin maintaining the unit's Hurricanes operating from Ta Kali as a temporary measure. Domestic accommodation was quickly taken over and on 8 November 1940 the airport became RAF Station Ta Kali. No 261 Sqn moved over permanently from Luqa on 20 November.

The airfield was bombed in March 1941, although no damage was done. At the end of April 'C' Flight of 261 Sqn moved to Luqa. In May, when construction work on dispersal tracks and aircraft pens began, the remainder of 261 Sqn disbanded, but was replaced by another unit, No 249 Sqn, whose Hurricanes now took on the enemy bombers. In an Axis attack on 25 May two Hurricanes were burnt out and three damaged. Groups of transitting Hurricanes were escorted away to the Middle East by Marylands through the summer months, but ten of the fighters which arrived in June were used to form 126 Sqn, which was based here until the following May. During the course of October Italian fighters strafed the airfield, but later in the month No 69 Sqn moved in from Luqa for a brief period, with seven Marylands and three Hurricanes. An unusual visitor in early November was Mosquito W4056 from the Photographic Reconnaissance Unit at Benson in the UK. December saw the formation of 1435 Night Fighter Flight from the Malta Night Fighter Unit, which had itself begun life here back in July with Hurricanes. In addition, there were occasional raids by 249's Hurricanes, armed with 20-lb bombs and escorted by Hurricane fighters, on Italian targets. The Hurricanes were extremely busy at this period in response to raiding Ju 88s and Macchis.

Throughout early January 1942 there were dive-bombing attacks by Ju 88s, intercepted by 126 and 249 Sqns together with Hurricanes of 242 Sqn temporarily attached from Hal Far. Later in the month the Hurricanes bombed Comiso airfield, starting fires. A neo-605 Sqn (there was still a unit with this numberplate slogging it out in the Far East) flew in from Hal Far with its Hurricanes during February, but disbanded around the turn of the month. The blitz on Malta continued into March, by which time 249 Sqn was engaging the Me 109s with its newly-received Spitfires. The raids reached such a crescendo on 21 March, when over 1,500 bombs excluding incendiaries fell on the airfield in 24 hours, that all personnel had to be evacuated from the Station. A huge army working party attempted to repair the runway by night, but next day 249 were forced to operate from Luqa, so great was the damage. The close-quarters nature of the fighting was graphically demonstrated by the Ta Kali rifle party which damaged a Me 109 on 10 May, on a day when in the air 65 enemy aircraft, including Ju 87s, Ju 88s, Me 109s, Cants and Macchis, were destroyed or damaged.

Meanwhile, in April, 603 Sqn had begun operating Spitfires alongside 249, and in June these forces were augmented by the Beaufighters of 89 Sqn's 'C' Flight from Egypt. Within the space of eight days the 'Beaus' had destroyed seven enemy machines, and went on to despatch a further twelve in July. The month also saw the arrival of 248 Sqn, whose Beaufighters were here temporarily to provide an air escort for the naval Force 'Y' and to shoot

Hurricanes at Ta Kali during the Second World War. The underwing tanks suggest they have recently been ferried in. (Nat War Museum — Malta)

up the odd Sardinian airfield. In August, on the other hand, the resources of 603 Sqn were used to form 229 Sqn on Spitfire Vcs, the latter unit moving to Krendi in December. Two other Beaufighter units were taken on strength during November 1942, No 227 Sqn in the shipping strike role, and No 272 whose specialities were attacks on Tunisian airfields and patrols for enemy aircraft in the Cap Bon area. These latter two squadrons moved on in February and June 1943 respectively.

Activity in 1943 was geared towards another important milestone of the war, the invasion of Sicily, and Ta Kali's part in the operation was to receive the Spitfires of Nos 81, 152, 154, 232 and 242 Sqns, forming 322 Wing, which flew patrols and escorted Allied bombing raids over the island. The RN, for its part, contributed No 828 Sqn whose Fairey Albacores flew anti-submarine patrols. When the Spitfire squadrons moved forward to Sicily in July their place was taken by other Allied units such as the USAAF's 47th Bomb Group, which began operations with its Bostons, and another FAA Albacore squadron, No 826, also here for anti-submarine ops. August saw the arrival not only of an ASR and Communication Flight Wellington which was soon busily searching for downed aircrew, but also an RN Fleet Requirements Unit, No 728 Sqn whose Boulton Paul Defiants remained until January 1944.

The Station now entered a quiet period in its history, with no operational flying to speak of between October 1943 and the end of hostilities. After responsibility for the airfield was transferred to the RN in February 1944 another FRU squadron, No 727, was based here with Defiants and Swordfish in November of that year, but disbanded in early December. RN ownership was formalized on 1 April 1945 when the base was commissioned for FRU use as HMS *Goldfinch*, and throughout the late 1940s it formed the shore base for a number of FAA embarked squadrons such as 802 with Seafires (November 1947/March 1948 period), and in 1949 Nos 807 (Sea Furies), 809 (Sea Hornets) and 810 (Fireflies). On a more permanent basis, No 73 Sqn was based here with Spitfires for island defence duties from 1946 until 1948, while No 1702 Sqn's Sea Otters provided an ASR service from July 1946 until disbandment two months later.

Handed back to the RAF in June 1953 the airfield was under Care and Maintenance for some time before reopening as an independent RAF station on 1 August 1955. With the arrival of 32 Sqn's Venom from Iraq in October and the temporary presence of 809 Sqn Sea Hawks, Ta Kali

The Ta Kali Station Commander had this gibbet erected on the Station in May 1942 as a warning to anyone who had ideas about impeding the war effort! (via C Bowyer)

EXTRACT :- D.R.O's DATED 14.5.42
R.A.F. STATION, TA-KALI, MALTA

A GIBBET HAS BEEN ERECTED ON THE CORNER OF THE ROAD LEADING TO THE CAVES. ANY MAN, WOMAN OR CHILD, CIVILIAN OR SERVICE PERSONNEL, FOUND GUILTY OF SABOTAGE, THEFT, OR IN ANY OTHER WAY IMPEDING THE WAR EFFORT AND SUBSEQUENTLY SHOT, WILL BE HUNG FROM THIS GIBBET AS A WARNING TO ALL OTHERS.

Above *Kittyhawks of 3 Sqn RAAF at Ta Kali. They are probably being bombed up to attack Sicily in 1943.* (Nat War Museum — Malta)

Below *Spitfire F22, PK326, of 73 Sqn Ta Kali, 1948.* (S Burge)

was once again back in business as a fighter station. The die was further set when, in February 1956, 26 Armament Practice Camp moved in from Nicosia and the Station began hosting regular visits from RAF fighter squadrons, particularly the UK-based Auxiliary units. In the period up to 1957 when the RAuxAF was disbanded, Nos 500, 501, 504, 600, 601, 604, 608, 612 and 613 Sqns all had summer camps at Ta Kali. When 32 Sqn left for Jordan in August 1956 its place was taken by 208 Sqn, flying Meteor FR9s. This unit and 111 Sqn (Hunters), which happened to be visiting Ta Kali during November, were placed on standby during the Suez crisis, although in the event neither squadron was needed. On 1 May 1957 the Levant Canberra Servicing Unit was formed, and was well placed to deal with Canberra WJ758 of 12 Sqn when it belly landed on the airfield in December.

The opening months of 1958 saw both gains and losses for the Station, the Canberra Servicing Unit moving to Cyprus in January, followed by 208 Sqn a month or so later. On the credit side, the Malta Communications and Target Towing Sqn (with Pembrokes and Beaufighters respectively) transferred across from Luqa in February. In addition, the Station now became a regular exercise destination for the navigation and other training schools in the UK, and as late as 1960 the airfield was rarely without visiting Varsities and Valettas from either Topcliffe, Shawbury, Thorney Island or Hullavington. Meanwhile, the Malta Comms and TT Sqn received its first de Havilland Devon in September 1958, and relinquished its last Beaufighter when RD788 was flown to Luqa. Meteor T7s and F8s were now used in the TT role. The RN was also prominent in October, with 848 Sqn (newly-formed at Hal Far with Whirlwind helicopters as the Amphibious Warfare Trials Unit) operating from here briefly alongside 898 Sqn's Sea Hawks.

In addition to Devons and Meteors, the Malta Comms and TT Sqn was, in 1960, operating the Valetta. In December the unit flew Dakota KN452 to Cyprus on a training sortie, soon afterwards to be ferried to the UK for a Royal flight. By October 1962 the Squadron had been downgraded to a Flight, and was Ta Kali's sole remaining unit. Even this had disappeared by April 1963, the Station then being put under Care and Maintenance. Eventually transferred to the Maltese Government, it does not feature in RAF records after April 1968.

Tengah, Singapore

Tengah's origins can be traced back to 1931, when the virtual state of war that existed between China and Japan began to sow the first seeds of concern about Singapore's vulnerability to attack. This particular airfield was one of the remedial defence measures set in train, but even then its development was leisurely and protracted. It was not until 1937 that contractors first began clearing the site of rubber and coconut trees, and over the following two years a 2,500 ft landing strip, hangars and buildings were constructed.

The first aircraft to land officially was 'a biplane' carrying Mr Bailey, the Landing Field Inspector, in July 1939, and on 5 August Wing Commander McFarlane took up post as the first Station Commander. During the same month Nos 11 and 39 Sqn flying Blenheim Is arrived from India, but left for Kallang in September to be replaced by Tengah's first permanent squadrons, 34 and 62, also with Blenheims.

At first the war in Europe had little effect on life at Tengah but by 1941 the threat of a Japanese invasion of Malaya and Singapore had resulted in hasty improvements being made to the Station; a tarmac runway was built over the original grass strip, and sandbag blast pens were erected to protect aircraft. Number 62 Sqn moved up to Alor Star in February. When war finally came to Singapore on 8 December 1941, Tengah was one of the main targets of the initial Japanese air attacks, bombs falling behind the Asian Sick Quarters and along the runway. Later in the month 34 Sqn was detached up to Butterworth in response to Japanese landings in North East Malaya.

During January 1942 approximately 50 crated Hurricanes had arrived in Singapore, a number of which found their way to Tengah. Conditions on the Station were appalling, for besides being bombed each day the airfield was within easy range of Japanese artillery sited across the Straits of Johore on the Malayan mainland. Morale, already very low, reached rock bottom as a result of an incident known as the 'Endau Raid'. In this, the Station was detailed to provide a Hurricane escort for bombers attacking a Japanese landing at Endau, 100 miles up the east coast of Malaya. However, when the pilots arrived at their aircraft they found that, due to an appalling oversight, no one had briefed the ground crews – who were nowhere to be found. None of the pre-flight preparations could be made and consequently the

Hurricanes were too late to rendezvous with the bombers, which were recalled. Summoned to Headquarters to explain the error, this was the last straw for the Station Commander who had watched the rapid deterioration of his unit, and he committed suicide on 26 January 1942.

When 34 Sqn's Blenheims were withdrawn to Palembang on 18 January, followed nine days later by 62 Sqn now using Hudsons, only Hurricanes remained on the Station. These were reinforced by additional aircraft of this type from HMS *Indomitable* on the 30th, but increasing artillery fire soon rendered the airfield unfit for use, and it was therefore decided to evacuate all remaining aircraft to Sumatra. By 10 February it was in the hands of the Japanese.

Throughout the remaining war years the base was operated by the Japanese Army, which repaired the runway and other facilities using a workforce of labourers and POWs. It was then used by front-line flying units of the Japanese Army.

Following the Japanese surrender in August 1945, the first Allied unit to return was 902 Wing. Amongst the damaged Japanese aircraft found on the airfield was a captured Dutch Curtiss Mohawk, which could still be taxied. The Station generally was in a very neglected state and a labour force of Japanese Surrendered Personnel (JSPs) was drafted in to carry out renovation work. It would be two years before the JSPs left, but the base became operational again much sooner than that with the arrival in September of 152 and 155 Sqn's Spitfire VIIIs. In January 1946, at the request of the Dutch, No 152 flew reconnaissance sorties over Indonesia to locate political extremists. No 155 moved to Sumatra in February, while 152 disbanded in March. One of the priority tasks on the Work programme was the laying of a 2,000 yd runway, a project undertaken by 3353 Airfield Construction Wing. Thus, by the beginning of 1947, 28 and 60 Sqns with Spitfire FR14s and 18s had been installed and were carrying out live bombing, photo-recce, and practice interception on visiting Lancasters. The new runway was allegedly christened by 60 Sqn's Harvard, which suffered a collapsed undercarriage in the process!

The first jets were seen here in June 1947 when Meteor F4s EE595 and '596 arrived for tropical trials. The Meteors gave several thrilling displays, which were ecstatically reported in the local press, before getting down to the trials proper. After visiting several bases in Malaya and being flown by pilots from the Singapore squadrons, the jets were dismantled for shipping back to the UK in July. Meanwhile, June had seen the unscheduled arrival of KLM Constellation 'Nijmegan', which had run short of fuel while on a flight from Amsterdam to Batavia.

Wearing its new (but only temporary) mantle of RAF Transport Command UK – Far East trunk route terminal, Tengah handled its first scheduled Avro York in October 1947. At the same time the Station took on a parallel civilian role and turned round its first Qantas Constellation from Darwin. More tropical trials, this time for the Vampire, began in February 1948, and the jet was also demonstrated throughout the Far East Command.

The Station was soon to be called to arms again though, for when the Malayan Emergency began in mid-1948 its units, both resident and detached, played a central part in the military campaign, Operation Firedog. Following their move to Sembawang at the beginning of the year, 28 and 60 Sqns had been replaced by two fresh units, 81 Sqn with Mosquito PR34s and a Flight of Spitfire FR18es, and 84 Sqn on Beaufighter Xs. Both units were soon involved in Firedog, sending detachments up to Kuala Lumpur as part of the Task Force formed there. No 84 Sqn's contribution to the campaign, during which its 'Beaus' carried out cannon and 60 lb rocket attacks, was brief, for in October 1948 it transferred to the Middle East.

Shortly after the 'Yangtze Incident' in 1949, three of 81 Sqn's aircraft took part in a flypast over HMS *Amethyst*, the centrepiece of this famous naval action as she steamed to the UK from Hong Kong.

The tempo at Tengah now increased, with the arrival in December 1949 of 45 Sqn flying Beaufighter Xs. This unit had already been on detached operations in Northern Malaya, and it now began to re-equip with Bristol Brigands. A further eight Brigands, this time from 84 Sqn in the Middle East, arrived on indefinite detachment in April 1950. In March a new chapter in the anti-terrorist air offensive had opened, with the arrival of eight Lincolns from 57 Sqn in the UK. This was the first of a series of Bomber Command reinforcement detachments to the Far East which would successively be performed by 100 Sqn in July, and 61/144 Sqn in December. The idea had first been trialled by 97 Sqn Lincolns under Operation Red Lion II back in April 1948.

Plans already in hand for the formation of a Malayan Auxiliary Air Force were accelerated by the Emergency, and recruiting for a Singapore squadron began at Tengah in June 1950. On its formation it was equipped with Tiger Moths, later supplemented by Harvards and Spitfires. This scheme had only limited success, however, the Squadron mounting the occasional reconnaissance sortie and leaflet drop on Southern Malaya in support of Firedog.

Tengah's varied and busy role at this time is vividly illustrated by the activity of July 1950. Highlight of the month was the arrival of 1 Sqn, RAAF, with four Lincolns, which, say contemporary records, 'Got stuck in quickly'. The Australian aircraft augmented the 'resident' Lincolns of 100 Sqn already operating in the heavy bombing role and which, during the month, trialled a new technique of night bombing involving the use of a searchlight to guide them to the target. For their part the Brigands of 45 and 84 Sqns had flown many bombing and rocket sorties, but the tragic record of this machine had already begun to manifest itself – both units suffering fatal crashes during the month. (Of interest, No 84 also operated the Bristol Buckmaster for conversion training at this point.) Finally, a fighter squadron, No 60 with Spitfire FR18s, was already into its second month of anti-terrorist operations from the Station.

There were to be seven more fatal crashes, including three in June 1950 alone, before the career of Tengah's Brigands was terminated. (In one of the crashes Flying Officer Mathews, a navigator on 84 Sqn, was killed when RH881 lost a wing and went down near the Officers' Mess. A keen athlete, his name was commemorated in the Station's Mathews Trophy.) As a result 45 Sqn was withdrawn from operations in January 1952 to convert to the de Havilland Hornet, while 84 was grounded the following December after one of its aircraft lost a wing over Kota Tinggi.

Before becoming the first jet fighter squadron in the Far East when it took delivery of Vampire FB5s in December 1950, No 60 flew the last operational Spitfire sortie in an attack on bandit positions near Kota Tinggi. The Sqn was now taken out of line until April 1951 for training in its primary role of air defence, and Venom FB1s replaced the Vampires in February 1955. On the last day of March 1955 the two Far East Hornet squadrons, 45 (here at Tengah) and 33 (based at Butterworth but controlled by Tengah)

Hornet F3 WB898 'OB-A' of 45 Sqn Tengah, in the 1952-3 period. (P Russell-Smith Colln)

45 Sqn's Canberra T4 WH706 at Tengah in 1960. (P Russell-Smith Colln)

were amalgamated as 45 Sqn for Hornet operations from Butterworth. The number of fighter squadrons now available for Firedog was brought up to three again with the arrival from Cyprus of 14 Sqn, RNZAF (Vampires), in April/May 1955, and the year ended with the replacement of the Lincolns by Canberras in the Bomber Command detachments, and with the transfer of the detachments to Butterworth.

No 45 (Venom) Sqn returned to Tengah in November 1957 to re-equip with Canberra B2s while another familiar unit, 81 Sqn, returned the following spring with Meteor PR10s in the photo-recce role. More Canberras, in the shape of 75 Sqn, RNZAF, arrived in July 1958 to replace the 'Kiwi' Venoms. During the closing months of Firedog, 60 Sqn, whose contribution to the Operation had been a long one, changed to the all-weather role, collecting Meteor NF14s from Leeming in the UK and flying them out ot Tengah in October 1959. The Emergency officially ended in August 1960, though 81 Sqn continued to fly photo-reconnaissance sorties until mid-1961.

In March 1958 Air Ministry approval had been given for Tengah to be developed as a medium bomber base. In addition, plans were made for a Royal Navy Aircraft Holding Unit (to service disembarked carrier-based aircraft) to be located here. These plans involved the provision of a new 9,000 ft runway, together with a taxiway, hardstands and domestic facilities. Extra

land was acquired and the work was virtually complete by 1962, the RNAHU having moved in during 1960. The airfield was now an extremely busy one with five resident operational squadrons. No 20 Sqn, a day fighter/ground attack unit with Hunter FGA9s, reformed here in 1961 and 60 Sqn re-equipped with Javelin F(AW)9s. All FEAF's reconnaissance work was performed by 81 Sqn's Canberra PR7s, disembarked RN Sea Vixens and Scimitars were appearing in increasing numbers, and Bomber Command Victor detachments had begun. Butterworth-based RAAF Sabres flew in for air defence exercises, and in June 1961 the Station handled four Vickers Valiant tankers supporting Vulcans flying non-stop from the UK to Australia.

Rumblings of political discontent now began to affect Tengah, this time in the shape of the Brunei Rebellion of December 1962. During that month Hunters and 45 Sqn Canberras were detached to Labuan for dummy attacks on rebels. The revolt was merely a prelude to the Indonesian Confrontation, which began in earnest in 1963 and in which Tengah's units were to play a key role. With incursions into Malaysian airspace increasing, Hunters and Javelins were detached to Borneo during December 1963. Simultaneously FEAF was reinforced by eight Victors of 15 and 57 Sqns which were based here, and an RAF Regiment Light Anti-Aircraft Sqn was added to guard the airfield. The year as a whole was a busy one, with visits from

Meteor NF14 WS755 'C' of 60 Sqn at Tengah in 1961. (P Russell-Smith Colln)

USAF F-100 Super Sabres, F-101 Voodoos, C-130 Hercules and C-124 Globemasters for Exercise Joss Stick, Australian Navy Sea Venoms from HMS *Melbourne*, USAF B-57s from the Phillipines, and RAF Comets.

After the Indonesians had made paradrops on Malaya in 1964, more reinforcements arrived, comprising Sabres from the RAAF's 3 Sqn, 73 Sqn Canberra B15s, 14 Sqn RNZAF Canberra B12s, 64 Sqn Javelin F(AW)9s and 893 Sqn 'Sea Vixens'. In addition, three PR Canberras from 58 Sqn bolstered 81 Sqn so that by September 1964 there were actually ten squadrons, or part squadrons, based here.

81 Sqn Meteor PR10 VS970 at Tengah in 1960. In the background are the tailfins of 45 Sqn's Canberras. (P Russell-Smith Colln)

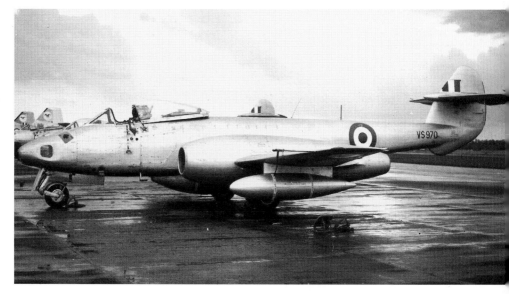

Javelin FAW9 XH839 'M' of 60 Sqn after a tropical downpour at Tengah in 1966. (P Russell-Smith Colln)

On top of its local activity, Tengah was tasked with mounting a detachment at Kuantan to prepare the camp as a forward operational strike airfield for detachments of Canberra B(I)8 squadrons from RAF Germany. Hunters flew rocket and cannon sorties in support of ground forces operating against Indonesian paratroops in Johore, and by the end of September most of the enemy had been eliminated. Later, in May 1965 when a party of Indonesian regular troops landed on the coast of Johore, Hunters directed by a Forward Air Controller dislodged the raiders with rocket attacks. (20 Sqn was using the disbanded 209 Sqn's cast-off Scottish Aviation

20 Sqn's Hunter FGA9 XJ683 'F' at Tengah in 1967. (P Russell-Smith Colln)

Pioneer CC1s of 20 Sqn's Forward Air Control Flight at Tengah in 1969. XL666 and XJ465. (P Russell-Smith Colln)

Pioneers for FAC work as late as 1970.)

Once peace returned to the area in August 1966 the Hunters and Javelins returned from Borneo, a timely move for the latter, which were beginning to suffer structural cracking. Medium bomber and photo-recce detachments to Tengah also ended.

The Defence Review of 1966 gave warning of planned reductions to the RAF in the Far East and the ailing Javelins were the first to feel the chill wind of contraction, 64 Sqn disbanding in June 1967 and 60 following a year later, after a memorable dusk flypast on 26 April 1968. Six Javelins that were not scrapped were sent to Seletar for the technical training of Singapore Armed Forces personnel.

In order to fill the air defence gap, 74 Sqn was deployed out to Tengah with its Lightning F6s in June 1967. The new Squadron took part in many exercises and in June 1969 four of its aircraft, refuelled by Victors and escorted by two Canberra weather ships, flew to Darwin to participate in Australian air defence exercises. The presence of the Lightnings also meant that 20 Sqn could be reduced in size and eventually disbanded. It was also 45 Sqn's turn to leave, and the two units put up a farewell flypast of six Hunters and six Canberras in February 1970. No 81 Sqn had disbanded the previous month after twelve years in the theatre, during which time it had flown the 10,000th Firedog

mission from Tengah back in December 1959, and had also operated Pembrokes in the photo-recce role.

A welcome 'breather' from the run down of forces was provided by the Far East reinforcement exercise Bersatu Padu in June 1970. For this, the Station hosted 54 Sqn's Phantoms which flew out from the UK.

The RAAF Jubilee celebrations of 1971 resulted in an invitation for four Lightnings to visit Australia in March of that year, where displays were given at the Edinburgh and Laverton bases. This trip was something of a swansong for 74 Sqn which disbanded on 25 August, its aircraft being ferried to 56 Sqn in Cyprus.

In January 1970 the training of Singapore Armed Forces personnel had begun here. Later in the year Britain joined Australia and New Zealand in the ANZUK pact, and in the autumn of 1971 the RAF forces earmarked for the pact were deployed to Tengah. These comprised eleven Whirlwind 10s of 103 Sqn, and three Shackletons (ex-205 Sqn) with 209's numberplate. A Nimrod detachment from 206 Sqn replaced the 'Shacks' early the following year. This arrangement was ended by the 1975 Defence White Paper, which announced Britain's intention to withdraw its ANZUK forces by April 1976. The last VC10 repatriating RAF personnel left Tengah in February 1976, and the RAF

Whirlwind HAR10s of 103 Sqn over Tengah Officers' Mess in 1972. (D Pells via C Bowyer)

Support Unit here disbanded in March. Since then it has been a main base for the Singapore Armed Forces.

Wildenrath, Germany

The first of the so-called 'Clutch' stations to be built (i.e. those close to the Dutch border – the other two being Brüggen and Laarbruch) Wildenrath was opened on 15 January 1952. Its role initially was to be that of fighter base, and in April two squadrons of Vampire FB5s moved in. These were Nos 3 and 71, and they were followed a month later by a third Vampire squadron, No 67, known collectively as 137 Wing.

The Vampires, however, were no match for the impressive MiGs facing them across the 'Iron Curtain', and in the absence of a comparable contemporary British-produced interceptor all three squadrons were re-equipped with Canadian-built North American Sabres as a stop-gap measure in 1953. In order to train RAF pilots for the new fighter in Germany as a whole, a Sabre Conversion Flight was first formed, the initial six aircraft for the Flight arriving at

the end of March. The squadrons then began re-equipping with Sabres in May. The Sabre Conversion Flight was later retitled Sabre Conversion Unit and by the time it had completed its task and disbanded in June 1954 some 353 pilots had been converted, with only one serious accident. Number 3 Sqn transferred to Geilenkirchen in July 1953, but Nos 67 and 71 remained here until they both moved to Brüggen in July 1955.

The 2nd TAF Communications Sqn had first appeared on the books with Ansons in December 1954, carrying VIPs and other personnel to all parts of the Continent and to the UK. By mid-1955 it was operating the Anson (Mks 12, 19 and 21), Valetta, Devon, Prentice and Vampire (FB5 and T11).

Nineteen fifty six saw the start of the Canberra era, with 88 Sqn reforming in January on B(I)8s, the first RAF squadron to equip with this mark of Canberra, with its distinctive off-set fighter canopy and belly-mounted gun pack capable of housing 20 mm or 30 mm cannon. Initially operating in the day and night interdictor role, the Canberra B(I)8 units as a whole were also given a low-level nuclear attack

Newly-arrived Sabre XB624 in the hangar at Wildenrath in 1953, with (left) the Vampire which it replaced and (right) a Meteor T7 used for training. (M Lines)

capability in 1959. A second Canberra squadron arrived from Wahn in April 1957, and this was No 17, equipped with the PR7 for photo-reconnaissance duties. No 88 Sqn, still with Canberra B(I)8s, was renumbered 14 Sqn in December 1962, while in February 1969 60 Sqn was reformed from the RAF Germany Communications Sqn. Types being flown on comms duties at this point included Pembrokes and de Havilland Herons.

The start of the 1970s was an extremely busy time for RAF Germany in general, and Wildenrath in particular. No 17 Sqn had disbanded with its Canberras at the end of December 1969 and 14 Sqn followed suit in June 1970. The Station now became the main operating base for the Command Harrier force, in the course of one of the most significant re-equipment moves ever made by the RAF in Germany. No 4 Sqn was the first to be reformed (on 1 June 1970) with this remarkable aircraft, followed in December by 20 Sqn. A third squadron, No 3, completed the Wildenrath Harrier Wing which was declared operational on 1 January 1972. Between October and November 1973 the three squadrons took delivery of the improved GR3 version

of the Harrier.

Designed as a ground attack aircraft to operate with a high degree of mobility right up at the front line, the Harriers were not ideally located at Wildenrath, which was some distance from any possible action. Gütersloh, on the other hand, the most easterly of the Allied airfields in Germany, was a far better proposition geographically, and in early 1977 the Harriers were deployed to this ex-Lightning base, where they were better placed to provide close support to the forward elements of the British Army of the Rhine. 4 Sqn left in January, followed by 3 Sqn in April. 20 Sqn, however, disbanded on 1 March to reform as a Jaguar squadron over at Brüggen, passing on its Harriers to No 3 and 4 Sqn to bring them up to the standard NATO establishment of eighteen aircraft.

In the meantime there had been changes to other squadrons on the Station. October 1971 saw 60 Sqn begin using Hawker Siddeley Andover CC2s as a temporary measure while the vintage Pembrokes were being re-sparred, an arrangement which lasted until November 1975. When, in 1987, it was time for the Pembroke to begin

Canberra B(I)8s of 14 Sqn at Wildenrath in 1968. (P Russell-Smith Colln)

bowing out for good, 60 Sqn again began re-equipping with Andovers. Both C1s and CC2 were taken on strength and the first machine, ex-Queen's Flight CC2 XS793, was delivered on 2 March. Still in the communications role, No 60's tasks included shuttle services to Northolt and Berlin and aeromedical evacuation flights.

The move of the Harriers to Gütersloh resulted in a complete change of role for Wildenrath, for the Station had been earmarked to take on the mantle of RAFG's main air defence base, now that the Lightning was coming to the end of its service in Germany. In anticipation of this, 19 Sqn (Designate) began training with Phantom FGR2 (released from the ground attack role by the introduction of Jaguars)

4 Sqn Harrier GR1 XV791 at Wildenrath in 1971. (P Russell-Smith Colln)

Phantom FGR2 XV472 'E' of 19 Sqn — Wildenrath 1982. (P Russell-Smith Colln)

in October 1976. The Squadron was declared operational in January 1977, at the same time as a second Phantom squadron, No 92, began working up prior to reforming in April. Armed with Skyflash medium-range, and Sidewinder short-range air-to-air missiles, two Phantoms were allocated to the permanently-manned Battle Flight positioned in Hardened Aircraft Shelters at the end of the runway.

The Station has also been home for a number of years for 12 Flight AAC, which, with its Gazelles, is the HQ BAOR and senior officer transportation unit. The Army aviation connection with Wildenrath dates back unbroken to December 1954 when 1912 Light Liaison Flight (under the RAF control) moved here from Bückeberg with its Austers in the light communications and reconnaissance roles. The Flight became 12 Independent Liaison Flight, AAC in September 1957 and remained in this guise until November 1964. Between November 1964 and July 1965 its title was 31 Flight, RASC, followed by a spell as 131 Flight, RCT until January 1970. From then until February 1971 it was known as 131 Aviation Sqn, when yet another change produced 669 Aviation Sqn/669 Sqn, AAC. September 1976 saw the final redesignation to the current 12 Flight, AAC. Austers plus the odd Chipmunk were flown in the period to

1960. Beavers were operated from June 1961 until 1975, together with Alouettes between December 1960 and December 1965. Scouts were on the inventory from 1965 until 1976, when the Gazelles arrived.

Like Gütersloh, Wildenrath is a busy transport airfield serving the 'Clutch Station' area. In addition to the activities of 60 Sqn, Britannia Airways Boeing 737s carrying MoD personnel and their families are handled on a twice-weekly schedule, while RAF Hercules, VC10s and TriStars are also regular visitors. Andover E3s from 115 Sqn in the UK have performed weekly aeromedical flights. On the logistic support side the RAF Germany Freight Distribution Centre is based here, receiving from the UK Equipment Supply Depots the vital spares and other equipment needed to keep the RAFG stations operational. Providing a low-level air defence capability for these diverse activities are the Rapier missiles of 16 Sqn, RAF Regiment which arrived in February 1976. The Squadron received Blindfire radar trackers in January 1980 which gave the Rapiers a 24 hour, all-weather capability. No 4 Wing, RAF Regiment which controls all the RAFG Rapier squadrons has also headquartered here since 1978. 'B' Flight of 25 Sqn with its Bloodhound SAMs was deployed at Wildenrath in the 1971-83 period, before the Squadron as a whole returned to the UK.

Index of units referred to in the text